THE SIGNS

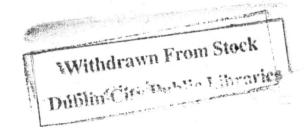

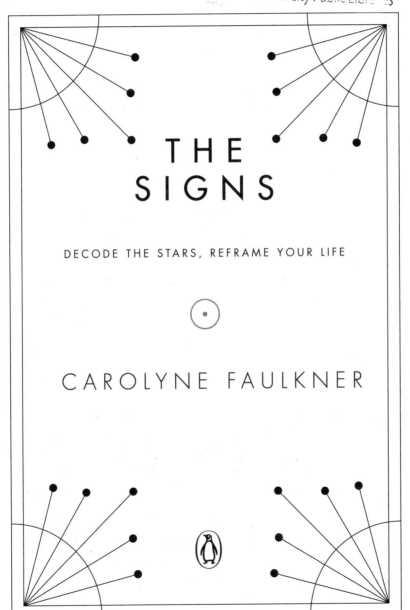

THE
SIGNS

DECODE THE STARS, REFRAME YOUR LIFE

CAROLYNE FAULKNER

PENGUIN LIFE

UK | USA | Canada | Ireland | Australia
India | New Zealand | South Africa

Penguin Life is part of the Penguin Random House group of companies
whose addresses can be found at global.penguinrandomhouse.com.

First published 2017

014

Typeset by Couper Street Type Co.
Printed in Great Britain by Clays Ltd, Elcograf S.p.A

A CIP catalogue record for this book is available from the British Library

ISBN: 978–0–241–30755–7

www.greenpenguin.co.uk

MIX
Paper from
responsible sources
FSC® C018179

Penguin Random House is committed to a
sustainable future for our business, our readers
and our planet. This book is made from Forest
Stewardship Council® certified paper.

This book is dedicated to my son Kam,
the real sun in my life. To all the people who
have woken up, this one's for you.

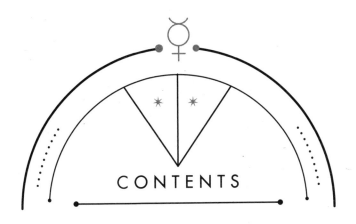

CONTENTS

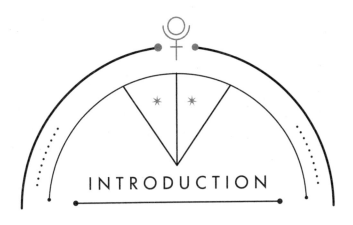

INTRODUCTION

If you, like so many people I know, find astrology interesting but are put off by confusing technical terms or esoteric trivialities, such as orders not to leave your house until Mercury moves out of its retrograde phase, I hope you will find this book refreshing, perhaps even enlightening, and, above all, useful. I wrote it for people like us (I include myself), who were looking for a book that made astrology accessible and fun, as well as practical. I believe astrology can be a powerful life-coaching tool, which everyone can learn to use for themselves. In fact, I'm on a mission to place its power in your hands. (I am Aquarius, after all, and Aquarians have a job to do here on Earth, in raising awareness and promoting equality.)

Let's clear something up right from the start. It cannot be possible, nor is it logical, to split the whole of humanity into twelve star signs and expect them all to be the same types of people experiencing the same things at the same time. Neither does it make sense to over-generalize. Assuming that all Leos are funny and outgoing or Scorpios are sexy but prone to jealousy is not realistic. Human beings are way more complex than that and our star sign (also known in astrology as the Sun sign) is only ever a rough guide to our personality and potential. As you'll see, learning the helpful and harmful traits of your sign and putting the former into practice will indeed enable you to shine with the brilliance of the Sun. Even so, astrology can never tell the whole story about who you are. After all, assessing anyone's character (including your own) solely on the basis of their star sign is like judging them on their looks. Sometimes we get lucky and nail them accurately, but very often we are mistaken – and this can lead to trouble!

And one more mistaken belief to get out of the way at the beginning: it's not set in stone that certain signs do or do not gel with others. The only way to make any kind of assessment of a relationship's durability is to assess both individuals' charts and study them alongside one another. Many of the successful couples I know have one person with the Sun in one sign and the other with the same sign as their Moon or rising sign. Traditional astrology would say that they wouldn't work out but, in my experience, it's rather like a game of snap: you just need to match signs with a potential partner (or friend or colleague) somewhere along the line. Two of my oldest friends are Leo and, as an Aquarius, they are my direct opposite. My other closest friend's star sign matches my rising sign. Astrology can yield fascinating insights, when you have the desire to dig a little deeper.

I have been studying astrology for more than eleven years. For the last nine I have also been using it to coach people to deepen their understanding of themselves and others, as well as to signpost ways for them to experience more honest and intimate relationships and enjoy professional success. The method I use, which I call Dynamic Astrology, helps to improve emotional, spiritual and physical health, and to increase overall well-being. You will notice that I use the word 'karma' frequently. Karma is cause and effect: for every action there is a reaction. Seeds planted in fertile soil are likely to yield a healthy crop; the opposite is also true. Try to think of karma as seeds that you plant. You cannot change past karma, but you can become more aware of every choice you make in the present and indeed alter the future.

I know that when Dynamic Astrology is used as a tool to enhance self-awareness, it helps us to navigate a much smoother path through our lives. It can bring about an empowering transformation and a deeper connection with the more authentic part of ourselves. This is vital because, as I see it, only our truest vibe attracts our real tribe.

My experience of working with people from all over the globe and all walks of life has taught me that astrology is essentially a framework for tuning in to the rhythms of your own life, a tool for managing human behaviour – your own and others'. I like to think of it as the scaffolding for a renovation only in this case the building being sympathetically restored is you!

Astrology has been practised by societies all over the world for thousands of years. It's a bit like the ancient world's forerunner to the modern science of psychology. And when you start to think of it in these terms then its incredible stoicism, even in our sceptical modern world, where most people have lost faith in anything other than what they see with their eyes (as opposed to what they feel with their hearts) begins to make sense. I believe that our own minds shape and then create our reality. Neuroscience has proved it. Nobody's future is written in the stars, it is ours to create.

So, as far as I'm concerned, astrology has nothing to do with fortune-telling or two-line daily horoscopes and everything to do with boosting your ability to grow personally, which increases happiness and enhances positive interactions with others. It also helps us to become more mindful, to make better-informed judgements about our abilities and limitations, and those of other people. And bear in mind that even a basic knowledge of astrology provides us with the opportunity to master our sense of timing. The best chefs will testify that timing is indeed everything!

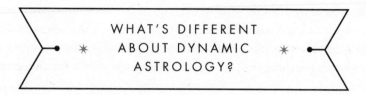

WHAT'S DIFFERENT ABOUT DYNAMIC ASTROLOGY?

Dynamic Astrology combines spiritual and astrological teachings with research into contemporary human behaviour from a life coach's perspective. In this framework, your chart is not a rigid description of who you are, or a set prescription for how you should live your life. Astrology becomes a tool for interpretation that puts you at the centre of the decision-making. Knowledge of the stars empowers you to work in harmony with their energy.

For me, astrology has become as much a part of everyday life as the electricity that powers our homes. As with electricity, I use it because it gives power and light when I need them. And I share it because I believe that this star language is one that transcends class, race, status and, most importantly, ego. Anyone can use it, and I like that.

With Dynamic Astrology, I wanted to create a method to show you how to use astrology yourself, with no need for an astrologer on a retainer to chart your every decision. I have a mission to empower other people's intuition. We are all intuitive to a greater or lesser degree, but our intuition is often so tightly wrapped up in logic that we end up being limited to a one-dimensional perspective.

Astrology is sometimes made to seem more complex than it needs to be. It's true that, at first glance, a full birth chart can look very complicated and even daunting, and some of the terminology takes a bit of getting used to, but I have simplified the process to make it fully accessible, and I know from coaching my clients that astrology doesn't have to be so difficult. In fact it is just like learning a foreign language: you pick up bits and pieces, a few words and phrases here and there, you weave the conversation together and then, with practice and patience, you begin to speak the language. Or in this case you learn to 'astrochat', as I like to call it.

Dynamic Astrology offers clues and turns you into the detective in charge of your own case. It realigns you with your soul (or mind, if you prefer) as opposed to the seductive but harmful snare of our ego. I believe that the soul (or mind) is infinite: it never dies. In fact, it goes on to create future lives, which is why our birth chart indicates strengths to embrace and issues that we need to resolve in this lifetime so that we can graduate to the next level. Nothing is fixed and everything is changeable. With awareness and an honest approach to your own patterns of behaviour, choice is always available and a better future is yours to create.

'GONE RIGHT'
VS
'GONE WRONG'

Years of working with my intelligent, successful and oh-so-demanding clients, and observing the way that particular star patterns correlate to their experiences, behaviour and characteristics, have made it clear to me that any trait associated with any aspect of astrology has the potential to be either helpful or harmful. I call this 'gone right' versus 'gone wrong', and we see these dualities over and over again.

At its heart, Dynamic Astrology is the practice of applying astrological know-how in strategic ways to increase the helpful traits ('gone right') and reduce the impact of the harmful ones ('gone wrong'). You can change things that fail to serve you or that you simply don't like. With awareness and greater self-knowledge come the power to bring more acceptance, happiness and soul contentment into your life. When you master new ways to handle traits that have previously been the bane of your life, you'll feel like giving yourself a fist bump. It's such a liberating feeling.

A word of advice: don't be frightened of your 'gone wrong' side, also known as the dreaded 'shadow'. After all, everyone has one. Time after time, when people read their 'gone right' sections for the first time I see them nodding or smiling, and then I wait for it: they suddenly go quiet. I know they're reading their 'gone wrong' traits and pennies are dropping all over the place. But this opening up to self-awareness is the first step towards any kind of real self-improvement. In my own experience as a student, the most compassionate teachers I ever had rarely handed me sweets, treats or easy truths.

So, to paint a picture of 'gone right' characteristics versus 'gone wrong', let's use Taurus as an example. A positive trait for Taurus is talent. Many Taureans love to cultivate their own talents, as well as other people's. A 'gone wrong' Taurus trait is jealousy (one they share with their opposite sign, Scorpio). It isn't that every Taurus is necessarily suffering with the green-eyed monster, but it is likely to be showing up somewhere in a Taurus's life because jealousy is a trait that Taurus people are here on Earth to learn to overcome. And to contextualize the 'gone right' versus 'gone wrong' further, I've observed that a Taurus who is genuinely working with his or her own talents rarely suffers with personal jealousy. If they attract it from others, they must strive harder to work with grace and humility (which are both words associated with Taurus).

HOW TO
USE THIS BOOK

I wrote *The Signs* with the aim of making a complex subject accessible to everyone by focusing on three main areas of astrology: planets, signs and houses. Inevitably this means that there are lots of things I can't hope to cover, but astrology is so powerful that even a little knowledge goes a long way. I hope the book will serve as your guide to using astrology in practical ways to make real, positive change in your life. And then when you 'crack the code' you can help others who may be struggling to get on the surfboard and ride the waves of life.

You can read the book in one of two ways. Either flip straight to the section on your star sign and read all about your sign's helpful and harmful traits – its 'gone right' and 'gone wrong' – then use the 'Fix' of practical suggestions to reduce the 'gone wrong' and increase the 'gone right'. (By the way, you can, of course, do the same thing to deepen your understanding of other people's behaviour. It's fun and often uncannily accurate. Try looking up your partner's sign, or your colleague's, and see if its characteristics shed some light on anything that baffles or annoys you!)

The second way, if you prefer, is to delve a bit deeper and use the book to learn how to read birth charts and make your own interpretations.

A birth (or natal) chart is a snapshot of the alignment of the stars and planets at the time of your birth. Learning how to decode your chart by reading about the role of your star sign, your Moon and rising sign, as well as the alignment of the planets and placements of the houses, is enlightening and empowering. For example, identifying your rising sign (the sign in your first house at the moment you were born) helps you to understand how you are perceived by others, and opens the door towards self-discovery. When you know your Moon sign (the sign the Moon was in when you were born), you can figure out how to take more care of your emotional well-being, which will in turn improve your emotional intelligence. Knowing your partner's or child's Moon sign helps you to nourish them on an emotional level. (My son has Moon in Taurus, and Taurus is associated with a healthy appetite for good food, so I always feed him before addressing any emotional issues I may have with him!)

I will never get tired of watching as my clients experience the mental click when some aspect of their personality or personal experience comes into focus. Those 'aha' moments are deeply satisfying to them, and they can be for you, too. When you understand your chart and those of the key people in your life, you gain an invaluable perspective. You become more compassionate; personal and professional goals are easier to achieve and everyday life becomes less of a din and more of a tune. You stop fighting against the tides and go with the flow and the rhythms of life. Everything from physical and emotional well-being to career goals and previously tense relationships can suddenly feel much easier. I am not saying that everything will change overnight. It takes a little work and, let's face it, some people will always annoy us, but we can take control of how we react by hitting the pause button and analysing the root cause of their behaviour and, indeed, our reactions.

Imagine that you are now standing in an airport with only your passport and a map in your hand. A private jet is waiting. You're not quite sure where you're going but you intuitively know that something life-enhancing awaits. I am showing you the door to self-discovery. The map will provide the clues to help you find your personal treasure chest, but you have to navigate your own journey and take responsibility for your own decisions.

I know from my own experience of learning through astrology, and from the successes of my clients, that great things are possible. Remember, your birth chart is only ever sketched in pencil: it really is down to you whether you want to take the pen and make your mark. Forget how you were in the past. Be in this very moment and tune into your highest potential.

The future is in your hands.

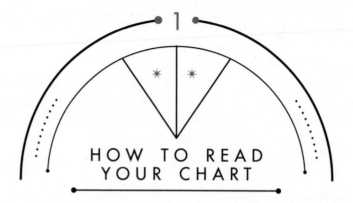

HOW TO READ YOUR CHART

Dynamic Astrology is based on the study and interpretation of birth charts, and the use of practical strategies to improve traits that do not work for us and boost the behaviours that do.

A birth chart is a snapshot of the sky, like an energetic scribble across space, at the moment when someone was born. A person's date, time and place of birth are used to calculate the position of the Sun, Moon and other planets, and to map how they fall into the signs and houses. (Don't worry, there are clear instructions on how to generate your own birth chart later in this chapter.)

This chapter shows you how to work with all the fundamentals you need so that you can interpret your own chart, and then, when you've figured out the way it works, you can move on to interpreting other people's charts. That's when things start to get really fun!

We will be working with three main areas: the planets, the signs and the houses. (Remember that everything in Dynamic Astrology works in threes.) When you've mastered the essentials of these three areas you'll be well on your way to deciphering the clues contained in your chart and cracking the most interesting code of them all: the code behind human behaviour.

Have a look at the example birth chart opposite.

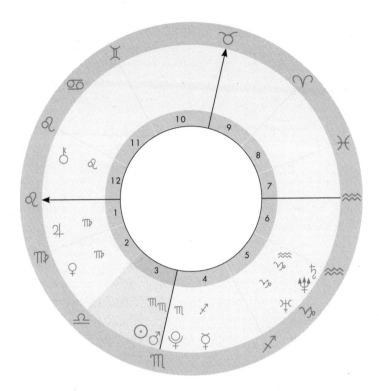

We will be breaking this chart down, step by step, so that you can understand the role of the planets, the signs and the houses, then begin to apply this knowledge to your own chart. We will return to this full example chart later in the chapter and reassemble it to show you how everything combines to build up interpretations.

Now have a look at the keys to the symbols for the different planets and signs, and start to familiarize yourself with them. At first you'll need to refer back to them every time you study a chart, but it won't be long before you start to recognize the symbols.

SIGNS	PLANETS
♈ Aries	☉ Sun
♉ Taurus	☽ Moon
♊ Gemini	☿ Mercury
♋ Cancer	♀ Venus
♌ Leo	♂ Mars
♍ Virgo	♃ Jupiter
♎ Libra	♄ Saturn
♏ Scorpio	♅ Uranus
♐ Sagittarius	♆ Neptune
♑ Capricorn	♇ Pluto
♒ Aquarius	⚷ Chiron
♓ Pisces	

I would suggest you pull up your own chart at this stage to refer to alongside the examples. (Just don't be alarmed if it all looks a little overwhelming: be patient!)

You can draw your own chart by going to the website www.dynamicastrology.com, then going to calculators and filling in the details of your date, time and place of birth. (Bear in mind that you will not be able to determine which houses the planets fall in if you do not have your time of birth to work with. In this instance, type 'time unknown' in the chart calculator. You will still be able to work with the planets and signs and I promise you there will be insights aplenty.) If it were me I would print the chart out and use a pencil to scribble notes about the effects of various elements, but I suppose I'm old school! Alternatively, here is a blank chart for you to record your birth chart, if you wish.

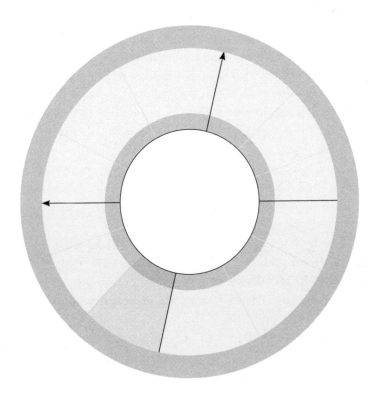

STEP ONE:
THE PLANETS

The first step is to identify each of the ten ruling planets and explore their relevance. Let's start with the Sun. The Sun, like all the planets, falls in a particular sign in your chart. Your star sign is the sign of the zodiac (Cancer, Pisces, Leo, etc.) that the Sun was in at the time of your birth. As you can see from the key to the planet symbols, there are nine other planets that we'll be working with but your star sign is the first one to use in order to begin your charting journey. Then you can move on to find out where the other planets fall in your chart. Please note that they are known as 'ruling planets' as each one is allocated to a sign. (And, technically, the Sun is a star and Pluto and Chiron are not in fact planets, but to make this as easy as possible we'll use the umbrella term 'planet' – just don't tell the astronomers!)

I call each planet in your chart the 'what'. As in, what does that planet mean for you?

Let's start by identifying your star sign in your own chart. Have a look for the Sun's symbol, using the planets key above and this example chart to guide you.

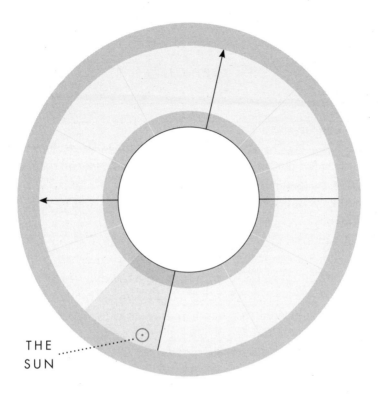

THE
SUN

What does this planet, the Sun, mean for you? In a nutshell, the Sun represents a person's ego, their self-identity. If you embrace the sign it falls in and use all of the 'gone right' characteristics of that sign, you are starred to shine with the brilliance of the Sun. If, however, you demonstrate the 'gone wrong' traits, you will be more aligned with your ego than your brilliance. Each of the ten planets we're going to be working with is associated with a particular area of your personality, with specific lessons to learn.

You will find much more detailed explanations of the role the Sun plays in your chart (as well as all the other planets) in 'The Planets' (pages 30–96).

STEP TWO:
THE SIGNS

The second step is to identify and explore the meaning and impact of the signs. You've already located the Sun in your chart. Now make a note of the Zodiac symbol in line with it, towards the centre of the chart. This represents your star sign.

Our example has the Sun, which is the planet, in Scorpio, which is the sign.

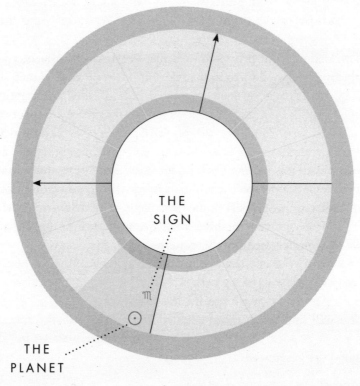

THE
SIGN

THE
PLANET

What does this sign mean? The sign in a chart represents the 'how'. How will this sign play out for this person?

Using our example, this person has the Sun in Scorpio, so they would flick to the section on Scorpio in 'The Signs' (pages 207–23) to find out more about how this sign plays out in relation to their ego and self-identity. To simplify, for Scorpio people to shine they must learn how to handle power, depth, transformation and change. 'Gone right', they have depth and stand confidently in their own power, using it to empower others and to make great changes both internally and externally. 'Gone wrong', they are weak-willed and often become manipulative and jealous of anyone they consider more powerful. They may attempt to steal power or disempower others ruthlessly with put-downs and manipulation tactics.

(Of course this is a simplified interpretation and there is more detail on Scorpio and all of the others in 'The Signs'.)

Throughout your process of learning to work with charts, you'll be flicking back and forth to the relevant pages for each planet, sign and house. It's a good idea to make a note of which descriptions resonate with you intuitively and you'll see that there are spaces for you to do so throughout the book. Be honest, especially when working with your own chart. Find an equal amount of helpful and harmful traits, jot them down, then read the 'Fix' to understand how to increase the 'gone right' and reduce the 'gone wrong'. Only then will you progress. I am a firm believer that when we write something down we remember it more readily and free up valuable brain space to collect more information.

STEP THREE:
THE HOUSES

The third step is to explore the areas of life affected by each house, by looking at the planets and signs within each one. You should have your chart in front of you, have identified your Sun and be aware of which sign it falls in. If you know the time you were born then you can also figure out which house your Sun falls in. The houses are identified by the numbers listed 1–12 on the inner rim of your chart.

So, what do the houses mean for you? Each house is associated with various areas of life, such as sibling relationships, or assets and personal finances. Taken together, the houses make up what I call the 'where'. 'Where' will each planet and its sign play out for you? In which aspect of your life? What are they trying to tell you?

You will find detailed information on each of the houses and their various associations in 'The Houses' (pages 286–331), but in a nutshell, and going back to our example, the third house is where you will learn about communication (among other things).

So, in this instance we are using Sun in Scorpio in the third house.

A person with the Sun in Scorpio in the third house needs to learn how to communicate with empathy and feeling. (Scorpio is all about empathy and feeling!) They should learn how to tune into their depth without being too intense or so secretive that it scares people away. They must grasp how to communicate in ways that empower themselves and others, to resist jealousy, manipulation and control, which are detrimental, and be confident enough to stand in their own power.

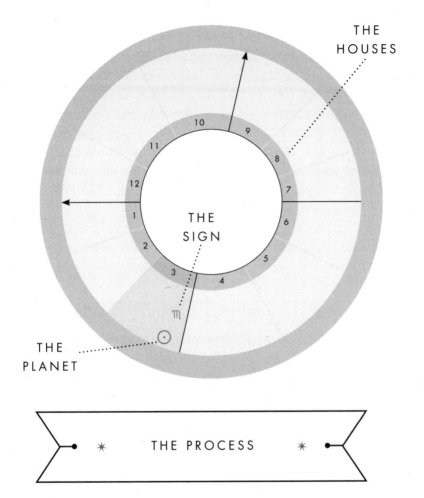

THE
HOUSES

THE
SIGN

THE
PLANET

THE PROCESS

In a nutshell, this is the process you'll be using throughout the book. You're going to need the symbol keys to interpret your chart. You first need to identify the ten planets. Then, working with each planet in turn, flick to its section in 'The Planets (pages 30–96) and read all about the behaviours associated with it. Use your intuition and jot down the traits that fly out at you. Then you need to identify the sign right next to each planet, as we did in the example of Sun in Scorpio, and flick to the relevant section in 'The Signs' (pages 97–285) to repeat the exercise and jot down any associations, 'gone right' and 'gone wrong', that particularly resonate. Finally, if you have your time of birth you can locate the houses that the planets and signs reside in, by checking the inner rim of numbers 1–12. Then flick to the relevant section in 'The Houses' (pages 286–331), making notes all the way. You'll be surprised at just how quickly you pick this up, and when the revelations begin, you will be hooked!

✳ NOW LET'S CHART! ✳

Pull up your birth chart and identify the line with the arrow tip pointing to nine o'clock, as if looking at a clock face. This line indicates your rising sign and marks the start of the first house in your chart. You're going to work anti-clockwise around the chart, making a note of which planet falls in which sign and within which house.

Let's go back to our example of the person with the Sun in Scorpio in the third house. Here's their full chart, the one we saw at the beginning of the chapter, with all the other planets and their signs distributed throughout the various houses. You'll see that the arrow tip is pointing to the Leo symbol in the outer rim of the chart. So this person's rising sign is Leo.

Perhaps some of your houses are empty and others are crowded with planets, as in the example chart. I always tell my clients when they have lots of planets in a certain house that the planets are

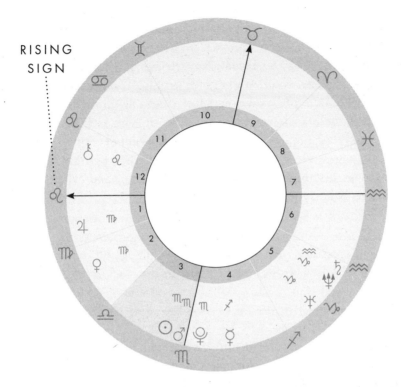

RISING
SIGN

trying to get their attention. They're telling the person that he or she needs to look more deeply at them, their meanings and the area of life governed by that particular house.

And if you happen to have an empty house, don't worry – it doesn't mean there's nothing happening in this area of your life. That would be impossible. If you have an empty third house, for example, does it mean you cannot communicate? No! We can all communicate, but some people are more skilled at it than others. When you come across an empty house, identify the sign (or signs) on the outer edge of the house and use the information in 'The Signs' (pages 97–285) for more clues on how to improve the area of life associated with that particular house. By identifying the clues (planets and signs) within the third house of your chart, for example, you will become more skilled in the art of communication as opposed to working mindlessly with the 'gone wrong' traits associated with the sign that governs the house.

I will tell you a quick story to paint a little picture. The second house is the house of assets (among other things) and one of my clients began visibly to panic as she gazed upon her empty second house. I had to remind her that she was actually in a position to buy a whole football team outright, so in her case she just needed fewer clues in that house than the rest of us! The sign around the edge of her second house was Leo and she made her fortune and found fame within the entertainment industry (a very 'Leo' profession).

In my experience, any planets above the line going through the centre of the chart (from nine to three on the clock face) describe behaviours and traits easily observed by others, or perhaps traits and skills of which a person is conscious and happy to display openly for others to see. Activity underneath the line is sometimes said to indicate hidden depths. Often, though, it signals traits that are hidden from the untrained eye, either by that person's choice or simply because they are unaware themselves of what's going on. Whichever way it goes, until that person is ready to do some work or 'come out', many skills (and great potential) lie dormant or are displayed as 'gone wrong'. It will be down to you as the codebreaker to decipher which is the case for each chart and person you study.

Learning to interpret birth charts requires a bit of practice, so don't worry if you need to take some time to read and reread this chapter, absorb the concepts – flipping between the chapters on the signs, the planets and the houses to familiarize yourself with the language – and take notes. It's not so complicated when you know how, and you soon will. Remember that Dynamic Astrology is a code, and a chart is a map brimming with clues to reveal the real you.

If you've ever learned to drive a car, you'll know that at first it feels as if there are way too many things to remember at once. You believe that you will never be able to grasp even the basics, let alone think about watching out for crazy drivers on the roads. Then, all of a sudden, the penny drops and off you go. Learning to navigate your astrology chart is a little like learning how to drive a car. *The Signs* shows you the theory of how to drive your vehicle but you have to practise on the road of everyday life!

THE GREAT INTERPRETATION

We're going to be using Salvador Dalí's birth chart to study in more detail how the signs, planets and houses need to be cross-referenced in order to understand what the chart is actually telling us. It has been labelled clearly so you can refer back and double-check anything you're unsure about.

FIRST HOUSE / RISING SIGN: CANCER

SECOND HOUSE: LEO (EMPTY)

THIRD HOUSE: VIRGO (EMPTY)

FOURTH HOUSE: LIBRA (EMPTY)

FIFTH HOUSE: SCORPIO (EMPTY)

SIXTH HOUSE: SAGITTARIUS –
URANUS IN SAGITTARIUS

SEVENTH HOUSE: CAPRICORN –
CHIRON IN AQUARIUS

EIGHTH HOUSE: AQUARIUS – SATURN IN AQUARIUS

NINTH HOUSE: PISCES – MOON IN ARIES

TENTH HOUSE: ARIES – JUPITER IN ARIES,
VENUS IN TAURUS

ELEVENTH HOUSE: TAURUS – SUN, MERCURY AND
MARS IN TAURUS

TWELFTH HOUSE: GEMINI – PLUTO IN GEMINI,
NEPTUNE IN CANCER

I have mapped out a few aspects from Dalí's chart and offer you my interpretations as an example.

SALVADOR DALÍ / MALE / 11 MAY 1904, WED /
8:45 AM UT +0:00 / FIGUERES, SPAIN

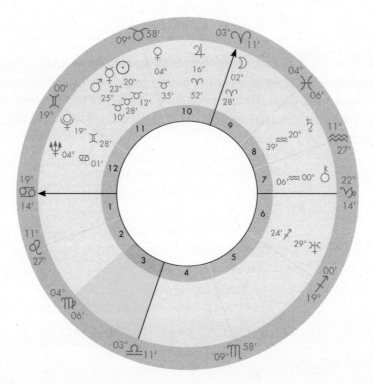

SUN IN TAURUS IN THE ELEVENTH HOUSE

The Sun represents our self-identity. If we unlock the innate potential associated with the sign in which it falls, this is how we are destined to shine. Taurus is all about learning to cultivate talent, and the eleventh house is the house of the masses – as in anything that connects to the masses and to the media. Dalí was a multi-skilled artist with great talent that was nurtured from a very young age by his parents. He enjoyed success across several media plat-forms, such as painting, photography, sculpture and film, and was indeed recognized and appreciated by the masses. He also recognized the talents of others and collaborated with other greats: all traits for Taurus 'gone right'.

MOON IN ARIES IN THE NINTH HOUSE

The Moon represents our emotions and, often, the sign it falls in indicates how we perceive our mother to be or have been. Dalí was famed for having terrible temper outbursts, which is quite common in this Moon sign. Aries can explode, then calm down quickly, wondering why everyone has run away. The ninth house is the house of foreign culture, overseas travel, academia, truth and spirituality (on some levels), then self-righteousness and ignorance on the 'gone wrong' spectrum. Dalí got into trouble at his art school when he declared that no teacher was good enough to judge his work, which is typical of a gifted ninth-house person with an explosive fire-sign Moon sitting within. Dalí's mother and father were very spiritual, though perhaps not always in an entirely healthy way: they took the young Dalí to his elder brother's grave and told him repeatedly that he was his brother's reincarnation. It seems likely that this had a significant impact on him. Spirituality, like anything else, can 'go right' or 'go wrong'!

SATURN IN AQUARIUS IN THE EIGHTH HOUSE

Saturn represents the authority in our lives and we need to learn patiently how to master the sign that it falls within. The eighth house reveals our attitudes towards power, sex, drugs and rock 'n' roll (among other things). Dalí's father shaped his attitude towards sex from an early age: he repeatedly showed him awful pictures of people riddled with sexually transmitted diseases to frighten him off all things sexual. This led to a rather detached and voyeuristic attitude to sex (all very Aquarian traits as Aquarians are also masters of long-distance and virtual relationships). He remained a virgin until he married, liked to watch his wife enjoying intimate relations with other people and, although he denied it at the time, before he met her he fell in love with a man, which is rather common for people with a strong Aquarian influence: they are often attracted to people of both sexes. Dalí was rebellious, shocking, eccentric and, in my opinion, an artistic genius, probably borderline crazy too: all traits associated with Aquarius. (You can decide for yourself which you think are 'gone wrong' or 'gone right' traits.) Dalí also seemed to have a gift for creating art that was verging on prophetic. I attribute this to his Uranus in Sagittarius (the sign of Truth, sometimes known as the Prophet) connected to his Neptune (planet of Intuition) and Saturn and Chiron falling in Aquarius, which is all about awareness of a higher dimension.

EXERCISE:
THE MAGIC THREE

Now here is a quick exercise for you. This will help to get you in the swing of interpreting things for yourself, and focuses on identifying and interpreting three key signs. You will need your planet and sign symbol keys to help you, along with the chart you wish to interpret.

Find your Magic Three:

1. **Star (Sun) sign.** This gives insight into your core nature, indicates your ego desires and the positive traits to embrace for soul contentment. Embracing the 'gone right' will help your brilliance shine through.

   ....
   ....

2. **Rising sign.** This sign directs you towards the path of self-discovery as it describes personality and character, and is the sign you wear outwardly. (You need your time of birth for this one, as the rising sign changes every two hours.) You can identify it by following the line that runs from the centre of your chart to the point at nine o'clock on the outer rim.

   ....
   ....

3. **Moon sign.** This indicates emotional intelligence and gives clues on how a person reacts to life, as well as showing how to meet your own or another person's emotional needs. It also reveals your experience of your mother, and if you're a woman, how you will mother your own children, if you have them.

   ....
   ....

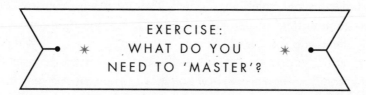

EXERCISE:
WHAT DO YOU
NEED TO 'MASTER'?

Another exercise, if you're feeling adventurous, is to find out which sign you are required to 'master' in this life by locating Saturn in your chart and identifying which sign it falls in.

Read more about Saturn on page 71, then flick to 'The Signs' (pages 97–285) to read about your Saturn sign. If you know your time of birth, you will also be able to see what house Saturn falls in so go to 'The Houses' (pages 286–331) and read all about it. Use the table below to make a note of the sign and house Saturn falls in for you. You can also jot notes as you're doing your reading, whenever you feel a truth hit you. Then read back over those notes and see what interpretations you can draw, from both an intuitive and a logical perspective.

PLANET	SIGN	HOUSE
Saturn		

....
....
....

You're now ready to begin the journey of self-discovery by interpreting your own chart and then moving on to the charts of people you know or wish to know on a deeper level. Remember that nothing is fixed, only loosely sketched in as potential, so do not judge anyone solely on a chart. They may have transcended their 'gone wrong' or chosen to ignore their 'gone right': we can never be completely sure. But as you become more skilled at interpreting, your own intuition will guide you towards insights that not only make sense to you but prove helpful in everyday life.

I have opened the door to astrology for many people and this book is your very own key, ready for you to use to unlock the secret code of the stars. Will you crack the code? I believe so!

This chapter is dedicated to Alan Turing,
one of the greatest codebreakers in our history.

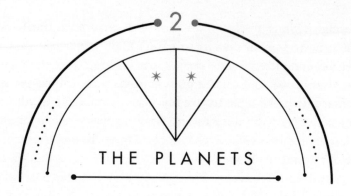

THE PLANETS

The first step in your star-based journey of self-discovery involves understanding the role played by the planets in your chart. In Dynamic Astrology each planet represents a facet of who we are. I call it the 'what', and the fundamental question you're asking is: '*What* does each planet represent and how does it impact on me?'

To answer this question you need, first, to know a little about the primary areas of character with which each planet is associated, then to cross-reference it with information about the sign each one falls in. Remember, if the planet is the 'what', the sign is the 'how'. As in, 'How may this particular area of my life play out?'

For example, if you wish to learn more about how you love, first study Venus (the planet that embodies our behaviour and attitudes towards romantic love) and then the sign it falls in for you: this will give you clues to interpret Venus's impact in your own life. To deepen your understanding of how you think and what interests you, study Mercury (associated with the mind, from intellect to decision-making style) and the sign it falls in for you. And so on. (If you need a reminder of how to identify the planets and their corresponding signs, take a look at the example chart on page 24, where I talk you through the process in more detail.)

The planets of our solar system are named after the gods of Roman mythology, all of whom had very different personalities.

Aspects of these personalities play into our astrological under-standing. So, Jupiter, the largest planet in our solar system, which at last count had at least sixty moons compared to Earth's one, is named after the king of the gods. Jupiter is the ruling planet of Sagittarius, the sign that typically likes to go large in all areas. Uranus, who ruled the skies and heavens, is the ruling planet of Aquarius, an air sign known for generating ideas: Aquarians are usually so ahead of their time that they feel as if they've been plucked from the heavens. Pluto, also known as Hades, is king of the underworld and rules Scorpio, which is all about power, transformation, depth – and 'gone wrong', the darker sides of life.

Every one of us has all the planets somewhere in our charts. Some work well for us. Others need a little more discipline to behave themselves. This chapter is full of the information you need about them and the practical tips that will enable you to master their influence. Remember that awareness is the first step. An action plan will soon follow.

HOW TO WORK
✳ WITH THE PLANETS ✳
IN YOUR CHART

Planets have an association with a specific sign and a specific house, a default setting, if you like. When you read the individual sections on the different planets, you'll see that their default setting is listed. The planet is said to be the ruler, or the ruling planet, of its natural home. So, for example, the Moon (primarily associated with emotions and your emotional well-being) rules Cancer and the fourth house.

For many people, the planets – or some of them – actually do fall into the default settings on their particular birth chart, but this isn't necessarily the case. For example, you might have the Moon in Scorpio in the seventh house: you would have an emotional need (Moon) for deep and intense (Scorpio) relationships (seventh house), with plenty of opportunities for transformation (Scorpio again). Avoiding frivolous hook-ups (because Scorpio isn't into superficial) will take care of your emotional well-being (Moon being strongly associated with how to take care of your emotional needs). The Moon (and all the other planets) will play out very differently depending on which sign it's in and in which house it falls.

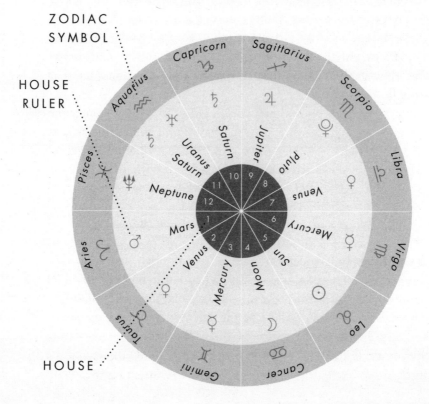

ZODIAC SYMBOL

HOUSE RULER

HOUSE

If you imagine that each element of your chart – planets, signs and houses – is positioned as if on its own clock face, then sometimes those three clock faces overlap so that the elements stay with their family members, but often they don't. When a planet falls in its natural sign, its influence is typically more powerful. But they may fall differently in your chart. For now, let's keep it simple and get started on figuring out which sign and house your own planets fall in.

Have a look at the example chart above. This shows you the Moon in Cancer in the fourth house, which is its default setting. By now you will hopefully be feeling more familiar with the layout of birth charts, but to remind you: the two symbols within each house are the planet and sign symbols, in this case Moon and Cancer. The inner section is what we call a house, the number of which is on the inner rim (in this case it's the fourth). And the sign symbol in the outer rim of the chart tells you which sign is resident in that particular house.

Now, turning to your chart, you're going to work through the steps laid out below to identify the main planets and their signs within your own birth chart so you may begin to interpret the clues they hold. At the end of the section on each planet there is space for you to jot notes, and a table where you can keep your own personal summary of each planet's 'gone wrong' and 'gone right' traits, according to its sign placement in your chart. Also, you should make a note of the house it falls in.

STEP ONE.   Using the planet symbol keys on page 12, identify all the planets in your chart and note the sign each one falls in.

STEP TWO.   Read the information in this chapter about what the planets represent. Pay attention to any details that seem particularly relevant to you. Make notes!

STEP THREE. Go to 'The Signs' (pages 97–285) and read about the sign for each of your planets, bearing in mind what you know about what that planet represents. Make a note of any of the traits ('gone wrong' and 'gone right') that jump out at you.

STEP FOUR. Check which house the planet falls in. (Don't worry too much about the houses for now. We will be working with them in more detail in 'The Houses' (pages 286–331). For now just jot them down.)

STEP FIVE. Create your personal rundown of each planet's influence in your life by filling in the tables with information on the 'gone wrong' and 'gone right' traits that seem to be playing out for you, according to what sign each planet falls in. Remember, you can only fully figure out whether a planet is going 'wrong' or 'right' for you by reading about the 'gone wrong' and 'gone right' traits of the sign in which it falls in your chart. So, for example, Moon represents emotions (among other things). If it falls in Aquarius in your chart you need to study Aquarius in 'The Signs' (pages 97–285), its 'gone wrong' and 'gone right' traits, and see how they apply to your emotional life. Having said that, the planets *do* exert their own energies, irrespective of which sign they fall in. So, although you must cross-reference each one with its specific sign to understand your own situation, it is possible to say that, for example, when Moon 'goes wrong' it *tends* to be defensive or over-emotional. When it 'goes right' it *tends* to be caring and emotionally intelligent. There are general clues that the planets give off, but these require attention when you cross-reference them with the traits assigned to their sign. Don't worry too much about this for now. Just get started and all will become clear. Listen to your intuition: it will tell you which traits matter most to you personally.

FAST TRACK
TO THE PLANETS!

Here's a summary of some prominent life themes that the planets represent in your chart. Please note that this is not an exhaustive list of all the astrological features that can influence a person's behaviour and life choices, but it's enough to give you a very full picture of what your chart is trying to tell you. And, as I said previously, three of these bodies (the Sun, Pluto and Chiron) are not technically planets at all, but for the purpose of keeping things simple, we'll let that label sit!

⊙ THE SUN
Associated with: experience of father and fathering;
ego and self-identity; soul-path.

☽ THE MOON
Associated with: past-life characteristics (especially
negative ones); emotions and emotional needs;
experience of mother and mothering.

☿ MERCURY
Associated with: the mind in general, including what
interests you intellectually; your sense of timing; how
you think and communicate; intelligence.

♀ VENUS
Associated with: love; style and appearance;
expectations; the female aspect of ourselves; how we
view money and other worldly pleasures.

♂ MARS
Associated with: sexuality; attraction; physical
energy; basic drive and motivation.

♃ JUPITER
Associated with: skills, talents and abilities; life
lessons; extreme behaviour and over-indulgence.

♄ SATURN
Associated with: past-life karma and life lessons;
attitudes to stability and commitment; maturing
and ageing.

URANUS
Associated with: awareness, especially self-awareness; change and rebellion; inventiveness.

NEPTUNE
Associated with: insight and intuition; our deepest fears and loss; faith, hope and dreams; the areas where we need to let go.

PLUTO
Associated with: power – our own and our relationship with other people's; motivations; transformations, including birth, death and rebirth.

CHIRON
Associated with: deep wounds; spirituality; healing.

THE SUN

ASSOCIATED WITH: EXPERIENCE OF
FATHER AND FATHERING; SELF-IMPORTANCE,
EGO AND SELF-IDENTITY; SOUL-PATH.

RULING PLANET OF: LEO THE LIONHEART

DEFAULT HOUSE: FIFTH

SUN 'GONE WRONG' IS: ARROGANT, SELFISH,
EGO-DRIVEN AND NARCISSISTIC

SUN 'GONE RIGHT' IS: GENEROUS, HUMBLE,
LOVING, BENEVOLENT AND NOBLE

The Sun is so large that more than 1.3 million Earths could fit inside it. Its rays are the energy source for all life on Earth: without them we could not survive. Although the Sun is at the centre of our solar system, most forms of Western astrology use Earth as the centre and look to the Sun in the heavens when calculating charts.

It takes twelve months for the Sun to move through all of the signs. During that time it illuminates the energy of the sign it's in, allowing us the opportunity to shine.

As we've already seen, the star sign is the single piece of astrology that most people are aware of, and there's a reason for that. Given its absolutely fundamental role in the existence of life on Earth, it should be no surprise that the Sun is a hugely influential presence in your chart, and on your life. It's also our starting point as we begin to delve more deeply into the role of the planets.

⊖ ASSOCIATIONS ⊖

I. FATHER AND FATHERING

The Sun has a masculine energy and can shed light on the relationship we have with our father or any male authority figure, such as a grandfather or an influential teacher. It often indicates traits that we have inherited from a father figure. So, for example, if a person has Sun in Pisces it might suggest either a very intuitive artistic or spiritual father or one that is completely absent in some way. (Both heightened intuition and, less helpfully, a tendency to duck out of life when it gets challenging are very Pisces traits.)

My own spiritual father, the late great Dr Akong Tulku Rinpoche, who was a key figure in bringing Tibetan Buddhism to the West, had the Sun in Sagittarius and was the very definition of Sagittarius 'gone right'. He embodied 'Truth', which is one of Sagittarius's defining traits, and was a man of few words but those he spoke penetrated the superficial and hit your core. He ran social projects and outreach programmes all over the world, so many that his own administrators could hardly keep up. When he died suddenly they were stunned to discover the extent of his work. And he always practised what he preached. Whenever I am in a tough situation, I ask myself, 'What would Rinpoche do?' and I follow the answer. I can think of no other person who embodies 'gone right', of the Sun in Sagittarius, like he did. I have the Sun in Aquarius, the eighth house, so my experience of father is one who works for humanity (Aquarius), with many charities (Aquarius), and the eighth house is often about transformational experiences. It is safe to say that Rinpoche woke me up on some level (Aquarius is all about waking up), changed my life and set me on a much deeper path.

2. EGO AND SELF-IDENTITY

The Sun indicates the ego in terms of who we 'think' we are and how we identify ourselves. When I speak of ego, people often initially think of a sort of peacock, but ego isn't just about showing off and buying fast cars and big houses. It's really about being trapped in a superficial reality. Ego is something that takes us away from our innate spiritual potential. It often drives how we wish to be perceived by others. I always say that it's fine to covet nice things and want to be successful, but what's the point of being successful if you have no good people to share it with? And when it comes at great expense to other beings, or indeed to our own true purpose, obsessive striving (whether for status, physical beauty or money) certainly isn't positive.

You don't have to shave off your hair and renounce all material pleasures to reduce ego but being the most authentic version of yourself and keeping your focus on what is actually important are both key to your journey towards self-awareness and your progression in life. I believe that we are spiritual beings having a physical existence, and living a purely selfish life is no life at all.

In my experience, and that of other people in my circle, when a person's ego becomes too inflated the rug is usually pulled out from under them. In this way the ego is brought down to size. Dr Akong Tulku Rinpoche used to say, 'Ego is like a weed: no matter how many times it dies, it just keeps on growing.' If you want to avoid the unceremonious rug-pulling, it is wise to stay humble, which is characteristic of the Sun 'gone right'.

To use the positive qualities of the Sun to their maximum, we must become aware of what holds us back and keeps us from growing, and learn more about ourselves in a non-egotistical way. For example, the Sun shows how you may shine in life by embracing the positive qualities of the sign it falls in, and also indicates how you love others. Of course, when you are truly ready to love another person you will be prepared to put their well-being before your own. Love for self is important (the opposite implies a lack of self-respect that is obviously damaging) but not when it turns into narcissism, which is pure Sun 'gone wrong', summed up by the selfie-obsessed folk who seem fuelled by ego, driven by how they 'wish' to be perceived.

Sun 'gone right' gives a person the ability to shine with all the 'gone right' traits of the sign the Sun falls in for them. Just as the energy of the Sun keeps us alive, people with a 'gone right' Sun are usually confident in their own skins, creative, fun to be around and extremely loving individuals, irrespective of their Sun sign. As soon as they walk into a room they light it up and make people feel happier with their generous natures and sunny dispositions.

3. SOUL-PATH

Our star sign is a strong indicator of our soul-path, and whatever sign it falls in will give us clues as to how we can fulfil our deeper purpose in life. I was taught that in order to fulfil our soul's potential and deeper purpose we must embrace the 'gone right' traits of our sign before we leave this life. There are 'jobs' each of our signs is tasked with here on Earth. You will pick up clues by finding the sign your Sun falls in and reading more about it in 'The Signs' (pages 97–285)! As a starting point, when you flick to the information about your star sign, take note of the 'name' allocated to it. For example, if you are Sagittarius you must strive to become 'The Inspiration' (having first found your own source, naturally).

─⊖ HOW IT PLAYS OUT ⊖─

To give you a fuller picture of how all this might play out, let's look at the example of a person with the Sun in Taurus in the second house (Taurus's natural house, or its default setting). 'Gone wrong' may mean that the person is very driven to accrue worldly possessions: their ego insists that they need tangible assets to help them feel valuable, whole and important. (Taurus is practical and loves to build and produce things, but 'gone wrong' has a tendency to focus too much on acquiring 'stuff'.) The deeper lesson for them is to check what they are building in life, in particular how they are making their money, and assess whether it makes them feel productive. For example, a person with this star sign in this house placement would not be content on a soul level to be a trust-fund baby. They would need to build something for themselves in life that adds to their sense of worth.

The Sun in Gemini, the ninth house, on the other hand, suggests a person who has the potential to shine in the area of communication and is usually smart, highly educated and cultured. They may seem almost prophet-like in their wisdom and their ability to connect and commune with others. (These are traits derived from a combination of Sun, Gemini and the ninth house.) That's the 'gone right' manifestation. If it's 'gone wrong', this person needs to study and to avoid ignorance and self-righteousness to reach their full potential.

The Sun in Scorpio in the third house indicates a person who has the capacity to be powerful and empathetic (Scorpio), to shine (the Sun) in the area of communication (third house). 'Gone wrong', someone with this alignment can be secretive, inclined to keep their thoughts to themselves (thoughts and mental processes are associated with the third house), manipulative and controlling (all typical of Scorpio 'gone wrong').

—⊖ HERE'S YOUR SPACE ⊖—

Studying the sign and house placement of the Sun in your chart can show you how to shine in life. By harnessing your star sign's energy and maximizing its 'gone right' traits you will nourish your soul and move away from being overly driven by the unconscious demands of ego.

Having found your Sun, flip to the relevant sign in 'The Signs' (pages 97–285) and read all about its 'gone wrong' and 'gone right' traits, bearing in mind what you now know the Sun represents. Use the space below to jot down anything that jumps out at you. You're looking for things that associate with your experience of fathers and fathering, anything related to ego and the way you've built up your sense of identity, and anything that connects with a sense of soul purpose. Trust your intuition to guide you. You can also make a note here of the house your Sun falls in, ready for you to build on your interpretations when you read 'The Houses' (pages 286–331).

And one more reminder for your learning: a 'gone right' Sun is simply defined as one that allies more with the 'gone right' than the 'gone wrong' traits of the sign it falls in, in relation to a particular aspect of your character or life. It doesn't matter what sign it falls in, so it's not that Sun in Aries is 'bad' or Sun in Gemini is 'great'. They can all be great! The crucial thing is that you try, when you examine your own chart honestly for clues, to identify the 'gone wrong' or 'gone right' traits of that particular sign in relation to your own experience. As always there are no black or white rules. You are the one who gets to decide what constitutes 'gone wrong' or 'gone right' for you because you are in control of reading and interpreting your signs. It's an intuitive practice that gets easier the more you do it and the more honest you are with yourself.

SUN GONE WRONG	SUN GONE RIGHT

THE MOON

ASSOCIATED WITH: PAST-LIFE CHARACTERISTICS
(ESPECIALLY NEGATIVE ONES); EMOTIONS AND
EMOTIONAL NEEDS; EXPERIENCE OF MOTHER
AND MOTHERING

RULING PLANET OF: CANCER THE GUARDIAN

DEFAULT HOUSE: FOURTH

MOON 'GONE WRONG' IS: REACTIVE, MEAN,
DEFENSIVE AND OVER-EMOTIONAL

MOON 'GONE RIGHT' IS: CREATIVE,
EMOTIONALLY INTELLIGENT, SENSITIVE AND KIND

The Moon spends approximately two and half days in each sign and moves around one degree every two hours so a full cycle takes less than one month. Relatively speaking, the Moon is not too far from Earth (only about 239,000 miles), which is why astrologers believe that it impacts us deeply.

Throughout history and across all cultures it has been believed that the Moon influences human behaviour. The term 'lunacy' dates from the sixteenth century when it referred specifically to a form of madness that came and went with the waxing and waning of the Moon. In many Asian countries, full and new moons, as well as eclipses, are believed to be sacred days when the results of what we do and say are magnified. For this reason many Buddhist monasteries take a vow of silence during these phases of the Moon to limit the potential for any bad karma to be generated. One thing is for sure: the Moon's gravity gives our oceans their tides and impacts on all large bodies of water. And up to 60 per cent of an adult human body is water. In my experience, the Moon is critically influential in astrology.

⊖ ASSOCIATIONS ⊖

1. EMOTIONS AND EMOTIONAL NEEDS

Throughout history the Moon has been associated with the energy of emotions and feelings. Its position in your chart can reveal a huge amount about what you need on an emotional level and, in particular, to feel safe and secure. Looking into the way the Moon's influence plays out in your life will certainly pay off as you boost your ability to nurture yourself and others.

A 'gone right' Moon (whatever the sign it falls in) tends to make a person emotionally strong and stable, protective and caring. These are its general planet-specific traits but, remember, you won't get a full picture of how it's playing out for you until you add in the all-important layer of traits from the sign it falls in for you. Of course, a 'gone wrong' Moon is likely to manifest in the other way. A 'gone right' Moon in a chart also tends to indicate a kind person with heightened emotional intelligence and strong intuition. Typically these people are balanced, in tune with the tides of life and in control of their own emotions.

2. PAST-LIFE CHARACTERISTICS

Some astrologers feel that your current Moon sign was the Sun sign in your previous life's chart. Irrespective of whether you believe in past lives or not, I can tell you that my experience of working with clients suggests that the Moon does indeed indicate negative tendencies by sign. So, if your moon sign is Aquarius, for example, it's particularly important that you move away from Aquarius 'gone wrong' traits and use the memory of Aquarius 'gone right' (which will certainly be lodged in your subconscious somewhere) for this life.

3. MOTHERS AND MOTHERING

Moon shows what type of experience one has with one's own mother or female guardian. The first relationship anyone has with a woman is with their mother and it's prudent to listen carefully when someone describes their experiences and relationship with her: a man with unresolved mother issues may be difficult as he may have become scared of emotion, making him either cold and devoid of it, or unable to control his emotions, like an immature child.

A 'gone right' Moon reveals a healthy relationship with and attitude towards one's own mother. A 'gone wrong' Moon often indicates a challenging relationship with the mother that may lead to uncontrolled emotions and a highly reactive person. The specific reactions are based upon the Moon's exact placement but, for example, a woman who over-sexualizes her appearance to gain attention usually has a 'gone wrong' Moon. A man who fixates on the breast usually has issues with his own Moon, which leads to dependence and unrealistic expectations in a relationship. For men, their Moon can indicate what characteristics they are searching for in a life partner.

The Moon may also hold clues as to how we mother our children, if we have them. For example, a person with a 'gone wrong' Moon in Aries is likely to push their children to their limits and be extremely competitive, wanting them to be first at everything. A classic 'tiger mum'. 'Gone right', they simply want the very best for their offspring and, if pushed, will fight for them to the very death – all very Aries traits. I have the Moon in Capricorn, and even though I was a very young mother, boundaries, bedtime and structure were implemented very quickly in our household – all very Capricorn traits.

By the way, if you're feeling alarmed by the focus on 'gone wrong' traits, especially in some of these very important and emotive areas, remember that the whole point of Dynamic Astrology is to increase your awareness and empower you to make positive changes where you want to. Nothing in the stars is written in stone! And, of course, it's not that all of this will apply to you personally, though some of it definitely will – if you're being honest!

⊖ HOW IT PLAYS OUT ⊖

To give you a sense of how this might work overall, take the example of a person with Moon in Libra in the tenth house, of status. This will often mean that the person is in need (remember, Moon indicates our emotional needs) of a relationship (Libra is all about relationships: they hate to feel alone) that bestows honour and status to them (all tenth-house traits). It's unlikely that this person would settle for a relationship that didn't enhance their status and make them 'look good' on some level. (We've probably all got a friend who's had a string of Burberry model-esque boyfriends, whom she loved to be seen with even though they were no good for her. All very Moon 'gone wrong' in Libra!) The deeper lesson for somebody with this particular alignment is the need to fine-tune the relationship they have with themselves and to nourish their own emotions without the need for external validation.

A person with the Moon in Cancer in the fourth house (all three astrological elements in their default setting) would likely be sensitive and kind (reactive if 'gone wrong'), nurturing and totally focused on providing security (traits of both Cancer and the fourth house) for him- or herself and their immediate family. Family (strongly associated with the fourth house) would be very important to this person and if their birth or immediate family unit was disjointed they would move to create an alternative family to satisfy their emotional need for a strong connection to a 'clan'. This person has an overwhelming need to 'belong' and that can be helpful or harmful, depending on what sort of people they align with. I call this placement the 'Mafia': it's all about 'family'.

If you don't know what house your Moon (or any of the subsequent planets) is in, don't worry: you can still uncover a huge amount by reading about the planet and the sign it falls in. For example, if a person has the Moon in Aries, you don't need to know its house placement to understand that, 'gone wrong', they would have an emotional need to compete with everyone and be the very best. I know a man with this placement and he cannot handle not coming first on any level. He literally has emotional meltdowns if he loses, even at tennis. I suggested he stop playing competitive sports! 'Gone right', a person with this placement would be driven by their own emotional need to be the very best version of themselves, dynamic and self-motivated.

—⊖ HERE'S YOUR SPACE ⊖—

Studying the sign and house placement of the Moon in your chart can give you clues as to how best to care for your emotional well-being and increase your gut-level intuition.

Having found your Moon, flip to the relevant sign in 'The Signs' (pages 97–285) and study its 'gone wrong' and 'gone right' traits, bearing in mind what you now know the Moon represents. Use this space to jot down anything that jumps out at you. You're looking for anything that associates with your own emotional well-being and emotional needs, your experience of mothers and mothering, and anything that suggests it might be connected with a negative past-life association. You can also make a note here of the house your Moon falls in.

MOON GONE WRONG	MOON GONE RIGHT

MERCURY

ASSOCIATED WITH: THE MIND IN GENERAL, INCLUDING THOUGHTS, WHAT INTERESTS YOU INTELLECTUALLY; YOUR SENSE OF TIMING; HOW YOU THINK AND COMMUNICATE; INTELLIGENCE

RULING PLANET OF: GEMINI AND VIRGO THE MESSENGER

DEFAULT HOUSE: THIRD

MERCURY 'GONE WRONG' IS: SUPERFICIAL, CRITICAL, IGNORANT AND DUPLICITOUS

MERCURY 'GONE RIGHT' IS: ADEPT, SMART, ANALYTICAL AND ELOQUENT

Mercury is the smallest planet in our solar system and the closest to the Sun. This means that in your chart it will always be in either the same sign as your Sun or the two signs just before or after it. My astrology teacher, the late Derek Hawkins, used to call Venus and Mercury the Sun's henchmen. (Venus is the next closest planet to the Sun, after Mercury.)

Mercury is overwhelmingly associated with matters of the mind, the intellect and thought processes. The position of Mercury in a chart shows how a person thinks, how they communicate and make decisions. It often gives clues as to what interests them and the concerns that occupy them.

Mercury (called Hermes by the Greeks) was depicted in Roman mythology as the 'messenger of the gods' and also known as the 'winged boy'. He was the love child of Jupiter and a nymph, and was able to move among mortals and gods alike. This was taken as proof of an elemental slipperiness. Those channelling Mercury 'gone wrong' are prone to lie and cheat and follow the ways of the 'silver-tongued messenger'. Just like Mercury, they are fluid, free, difficult to pin down and impossible to rely on. On the other hand, Mercury 'gone right' is all about flexible thinking, sharp analysis and a natural gift for eloquence.

A quick note on the famous 'Mercury Retrograde' before we move on. It happens roughly three or four times a year and lasts a few weeks, on average. It is often blamed for all sorts of chaos, from travel problems to technology malfunctions and periods of foggy thinking when we just can't seem to get our ideas in order. How on earth can it be possible for such a small planet to cause all that disturbance? The answer is: it's not.

First, Mercury doesn't move backwards (or into 'retrograde'). This is just an optical illusion. Second, we suffer with this sort of issue all the time, so why blame Mercury?

That's not to say there's nothing in it. To my teacher this phase was like being stuck on a plane that's delayed for take-off. You know it's going to leave eventually, so you may as well be patient and read a good book. I agree. I smile when I hear that folk will not sign contracts or buy property under this phase. I mean, sure, things are likely to be a tad more challenging, but I don't believe that any astrological phase should prevent us from living our lives and doing what we need to do when we need to do it. Cosmic excuses! Perhaps it may be wise to do more due-diligence under these phases, to adopt an attitude of patience and to allot more time for journeys, but if you would even consider signing a contract without legal protection at any time other than Mercury Retrograde, you're asking for trouble. You would be wise to do as you like under these phases. Just do it with awareness.

ASSOCIATIONS

1. TIMING

People with Mercury 'gone right' have a great sense of timing in general. They are brilliant with their delivery of words and sense of timing, which roll out into every area of their lives, on time and on point. When Mercury is 'gone wrong', that person typically has no sense of timing: they are late for everything and frequently say the wrong thing at the wrong moment, often offending people unnecessarily with their poor judgement.

If this sounds harsh, please bear with me. The thing about Mercury is that, because it rules some integral parts of our lives and characters, the repercussions of a 'gone wrong' manifestation can be pretty serious. But, as with everything in Dynamic Astrology, even the most wayward Mercury can be tamed, first with awareness, then with patience and effort. I like to tell people that 'He is from Mars, she is from Uranus,' so we all communicate and think like people from other planets, which is why mastering your Mercury will help you no end. It can be done – I have done it and so have many of my clients. Every now and again we slip, but for the most part we are on point!

Mercury is all about timing so you need to train yours. Simple things can make a big difference. If you are inclined to say the wrong thing or take impulsive decisions, try to take one deep breath before you respond and ask the little voice that resides within (a.k.a. your intuition) if you should say what you have in your mind, send that email or leave the party. In my experience, a lot can be achieved by slowing down and becoming more mindful.

2. COMMUNICATION

Those with Mercury 'gone right' are fabulous with communication and view interaction almost as an art form. They know what to say and when to say it. They also know when to listen. So many people think that talking makes them good communicators but, in my opinion, the best are adept listeners who think deeply before responding rather than mouthing off for the sake of it. They also seem to know almost instinctively when to pitch projects or when to ask for a date – and when to wait!

'Gone wrong' is a different story. In this scenario they talk incessantly about nothing – just a load of shallow trivia and gossip, which results in their character reaching an all-time low. We've all met people like this, who seem only to care about the latest fashion fad or celebrity gossip.

3. INTELLIGENCE

Intelligence is never a simple matter, and it certainly doesn't always boil down to exam results. It's by no means a given. In fact it can be cultivated with study and hard work. (There really is no excuse for ignorance in this time of free information.) I always think that intellectual curiosity is the most important marker of intelligence – that and not being afraid to admit you don't know something.

So, in that context, Mercury 'gone right', whichever sign it falls in, is curious, intelligent and smart. People with this configuration take pleasure in researching ideas and are discerning with their opinions, making sure to find facts to back them up before sharing with the wider world.

Mercury 'gone wrong', on the other hand, displays its own ignorance without even noticing. Anyone who's banging on without any facts or proof to back themselves up is certainly channelling Mercury 'gone wrong'! I think we probably all know the type. I have come across a few who hold very strong negative opinions about astrology, for example, based solely on the daily horoscopes found in so many publications. They have no knowledge of individual or personal astrology but that doesn't stop them telling me it's all nonsense. I am now so used to it that I rarely react. Classic example of Mercury 'gone wrong': little fact, big opinions.

─⊖ HOW IT PLAYS OUT ⊖─

As an example, Mercury in Capricorn will often mean that the person in question is practical, and often extremely ambitious. These people usually have good business brains and the nous for creating structure and making things work. They are fixed and single-minded at times, courtesy of Capricorn. They are usually interested in the finer things in life and are quite serious people in terms of how they communicate and what interests them (unless they are impacted by their lighter next-door neighbours Sagittarius or Aquarius).

Ensuring that they are not blinded by the need for personal and professional success and that they figure out what actually interests them in life is their deeper lesson. That, along with the need to keep their arrogance in check.

Mercury in Virgo in the sixth house is half in its default setting

(Virgo and the sixth house) and usually indicates a very smart, logical, positive and cool person when it's 'gone right', all courtesy of Virgo. They also have great healing abilities, a strong work ethic (sixth house) and a fantastic sense of timing (Mercury). 'Gone wrong' they are anxious worriers who suffer from obsessive-compulsive disorders, hypochondria, and can over-analyse everything to the point of self-destruction. I usually sing them the song from *Frozen:* 'Let It Go'!

—⊖ HERE'S YOUR SPACE ⊖—

Studying the sign and house placement of Mercury in your chart can tell you how to boost your powers of decision-making and timing, as well as your ability to communicate effectively. Once you've identified it, flip to its section in 'The Signs' (pages 97–285) and study its 'gone wrong' and 'gone right' traits. Use this space to jot down whatever jumps out at you. You're looking for anything that associates with the way your mind works, whether that's the way you study or think, your decision-making style or the issues that fascinate you. Make a quick note of the house Mercury falls in so you can come back to it later.

MERCURY GONE WRONG	MERCURY GONE RIGHT

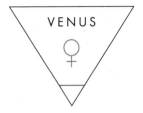

VENUS

ASSOCIATED WITH: LOVE; STYLE AND
APPEARANCE; EXPECTATIONS; THE FEMALE
ASPECT OF OURSELVES; HOW WE VIEW MONEY
AND OTHER WORLDLY PLEASURES

RULING PLANET OF: LIBRA AND TAURUS THE DIPLOMAT

DEFAULT HOUSE: SEVENTH

VENUS 'GONE WRONG' IS: VAIN, DEPTHLESS,
EXTRAVAGANT AND MATERIALISTIC

VENUS 'GONE RIGHT' IS: BEAUTIFUL, GRACIOUS,
ACCOMMODATING AND ARTISTIC

Venus takes around 225 days to orbit the Sun and is the hottest planet in our solar system. It has been suggested that Venus once had oceans like ours, but they vaporized due to the heat. Three leading climate-change scientists recently said that, if we do not combat climate change, Earth could turn into a Venus. Nevertheless, it has to be said that a person with Venus 'gone right' is smoking hot, just like the planet!

Venus was the Roman goddess of love and beauty, the ultimate symbol of femininity. She was known in ancient Mesopotamia as Ishtar, which literally means 'bright star' and makes sense as Venus is usually bright enough to be visible to the naked eye. Venus (or Aphrodite in Greek mythology) was the goddess who caused strife and competition between gods (such as Ares the Greek god of war and Adonis), and mortals alike. She is said to have had many affairs and several children as a result. It's undeniably true that something about her potent association with all things connected to love, beauty and general gorgeousness means that her name is still a byword for powerful femininity.

—⊖ ASSOCIATIONS ⊖—

I. LOVE

The planet Venus is all about love, and its position in a chart shows how a person expresses themselves in intimate relationships and affairs of the heart. Its sign gives clues as to our expectations in relationships, such as marriage, and the way we approach love in general, and behave when we are in love.

It also offers clues as to how we can attract the right kind of intimate partner and retain their attention and affection. As Mars and Venus represent the masculine and feminine aspects of ourselves, they show where we are likely to be attracted (Mars) and attractive (Venus). (As we all know, opposites attract.) This is the case for both sexes. If you have Venus in Cancer, for example, you will be attractive to partners looking for Cancer 'gone right' (kind, nurturing, creative). If you have Mars in Cancer you will be attracted to someone safe, secure, kind and emotionally intelligent. If you have Mars in Aquarius you'll be attracted to someone crazy – I can make that joke: I'm Aquarius! Of course this can all go wrong, too. If you have Mars in Aquarius 'gone right', crazy, funny, or Mars in Cancer 'gone wrong', ice cold, detached, until you actively crank up the good traits yourself, you may attract someone who is reactive, moody and emotionally damaged.

'Gone wrong', Venus can be rather selfish. She tends to fall in love with those who fall in love with her first, especially if they can offer her a beautiful life. She knows how to give pleasure to attract adoration and will often use her body to capture the attention of her target.

Peace, harmony and balance are all qualities associated with Venus 'gone right', unless there is a love rival in the equation. Then Venus goes all-out to win the object of her affections and elbow her competitor out of the picture.

2. STYLE AND PERSONAL APPEARANCE

Venus rules style, clothes and physical beauty. Many of the most physically attractive or self-confidently stylish people I know, of both sexes, exhibit Venus 'gone right' traits. Seriously beautiful inside and out, these people beam with grace and, with one kind word, can make you feel just as gorgeous as they look. Sincere and genuine, you can tell when a person has Venus 'gone right' by the way they make you feel in their presence. Even after they have left you, you still feel as if you've been touched by something rather angelic.

But 'gone wrong', Venus can manifest as self-indulgence and vanity, producing a person who is shallow and lazy, motivated by their need for admiration. Vanity, in its original sense, means 'empty'. Empty inside and lacking in depth are typical qualities of Venus 'gone wrong'.

3. EXPECTATIONS

Venus indicates, first, how we expect ourselves to be as people, and second, the expectations others place upon us. It is usually reserved for intimate unions but a 'gone wrong' Venus places over-the-top expectations on everyone, including friends. The thing is, Venus is a goddess so has extremely high expectations. She likes the finer things in life, and to be adored and pampered. All of which can make it hard if you were not born a princess in this life! (I have worked with an actual princess and her expectations were enormous, sometimes unreasonably so!)

A person with Venus in Libra (its default setting), for example, has seriously high expectations in the love arena. Basically, they wish to be treated like a god or goddess. Now, there's obviously nothing wrong in expecting to be treated well, but the problem is that Venus's 'gone wrong' tendency to focus on the superficial things in life means that a person with this configuration risks attracting shallow partners who are only interested in their physical appearance. By the same token, Venus in Capricorn would expect their partner to be successful and in some way add to their own 'status'.

4. FEMALE ASPECT

Venus indicates the softer side of our self, in both men and women. If we are channelling Venus 'gone right' in, say, its default setting of Libra or Taurus, we would hope to embrace grace and beauty as a given. If a man is very effeminate it usually turns out that he tunes more into his Venus than his Mars sign (which is all about masculinity). As with all of this, everything needs to be balanced, so if a man tunes more into his Venus energy he may attract very masculine or dominant partners to even things out, which is clearly fine if both sides are happy. From my experience, though, the Venus-led man often needs to combine the energy of Mars and Venus by channeling all of their 'gone right' traits.

When I look at successful couples' charts, I often see the 'gone right' traits of one person's Venus sign playing out in the person's chosen partner. So, for example, if a heterosexual man has Venus in Cancer and he's channelling Cancer 'gone right' energy, he will attract all the positive traits of Cancer in his woman (kind, nurturing, creative and sensitive).

5. MONEY AND OTHER WORLDLY PLEASURES

As well as being generally indicative of your attitudes to worldly pleasures, luxury and money, your Venus offers particular clues as to how you will earn your living. If you have Venus in its default setting of Libra or Taurus, you may be drawn to work in the beauty industry or fashion, or in construction (Taurus is the architect). If Venus is in Pisces, you may aspire to be a designer or an artist. Venus in Capricorn typically wants to be their own boss.

HOW IT PLAYS OUT

Let's have a closer look at the example of Venus in Cancer, which will often mean that the person is extremely sensitive in their love relationship. (Water signs' feelings are generally easily hurt and misunderstood.) Venus in Cancer people are usually very domesticated, enjoying the art of homemaking, and are usually driven by their need for security in relationships, striving to achieve the stable home, partner and family that they need. 'Gone wrong', this configuration can be touchy, demanding and anxious. But 'gone right', they are empathetic, considerate and gracious. The deeper lesson for them is to ensure that they are not held back by past hurts or insecurity, to keep their desire for security in check and to retain their kindness and generosity of spirit in life.

Venus in Aquarius, by contrast, needs plenty of freedom and space in relationships. If you leave the door open and give them trust you will be rewarded with their loyalty, but if you trap them they will cause chaos. 'Gone wrong', they become rebellious or cold when hurt in love, and are also prone to be detached and extreme, even sulky. 'Gone right', they are compassionate, intuitive, caring and extremely creative. The deeper lesson for them is to learn about compassion and not to see compromise as a form of entrapment.

—⊖ HERE'S YOUR SPACE ⊖—

Studying the sign and house placement of Venus in your chart can reveal a huge amount about how you operate in love, as well as how you deploy your feminine side and feel about the pleasures of life.

Identify Venus in your chart, flip to its section in 'The Signs' (pages 97–285) and study its 'gone wrong' and 'gone right' traits. Use this space to jot down anything that jumps out at you. You're looking in particular for anything that associates with your love life, as well as the way you set expectations for yourself and others, express your sense of style, etc. As always, don't over-analyse; just trust your gut instincts or the first thing that jumps out at you to guide you, and try to be as honest as you can.

VENUS GONE WRONG	VENUS GONE RIGHT

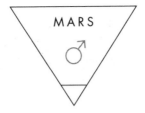

MARS

ASSOCIATED WITH: SEXUALITY; ATTRACTION;
PHYSICAL ENERGY; BASIC DRIVE AND MOTIVATION

RULING PLANET OF: ARIES THE PIONEER

DEFAULT HOUSE: FIRST

MARS 'GONE WRONG' IS: ANGRY, AGGRESSIVE,
COMPETITIVE AND RASH

MARS 'GONE RIGHT' IS: PIONEERING, BRAVE,
DIRECT AND INDEPENDENT

Mars was the Roman god of war and indicates a masculine (and potentially aggressive) energy in both men and women. The planet takes approximately 687 days to orbit the Sun and spends approximately six weeks in each of the twelve signs. When Mars enters the same sign as your own Mars sign, it's known in astrological circles as your Mars Return, and gives you an energetic boost. I liken this transit to walking for miles, lonely and thirsty, through a dry and desolate desert, then suddenly finding an oasis with refreshing pure water. If your car has ever been running on empty and you miraculously find a petrol station to refuel, you'll know the feeling of unexpectedly boosted energy that a Mars Return brings with it. So, for example, if you have Mars in Taurus in your chart, it will mean that when Mars moves into Taurus in the sky you will be in for a serious energy boost. It can be almost euphoric when it goes right, but 'gone wrong', you will be in for more battles than usual. After all, Mars is the god of war! If you want to prepare for Mars' return in your own life, you first need to identify your Mars sign, then use the internet to find out when Mars is next moving into that sign in the heavens. You will be astonished at your ramped-up energy levels and your powers of attraction. Use the knowledge wisely.

In short, Mars is all about competition, passion, attraction and energy. When we have a Mars boost we are usually full of energy, more attracted and attractive to others, and also, on a very base level, prone to crave physical encounters, as virility levels are higher than usual under this influence. Mars strengthens the energy of the sign it moves into, so we have the opportunity to crank things up when Mars steps into our arena.

—⊖ ASSOCIATIONS ⊖—

I. SEXUALITY

Mars gives us sexual energy and passion. Its sign placement provides clues about what type of sexual partner we are attracted and attractive to. Very simply, a Mars in Libra person, for example, would be attracted to beautiful physical looks or someone involved in the arts. Mars in Capricorn would want a successful or trophy partner or perhaps just someone with a highly charged sexual drive.

Mars causes the sort of sizzle that happens when you meet someone you are sexually compatible with. If you are instantly attracted (remember that Mars is fire!) to someone, you can bet that you have a Mars connection. You might, for example, find that one of you has Mars in Aries and the other has Mars in Libra, which are opposite signs. Opposites very often attract and complement one another. A Mars connection means you're starred for an intense and steamy experience.

I generally advise my clients to practise self-awareness and exercise caution when it comes to Mars and sex, though. It is such a powerful driver that in some configurations it can get overly dominant. If we focus too heavily on this to attract a partner, we are unlikely to build anything significant. If you are looking for something more long term, it would be wise to check for other astrological matches in your combined charts, as Mars tends to burn bright and pursue ardently, then fizzle out if the passion dies or real life steps in. You would need a Saturn connection, to ensure you both work hard to sustain the union, and preferably a Moon connection, to help you work together on an emotional level.

2. ATTRACTION

Your Mars sign shows what sort of people and situations you attract. For example, if you channel Mars in Gemini 'gone wrong', you may attract intellectual battles with others. On the other hand, you may attract smart, intelligent people both as friends and potential partners. If you have Mars in Taurus, you are likely to go. for good looks (Taurus is ruled by Venus and both appreciate beauty.) If you have Mars in Leo, loyalty and humour would be of paramount importance.

To gain clarity about the kind of person you're attracted to and boost your ability to attract them, study your Mars sign's 'gone right' traits. People with these characteristics are likely to be just your type and, correspondingly, they will be attracted to you if you work on developing those traits.

3. PHYSICAL ENERGY

In order to maintain your energy levels you need to ensure that you are giving your Mars the right fuel. For example, Mars in Cancer needs security and a safe base to retreat to. Mars in Gemini needs intellectual stimulation and the ability to switch off and calm down. Mars in Taurus needs physical exercise and natural foods eaten little and often. Think of Mars as your engine – you need to figure out what fuel it takes to keep it running smoothly.

4. BASIC DRIVE AND MOTIVATION

Mars points to what drives and motivates us, especially when we seek a partner or a career. I have Mars in Taurus, so even though I am an ideas-led Aquarian, I have to make those ideas tangible to satisfy my Mars. I am also attracted to grounded, practical partners to offset all the air in my chart! A client I know has Mars in Pisces and, until she stopped to think, was always attracting Pisces 'gone wrong' in partners (drinkers, unfaithful and slippery). When she ramped up the softer side of her nature she changed the kind of man she attracted and is now with someone gentle, who plays the guitar and sings to her when they argue.

Mars 'gone right' gives a person enough power to attack anything and win, supplying the energy to achieve and the ability to drive initiatives forward with gusto. These people are hard to miss. They radiate energy and innate power, are usually competitive in a healthy way and are often highly charged sexually.

'Gone wrong' they can become addicted to physical activities. A person with a Mars 'gone wrong' will be aggressive with a very short fuse and ready to attack at the tiniest slight. Occasionally they are even capable of being violent if they fail to get their way. Sometimes this plays out for people with this alignment, not in their own behaviour but in the behaviour of the people they have attracted, whether it's romantic partners or business associates.

HOW IT PLAYS OUT

For example, Mars in Aries often means that the person is extremely fiery and assertive. They do not sit still for long enough to realize that their behaviour could cause harm, to themselves and others. They are usually very driven and dynamic and love to indulge in the art of 'war' on some level. They are always in battles with others, and are usually driven by their need to win.

So, the deeper lesson for people with Mars in Aries is to ensure that they are not alienating gentle folk with their temper or, indeed, attracting these types with their passive-aggressive behaviour. They must keep in check their desire to beat opponents, to win at any cost, and must also retain their playful zest for life and use their enthusiasm for fighting and winning in the service of higher causes, not just for themselves.

To give you a different picture of how Mars can play out, consider the example of a person with Mars in Virgo. They will attract (Mars attracts) all the traits of Virgo into their life. 'Gone right': clever, pure, logical and pragmatic. 'Gone wrong': controlling, critical and even cruel. They need organization and order to best manage their energy (energy is governed by Mars) so that they can achieve their potential. I know a few doctors with this placement and, since Virgo rules health and healing, that makes sense!

⊖ HERE'S YOUR SPACE ⊖

Studying the sign and house placement of Mars in your chart shows you how to manage your energy and control it so it's flowing in the right direction and working to attract more of what you want and less of what you don't.

Identify Mars, find the sign it falls in, then flip to its section in 'The Signs' (pages 97–285) and study its 'gone wrong' and 'gone right' traits. (Bear in mind that because Mars represents the energy we are most likely to attract, your Mars configuration may play out not in your own behaviour but in that of other people in your life.)

Then jot down any words that seem especially significant. You're looking in particular for anything that associates with your sex life and the kinds of events and people you attract into your life, especially if they tend to appear over and over again. As always, be as honest as you can be and trust your instincts.

MARS GONE WRONG	MARS GONE RIGHT

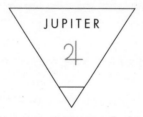

JUPITER

ASSOCIATED WITH: OUR SKILLS, TALENTS AND ABILITIES; OUR LIFE LESSONS; EXTREME BEHAVIOUR AND OVER-INDULGENCE

RULING PLANET OF: SAGITTARIUS, 'THE INSPIRATION'

DEFAULT HOUSE: NINTH

JUPITER 'GONE WRONG' IS: SELF-RIGHTEOUS, JUDGEMENTAL AND LACKING IN EMOTIONAL INTELLIGENCE

JUPITER 'GONE RIGHT' IS: ENTHUSIASTIC, INSPIRATIONAL,
OPTIMISTIC AND GENEROUS-SPIRITED

In Roman mythology, Jupiter (Zeus for the Greeks) was the king of all the gods. He was believed to rule the earthly realm and, of course, the heavens. (Perhaps the old saying 'by Jupiter' came from the fact that we humans used to perceive lightning and other natural forces as signs from Jupiter himself.) He was judgemental, sanctimonious and notoriously promiscuous. I always liken Jupiter to a stern but benevolent judge who likes to drink rather a lot of fine red wine, eat too much (now he's sounding more like Henry VIII!) and be entertained by pretty girls and handsome boys. Fortunately, Jupiter doesn't feel the need to chop off anyone's head – that would be more of a Saturn trait!

Jupiter takes about twelve years to orbit the Sun and is the largest known planet in our solar system. It's over three hundred times the size of Earth and, at last count, had sixty-three moons, compared to our one.

Jupiter in a chart is all about expansion and growth, but be mindful: it's also out to encourage overindulgence. Jupiter spends approximately a year in each of the signs and during this time you can expect to expand your mind or your waistline, depending on how you handle growth! When the planet Jupiter enters the same sign as your own 'Jupiter' sign, it's known in astrological circles as your Jupiter Return and causes an energetic shift. Many astrologers would say that it will usher in a year brimming with opportunity but in my experience it's more about lessons, and tough ones at that. I call Jupiter the 'great teacher' and I believe that life throws up the very best lessons under these phases for us to expand our knowledge, awareness of self and overall wisdom. Sure, fabulous opportunities are often presented, as Jupiter usually bestows luck, but there can be no better gift than wisdom.

⊖ ASSOCIATIONS ⊖

1. SKILLS, TALENTS AND ABILITIES

Jupiter shows where we are skilled in life. It's a cool planet to know. These skills are innate and we all have the capacity to tune in to them by looking to the 'gone right' traits associated with our Jupiter sign with as much awareness as we can muster. Given that Jupiter takes approximately twelve years to orbit the Sun and spends about a year in each sign, the Jupiter sign is the same for people born in the same twelve-month period. So, for example, one person with Jupiter in Virgo may be the most organized and smart PA on the planet; another born in the same year may be the most detail-focused brain surgeon. In both cases they're exhibiting traits of Jupiter in Virgo. Now you just have to find yours!

2. LIFE LESSONS

Many astrologers believe that your Jupiter Return (every twelfth year, when Jupiter is revisiting the sign it was in at your birth) is a most fortunate time, and indeed it can be, if you have planted good seeds in fertile soil. Jupiter comes to spiritualize your life and help you get on track with your soul purpose. For many who are living ego-based lives based on superficiality, Jupiter coming home to roost can really shake things up, pressing them to begin to realize what's really important in life. I got my first break on TV under my Return and my Jupiter is in Aquarius (Aquarius is all about con-necting to the masses). On the 'gone wrong' side, I have been at my most fanatical about astrology during my Jupiter Return year!

3. EXTREME BEHAVIOUR AND OVER-INDULGENCE

On the one hand, Jupiter shows us our skills, but on the other it shows us which sign's energy we use to go over the top, or where we become fanatical (both traits of Jupiter). I have a client with Jupiter in Sagittarius (its default setting) who is very academic but lacks emotional intelligence. She comes across to her loved ones and colleagues as self-righteous, which causes her no end of grief. It was an eye-opener for her to hear this and she's now working on it (hard!). The problem is she is usually right (a very Sagittarian trait), and even though her star sign is Virgo, she goes over the top with Sagittarius energy, which she is now learning to tame.

A guy I know has Jupiter in Gemini, and although he is very clever, he doesn't stop talking. (Classic Gemini 'gone wrong'.) I had to tell him one day that he was making my ears bleed! I also know a lady with Jupiter in Virgo who is pure OCD (I think we probably all know one). She is a hypochondriac, has every allergy under the Sun and talks non-stop about her work, keeping fit and nutrition (all Virgo obsessions). Now, clearly, looking after yourself is great and most of my group likes to exercise, but we also like to have fun, forget work and frequent the pubs and bars of London. Which we do without her because she says they're too dirty!

If there's a behaviour, from the serious to the trivial, that you suspect is playing way too big a part in your life, try viewing it from the perspective of your Jupiter sign. I can virtually guarantee that you will find it illuminating!

HOW IT PLAYS OUT

For example, having Jupiter in Aquarius 'gone right' will often mean that the person is very friendly, social, and is learning about humanity in general, compassion and awareness in particular. Although these people usually have plenty of awareness they must still learn how to handle it and put it to good use. Those who are fanatical about their beliefs (Jupiter is also all about beliefs) are dangerous and not content to believe quietly. They frequently wish to convert others and will resort to extreme measures to do so.

On a more worldly level, many people I know with this placement work for organizations that incorporate a vision, such as charities, good causes, activism, journalism and, indeed, the media industry as a whole. (Nope, reality TV doesn't count in this context.)

⊖ HERE'S YOUR SPACE ⊖

Studying the sign and house placement of Jupiter in your chart can be totally fascinating as it's associated with so many crucial areas that respond really well to focused attention. When you raise your awareness around Jupiter's influence you learn powerful life lessons, curb your excesses and nurture your innate skills.

First, identify Jupiter in your chart, find the sign it falls in, then flip to its section in 'The Signs' (pages 97–285) and study that sign's 'gone wrong' and 'gone right' traits. Then jot down any words that seem especially significant. You're looking out for anything that associates with skills you have a hunch you may possess (or know you'd like to develop), as well as any area that speaks of excess you'd do well to curb, and any clues to life lessons you need to learn. Some of this may be uncomfortable, but working with Jupiter can be a powerful catalyst for change: try to stick with any discomfort and trust that the search will be worthwhile.

JUPITER GONE WRONG	JUPITER GONE RIGHT

SATURN

ASSOCIATED WITH: PAST-LIFE KARMA AND LIFE LESSONS;
ATTITUDES TO STABILITY AND COMMITMENT;
MATURING AND AGEING

RULING PLANET OF: CAPRICORN, 'THE MASTER'

DEFAULT HOUSE: TENTH

SATURN 'GONE WRONG' IS: COLD, CALCULATING,
EMOTIONALLY RESTRICTED, AUTHORITARIAN, RUTHLESS

SATURN 'GONE RIGHT' IS: SELF-DISCIPLINED,
AUTHORITATIVE, COMMANDING, POWERFUL

According to Roman mythology, Saturn, also known as Kronos, the son of Uranus and Gaia, was the father of Jupiter and Venus. Saturn and a few of his brothers castrated their father, who was then the king of the universe, to take his power. Out of the ensuing chaos came the goddess of love, Venus. On some level this story has always appealed to me as it makes a perfect kind of sense. Anyone who has ever been in love can testify that love is often born, and certainly often created, from chaos.

Saturn takes twenty-nine years to orbit the Sun and spends around two years in each of the signs, so everyone born within two years of each other has the same Saturn sign placement. The sign may not vary so much from one individual to another but the house placement continues to vary enormously, so it's well worth making a note to yourself to pay particular attention to Saturn's (and all the even-longer-staying planets that come after it), when you get to 'The Houses' (pages 286–331).

The planet Saturn has an ice-cold atmosphere and this is in keeping with the astrological effect of Saturn in a chart. Wherever your Saturn sign falls shows the area where you have often been restricted from an early age and, depending upon the sign it's in, shows what you must master in this life to be successful and content.

In astrological circles Saturn is known as 'Old Father Time' and Saturn does concern itself with time (with maturing and ageing, in general). But I renamed him several years ago. He is now a she, and we call her Queen Saturn. She rules her subjects, always taking the regulations into consideration, presiding over empires and being ever concerned with status, tradition and the establishment of order.

Saturn 'gone right' (remember that it can 'go right' or 'go wrong' whichever sign it falls in) gives a person stability and maturity, even at a young age. People with Saturn 'gone right' build structure out of chaos and discern what will work in practice as opposed to what they wish would work in an ideal world. They are practical, disciplined, logical and honest, with plenty of nous for business.

People with Saturn 'gone wrong' may come across as authoritarian parent figures at best, and cold, way too serious and ruthless at worst.

⊖ ASSOCIATIONS ⊖

1. PAST-LIFE KARMA AND LIFE LESSONS

In my opinion, Saturn often indicates past-life karma, the result of our actions in the past. We need to overcome the results of these actions and change deeply ingrained negative patterns of behaviour in this lifetime. Whether or not you believe in past lives, most astrologers agree that Saturn provides clues to the areas that we must master. If a person has Saturn in Gemini, for example, they may need to embrace depth, perhaps of knowledge. These people may need to learn how to study subjects deeply and not skim information or form an opinion too quickly.

If a person has Saturn in Capricorn, the lessons usually lie within the realms of commitment and the need to avoid being ruthlessly ambitious. Capricorns have a tendency to trample over others to achieve. They also run the risk of repeating old patterns and not progressing.

Saturn 'gone right', in whichever sign we're talking about, shows a person who is committed to learning, growing and becoming a better person.

2. ATTITUDES TO STABILITY AND COMMITMENT

Saturn 'gone right' shows a person who is not afraid to commit to projects, people or beliefs. They are stable, authoritative and have no problem in getting other people to work for them and their goals. I call Saturn 'the boss' and a good boss will always work with Saturn 'gone right'. If Saturn is in its default setting of Capricorn, the person has great potential to achieve, so long as they act with self-awareness and integrity.

As with everything in Dynamic Astrology, that which can be helpful in some contexts can be harmful in others. Saturn 'gone wrong' often manifests as a tendency to coldness or authoritarian behaviours, but may also show as an exaggerated sense of responsibility, a kind of dogmatic commitment even in unhealthy situations. I once knew a woman with Saturn sitting right on her rising sign (the line at nine o'clock on your chart, which indicates the sign that governs your personality) and she sacrificed her own personal path to dedicate her whole life to her ungrateful family. She allowed opportunities for love to pass her by and became miserable in the process. I tried to remind her that she needed to balance her Saturnian sense of responsibility to her parents and brothers with her commitment to herself. She chose not to hear.

3. MATURING AND AGEING

Those with Saturn 'gone right' are mature from a very young age. They stand tall even when they're too young to stand at all. They have a healthy and sustainable attitude to ageing, too, preferring to be seen as wise than look ten years younger than they actually are. Those with Saturn 'gone wrong' are terrified of ageing and will do all they can to halt the process. You probably know the type, with a new face and a frozen smile. To be able to live and grow old is a blessing not awarded to all of us, and those with Saturn 'gone right' accept the process and embrace the grey hairs that come with experience.

─⊖ HOW IT PLAYS OUT ⊖─

If you have Saturn in Gemini, for example, you will need to master the art of communication (strongly associated with Gemini). I sometimes call this placement the 'shadow'. It can be extremely annoying for those who have it as, for every positive thought in the person's head, in steps the deliberation jury to tear it apart. People with this placement need to learn how to tame their negative thoughts and become more adept at the art of communication, which includes how they speak to themselves.

If you have Saturn in Sagittarius, you will need to learn how to back up your beliefs with plenty of knowledge and hard facts. Sagittarius is very driven to search for and tell the truth, which is highly beneficial in many contexts. But 'gone wrong' there is a tendency to be a know-it-all who actually knows very little and to be self-righteous, ignorant and pompous. 'Gone right', this placement is superb: truthful even in the face of loss, totally dependable, smart, logical and decent. These folk are refreshing, like freshly squeezed iced lemonade on a very hot day. They know how to make lemonade out of life's most bitter lemons, and they do it with optimism and a positive attitude.

HERE'S YOUR SPACE

Studying the sign and house placement of Saturn in your chart can feel a little daunting. Saturn can be a strict teacher and a severe presence, all about lessons to be learned and linked to ageing, which is, of course, something that many of us don't want to face. The lessons of Saturn can be particularly deep as they are usually linked to past-life issues. But if you pay careful attention to your Saturn clues, you have a chance to clear up a lot of negativity in your life by addressing your own behaviour and taking personal responsibility, which leads to deep progress.

Saturn rewards your diligence with clues as to how you can bring more authority and self-discipline into your life. Rather than thinking of it as a disapproving, fun-killing parent, I see it as a means to fire up your power and command, and to learn how to use these well.

Once you've identified Saturn and the sign it falls in, flip to 'The Signs' (pages 97–285) and study its 'gone wrong' and 'gone right' traits. Remember, Saturn is all about learning so take your time and really focus on teasing out the lessons. Then, as always, jot down any words that seem especially significant. You're looking out for anything that associates with past-life karma or lessons you need to learn, as well as areas of your life you know you need to master and the ageing process in general.

SATURN GONE WRONG	SATURN GONE RIGHT

URANUS

ASSOCIATED WITH: AWARENESS, ESPECIALLY
SELF-AWARENESS; CHANGE, REVOLUTION AND
REBELLION; INVENTIVENESS

RULING PLANET OF: AQUARIUS, 'THE CONNECTOR'

DEFAULT HOUSE: ELEVENTH

URANUS 'GONE WRONG' IS: FANATICAL, REBELLIOUS FOR
THE SAKE OF IT, EXTREMIST

URANUS 'GONE RIGHT' IS: NONCONFORMIST,
IDEALISTIC, INVENTIVE

Uranus, or Ouranos as he was also called, was father of the sky and husband of the goddess Earth (or Gaia). In Greek mythology, he was known as the son born of Gaia alone, and then became her husband, which seems odd – but who are we to question mythology? Uranus fathered twelve children with Gaia, who were known as the Titans. Some astrologers have suggested that they were also the genesis of the Zodiac signs. In any case the family relationship was not a good one as they all hated each other and one of the Titans, Saturn, decided to rob his father of his immortal power (see page 72). Uranus was sometimes described in the myths as the ultimate creator and founder of the universe, holding power to create life-force unrivalled by any of the other gods.

The planet Uranus takes around eighty-four years to orbit the Sun and it orbits in a strange flip-flop tilt, which is very different from the orbit of other well-behaved planets and stars. It was discovered by an amateur astronomer in 1781, around the time that several revolutions were kicking off. France and America were in total chaos and the Industrial Revolution, which began in Great Britain towards the end of the eighteenth century, was in the process of introducing the delightful age of polluting factories and mass-production.

Uranus influences revolution, change and rebellion, and is known as the 'great awakener' for its ability to wake us up to things we need to be aware of. When we pay attention to what Uranus is telling us, we progress our awareness and break free from self-imposed restrictions.

A note on how to deepen your understanding of Uranus: since it is a slow-moving planet it takes a long time to orbit the Sun and therefore stays in each sign for about seven years. It is the first of the slower planets (the others are Neptune and Pluto), which are known in astrology as 'generational planets'. So although you can still gather information via the sign it falls in, you are likely to gain at least as many clues from its house placement.

ASSOCIATIONS

1. AWARENESS, ESPECIALLY SELF-AWARENESS

Uranus 'gone right' shows a person who is committed to improving through their own self-awareness and raising the awareness of important causes. Most of the game-changers in the human-rights arena have Uranus featuring prominently in their charts. Nelson Mandela and Rosa Parks, for example, both shared the generational placement of Uranus in Aquarius (its default setting, so extra powerful) and Parks, who has been called 'the mother of the Civil Rights Movement', also had her star sign in Aquarius. 'Gone right', they are humble, observant and always ready to accept when they may be wrong.

Uranus 'gone wrong' is a different chariot of carrots entirely. These people lack any kind of self-awareness and can be utterly asleep on the job of life. Lights on, nobody at home!

2. CHANGE AND REBELLION

If Uranus falls in its default setting of the eleventh house it is more likely than not that the person is some sort of activist, rebel or game-changer. Some people with a pronounced influence from Uranus walk a fine line between genius and insanity. 'Gone right', they are the activists who rebel against conventional wisdom or established power to bring about change and progress in ingenious ways. They are super-smart and inventive, brimming with solutions to the complex issues faced by humanity. 'Gone wrong', they veer towards fanaticism and extremism.

In fact, a person with Uranus 'gone wrong' can be borderline insane and very hard to handle. With discursive minds and random thought patterns, they rebel simply for the sake of it and are always trying to achieve a reputation for being 'different'. I tend to think that people who are genuinely different do not need to try: it's innate and cannot be faked. And, of course, keeping up this sort of pretence takes a lot of energy that may be better spent on other things. Ultimately, it's exhausting.

3 . INVENTIVENESS

Uniqueness and the ability to think outside the box are absolutely characteristic of people exhibiting Uranus 'gone right'. It's almost as if they cannot see either box or ceilings. Uranus rules the expansive sky! Some are borderline geniuses. Ever creative, they have lightning flashes of insight, coming up with plenty of ideas from which they can often make a lot of money. Some are not materially minded and prefer to leave little flashes of wonder for the rest of humanity to collect. I once worked with a very cool guy who had Uranus sitting right in his first house (house of self and self-expression) and he had flashes of insight that left us all in awe. He pulls ideas out of his mind like a magician, runs a super-successful innovation company and seems to have the Midas touch, but will readily admit that his grounded Virgo wife keeps him in touch with reality and prevents him from going insane! You, too, can tune in to your inner inventiveness if you study your Uranus.

So, although Uranus is a generational placement, meaning that it affects a whole group of people at the same time, you can still glean a lot of information from the placement of Uranus in your chart. It shows you how to progress your awareness by embracing the 'gone right' traits of the sign it's in. And awareness, as I hope you've already figured out, really is the key to working successfully with Dynamic Astrology across the board.

So, imagine you have Uranus in Scorpio. This is usually indicative of embracing power in some way (preferably for the greater good) and of learning about empathy, both Scorpio-associated behaviours 'gone right'. It also indicates becoming aware of your sexuality and how you use it. 'Gone wrong', a person may use sex to get what they want in life or close off their sexuality completely, which could lead to it coming out in inappropriate ways. The point here is that, whichever sign Uranus falls in, its energy is to push for you to explore that sign and its house placement as much as possible to deepen not only your awareness of the role of Uranus but also your self-awareness in general.

—⊖ HERE'S YOUR SPACE ⊖—

Studying the sign and house placement of Uranus in your chart will yield significant insight if you approach it with honesty, attention and patience. When you focus on the influence of Uranus you are building skills in (self-)awareness, one of the key areas that underpins the whole practice of astrology.

Identify Uranus in your chart, identify the sign it falls in, then flip to its section in 'The Signs' (pages 97–285) and study its 'gone wrong' and 'gone right' traits. You're looking for anything that associates with rebellion and revolution, and generally hunting for clues to set you on a path to greater awareness. If you get any moments of insight, trust them. Paying attention to anything that niggles you here will reap dividends.

URANUS GONE WRONG	URANUS GONE RIGHT

NEPTUNE

ASSOCIATED WITH: INSIGHT AND INTUITION, OUR DEEPEST DREAMS, FEARS AND LOSS (IN SOME AREAS, DEPENDING ON WHAT HOUSE IT FALLS IN), SPIRITUALITY IN GENERAL, INCLUDING HOPES, DREAMS AND FAITH; THE AREAS IN WHICH WE NEED TO LET GO AND THOSE IN WHICH WE MAY HAVE TO MAKE A SACRIFICE TO ACHIEVE OUR DREAMS

RULING PLANET OF: PISCES, 'THE VISION'

Neptune is another slow-moving planet, taking 164 years to orbit the Sun. It stays in each sign for around seven years so, as with Uranus, it is a generational influence on a great number of people. Since the house placement can be particularly rich in insight with these longer-staying planets, you may like to flick to 'Fast Track to the Houses' on page 295 to get a feel for the associations of the house in which Neptune falls for you.

Neptune (known as Poseidon by the Greeks) was the king of the oceans and seas, who was much inclined to smash down his trident to cause a huge wave of destruction if people upset him or troubled his underwater life. Many moons ago people would pray to him for safe passage on the high seas, and shipwrecks were attributed to his wrath.

Neptune in our chart shows the power of intuition and the flow of instincts. Its watery associations are a particularly profound influence on the water signs (Cancer, Scorpio and Pisces) but they affect us all to a greater or lesser extent. The gentle sound of water is almost universally calming and can help us relax our hectic minds and realign with our intuition.

⊖ ASSOCIATIONS ⊖

1. INSIGHT AND INTUITION
Neptune 'gone right' usually gives a person a heightened sense of intuition and the ability to see and feel things that other people

often miss. However, it can also turn people into dreamers who never produce anything tangible, such is the haze in their minds. Depending on which house it falls in, they need to strengthen their intuition in that area to achieve their dreams. So, for example, if you have Neptune in the fifth house, you would probably have to use your intuition in the areas of love, creativity and children.

2. OUR DEEPEST FEARS AND LOSS

Neptune can indicate our greatest fears. For example, if a person has Neptune in the fifth house, of children, creativity, play and fun, they may have fears around children or even have suffered losses. Perhaps they've had to make great sacrifices for their children. (I have Neptune in the fifth house and was a teenage mother, so in a way I sacrificed my teenage years for the person who is now my favourite human being on the planet!) Neptune in the second house would perhaps indicate that someone had lost assets and had had to rebuild them to follow his or her worthy dreams (all very Neptune-in-the-second-house traits).

3. FAITH, HOPE AND DREAMS

Neptune 'gone right' shows a person with an innate sense of spirituality and a good ethos in life. Such a person is almost ethereal, gentle, spiritual and kind, with an otherworldly sense of sometimes mind-blowing intuition. Many have prescient dreams fuelled by Neptune. The children born from 2012 (and for the following thirteen to fourteen years) possess a particular ability to tune into these qualities as they have Neptune in Pisces (its default setting). I have looked at several of these children's charts for curious parents and they have all displayed an outstanding ability to see and feel things hidden to other people. Many are sensitive to others' moods and energy. They can sense when people are struggling. This puts pressure on the parents to equip them with tools to manage their heightened awareness. One little girl had a dream in which she conversed with her late grandmother (she had never met her), later describing many things that would be classed as 'otherworldly'. But, for all of us, if we are aligned with our Neptune we have faith in a higher vision and hope in a better future.

4. THE AREAS WHERE WE NEED TO LET GO

Neptune also shows the areas in life where we need to let go and have a little more faith. Neptune in the first house usually shows a highly intuitive, inspirational, artistic and spiritual person, but 'gone wrong' they are flaky dreamers who risk never achieving anything. Neptune in the third house would show a person who communicates intuitively ('gone right') or someone who gets lost in their own mind easily. Neptune in the fifth would show a person who needs to let go of ego ('gone wrong') and one who needs to embrace love for all ('gone right'!).

HOW IT PLAYS OUT

Although many people will have Neptune in the same sign, because it stays in each sign for about fourteen years, you can still glean a lot by studying the sign and the house placement of Neptune, as it shows you how to understand your fears and which sign's 'gone wrong' traits you particularly need to let go of.

For example, those born between 1970 and 1984 have Neptune in Sagittarius. They need to trust in their own truth and have faith in a higher vision, which are both very Sagittarius lessons. They need to find their own way outside organized, traditional religion, and learn how to reach inside themselves for inspiration.

If you were born between 1984 and 1998, you have Neptune in Capricorn. It's usually indicative of needing to let go of any ambition that's held in an unhealthy, selfish way and also of giving up the need to control everything, both Capricorn traits 'gone wrong'. People with this alignment can be arrogant, haughty and imperious know-it-alls, though 'gone right', they are discerning, sensible, reliable, purposefully goal-oriented and extremely accomplished.

If Neptune falls in the first house, of 'self', then that person 'gone right' is very likely to become a rather inspirational human being in some way. These people often find it easy to motivate and comfort others. People with 'gone right' Neptune alignments are the natural healers of the Zodiac and often work as nurses and carers. In short, those with a tendency to help others will have Neptune 'gone right' in their birth charts. 'Gone wrong', they are big dreamers who have the tendency to get lost in a fantasy world of their own making. Marilyn Monroe, who had Neptune in Leo in the first house, grew up with various foster-parents who sent her to the cinema to get her out of the house. She began to dream of becoming an actress at the age of five and, though her life was tragic, she continues to intrigue and inspire people years after her death. She was idealistic about love (Neptune = ideals, Leo = love) and suffered greatly in that arena. She eventually became addicted to drugs to escape reality (which is very Neptunian).

Neptune in Pisces (its default setting, where its influence is particularly strong) has a higher vision and helps to shift the vibration of the planet to one in which we are more in tune with the compassionate and spiritual side of our natures. (Of course, 'gone wrong', these people embody all that is wrong with Pisces: they dream big but lack focus!)

HERE'S YOUR SPACE

When you study the sign and house placement of Neptune in your chart you are dipping into some really big subjects: loss, fear, faith, hope and dreams. Above all you are tuning into your own intuition and bringing focus to your insights.

So, first, find Neptune in your chart, identify the sign it falls in, then flip to its section in 'The Signs' (pages 97–285), and study the 'gone wrong' and 'gone right' traits. Then jot down any words that seem especially significant. You're on the lookout for things that resonate with your anxieties and griefs, your religious sense or your deeply cherished dreams. Like Uranus, Neptune is strongly associated with insight and intuition, so abandon the need to have everything spelled out for you and give free rein to yours. Make as many notes as you need, and remember that it might be helpful to check out the basics of the house alignment.

NEPTUNE GONE WRONG	NEPTUNE GONE RIGHT

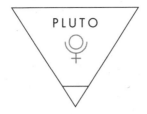

PLUTO

ASSOCIATED WITH: POWER – OUR OWN AND OUR RELATIONSHIP
WITH OTHER PEOPLE'S; MOTIVATIONS; TRANSFORMATIONS,
INCLUDING BIRTH, DEATH AND REBIRTH.

RULING PLANET OF: SCORPIO THE POWER

DEFAULT HOUSE: EIGHTH

PLUTO 'GONE WRONG' IS: POWER-HUNGRY,
MANIPULATIVE AND CONTROLLING

PLUTO 'GONE RIGHT' IS: TRANSFORMATIVE,
SEDUCTIVE, INFLUENTIAL

According to science, Pluto is too small to be a planet. It was recently downgraded and has been reclassified as a 'dwarf planet'. (The NASA website informs us that it's smaller than Earth's moon.) It takes around 248 years to orbit the Sun and it stays in each sign for between fourteen and thirty years so it's a really long-stayer, a true generational mover.

In mythology Pluto is also known as Hades, the king of the underworld, and the 'reaper of death'. Many people regard death as an evil force but I do not: it is simply another opportunity to transform – a very powerful Pluto association and one that derives from the famous story in which Hades stole the goddess Persephone and, thus, dark stole light. After making a deal with the other gods, he agreed to keep her in his underground kingdom of the dead for a few months, then to let her out each year in time for the buds to bloom, signalling the beginning of spring: dark becomes light again.

If you're wondering how a mere dwarf planet, such a comparatively small formation of rock, could wield any astrological power at all, let me tell you, Pluto is all about power (for good and bad). Speaking as one who has studied its transits (the impact upon us on Earth), I know it doesn't mess around! For example, at some point in our late thirties, Pluto in the sky connects to Pluto in our birth chart. It's called a Pluto square Pluto transit, and I began to notice that many new clients were under this influence. It can be devastating: people leave their jobs and partners in a desperate bid to transform. Pluto is like the bulldozer of the Zodiac and will trash everything that has become stagnant. I have seen its powerful effects time and time again. I usually ask people to transform internally before making any life-changing decisions under this transit. I told a client recently not to trade in her car for a Porsche or her husband for a toy-boy until she had worked on herself!

Pluto is all about birth, death, rebirth, transformation and change. Don't be fooled: Pluto might have been relegated but that in no way means its power has diminished.

⊖ ASSOCIATIONS ⊖

I. POWER

If you encounter people who have an uncanny ability to read others' minds, then use what they have learnt to manipulate them and twist situations to their own advantage, you can bet they're channelling the energy of Pluto to do so. They are also manipulative and controlling, only ever making moves to gain more power or to take someone else's from them. If you see people misusing power, this is a classic signal of Pluto 'gone wrong'. You can gain a lot of insight on how to deal with them if you can find out what sign it falls in for them.

Pluto 'gone right' is comfortable with power and has the ability to sensitively change people's lives for the better. I know a millionaire who invests in people he feels are making a difference to the planet. I have introduced a few people to him and it's incredible to watch as he uses his power as a force for good. Power corrupts the weak but those who are at ease with it stay pure and drive progress for us all.

Find your own power and stand in it, no matter what!

2. MOTIVATIONS

I once asked my teacher a question and he answered me with a line that changed my life. (After a while I had quite a collection of these lines!) He said, 'Check your motivation in all you do and say.' That line has stayed with me ever since he said it, more than ten years ago. I understood it to mean that, if we're honest, we know when we're working from a place of sincerity and when we're not. Sometimes it's not so much *what* we do or say as the attitude behind it (or the goal we're trying to advance towards) that reveals our true motivation. And sometimes that motivation is not so great, not so pure.

Pluto 'gone right' has the ability to penetrate the surface of your fears and is able easily to motivate and comfort others.

3. TRANSFORMATION

If you are faced with situations that literally strip away your ego and force you to rebuild, you can safely bet all your money that Pluto is impacting upon you. It's not that Pluto is negative – far from it: its impact helps us to break free from any rut we may have created for ourselves. A few red flags are shown, and if we ignore those warning signs, Pluto goes in and smashes down the current stale infrastructure to build anew, something better, based on humility and not ego. Pluto doesn't like ego very much, as a rule.

⊖ HOW IT PLAYS OUT ⊖

Because Pluto takes such a long time to orbit the Sun, it spends years in each sign, so there is less variation in signs across different people's charts than with many other planets. But as with other generational planets, there is room for individual interpretation within the house placement. For example, if Pluto falls in the ninth house, of travel and foreign cultures, then that person is likely to be in their power overseas. I can think of two incredible clients for whom this rings true: one, whose glittering career in film literally began to shine as soon as he left the shores of his hometown in Brazil; and another, who was in his famous father's shadow, met an American woman, married her within months, moved to be with her and built his own art empire.

Anyone born between 1939 and 1957 has Pluto in Leo and theirs is the power of love. 'Gone wrong', it's all about selfishness.

Anyone born between 1957 and 1971 has Pluto in Virgo and a powerful sense of discernment. 'Gone wrong', they are negative, critical and use their power to wound.

Anyone born between 1971 and 1984 has Pluto in Libra and will find great power by joining forces with others and bringing about peace. 'Gone wrong', they are judgemental.

Anyone born between 1984 and 1995 will have Pluto in Scorpio: these guys are highly intuitive and have the potential to exert serious power as Pluto rules Scorpio, so it's a double whammy! They are also known as the millennials, here to shake things up.

Those born between 1995 and 2008 have Pluto in Sagittarius: they are motivated by truth and can inspire positive change and even transform society.

After November 2008 comes Pluto in Capricorn: these guys are not messing around and are ambitious beyond belief! They have the power to bring about a new order to the structures and rules that are no longer serving the whole world.

Pluto remains in Capricorn until 2023 and will then be moving into Aquarius, where it will stay until 2043.

─○ HERE'S YOUR SPACE ○─

Pluto's sign and house placements have a lot to tell you about how to step into your power and use it for your own good and the good of others. Pluto's influence can feel pretty unsubtle (that bulldozer again) but its impact can be transformative. In some ways it's the planet of crisis, but that just gives you an even bigger reason to get to grips with it!

So, first, identify Pluto in your chart (or you can just check your year of birth in the list above), then flip to the appropriate section in 'The Signs' (pages 97–285) and study the sign's 'gone wrong' and 'gone right' traits. As ever, you'll be jotting down any words that seem especially significant. You're looking out for anything that associates with power or transformation, including death and rebirth. Remember to think widely here as the birth or death in question may not necessarily be a literal one.

PLUTO GONE WRONG	PLUTO GONE RIGHT

CHIRON

ASSOCIATED WITH: DEEP KARMIC WOUNDS,
SPIRITUALITY, HEALING

CO-RULER OF: VIRGO AND PISCES

DEFAULT HOUSE: SIXTH AND TWELFTH

CHIRON 'GONE WRONG' IS: LED BY PAST WOUNDS;
A MARTYR; LACKING IN SPIRITUALITY

CHIRON 'GONE RIGHT' IS: HEALING,
SPIRITUAL, SELFLESS

Chiron has an orbital period of about fifty years and, as far as I can tell, it's a bit of an enigma. First discovered in 1977, although images date back as far as 1896, Chiron was initially classified by astronomers as an asteroid and then as a minor planet, but it displays bizarre, comet-like behaviour.

In astrology Chiron is known as 'the wounded healer' for the part he played in the myth of Prometheus. The centaur Chiron became a mythological prophet, astrologer and great teacher. He was once immortal but sacrificed his immortality to save Prometheus, who had been damned by the gods to eternal torment for giving the secret of fire to the ungrateful human realm. Chiron was wounded by an arrow dipped in the blood of the Hydra, a wound that would never heal but turned him into a powerful healer of others.

There is much controversy over the question of which signs Chiron influences most, but in my experience it is Virgo and Pisces. Its placement is powerful for all of us, though, as it indicates where we are personally wounded, so that with awareness we may heal. My astrology teacher, the late Derek Hawkins, used to say that understanding Chiron was the key to finding the things that are missing from a person's life.

ASSOCIATIONS

1. DEEP WOUNDS

Chiron's placement in your chart shows where the deep wounds lie and how you may heal them by learning more about the sign and house it falls in. Studying the traits of your Chiron sign will reveal a lot about your vulnerabilities and, if you check its house, you'll begin to see where these vulnerabilities are prone to play out. For example, a person with Chiron next to their Sun may have a deep wound to do with self-identity and perhaps even a deeply upsetting experience with their father or father figure; on the other hand they may have had a particularly healing experience with their own father (or father figure) and thus inherited healing skills from him. Either way, the wounded can recognize the wounds of others and go on to become the healer for those who suffer similar wounds.

2. SPIRITUALITY

Chiron shows a person's potential for spirituality throughout their lives and, indeed, how they can become better people. A truly spiritual person is no pushover: they stand in their own power and gently assert their healing skills when and where they are needed, without feeling the need to boast about their successes. In my experience, there are plenty of true gurus who walk among us but they are humble; they do not crow. Chiron 'gone right' folk teach what they have learned generously and share their skills without fear of being taken advantage of. The real spiritual players know that the eye of karma never sleeps: no good deed is ever missed in life. It is logged and deposited in your karma bank of good deeds. To give with expectation of reward is not giving, neither is it pure: it is merely another transaction. People who feel they are never rewarded for good deeds and kindness in general need to work harder to clean up their own motivations and expectations. It is that simple. We all need to give more freely and expect less in return.

3. HEALING
Chiron 'gone right' are usually the unsung heroes: the firemen who risk their lives to save others (many are likely to have Chiron in Aries: Aries is fire), those who volunteer to help others in need – animals, vulnerable children and adults – and do so because they are driven to, rather than to gain recognition. I have long felt that Jesus embodies Chiron 'gone right' since he was a powerful healer who just got on with it, helping when and where he could. The friend or partner who listens and soothes you when you are hit by a dark night of the soul, without judgement or expectation of anything in return, is displaying Chiron 'gone right'.

HOW IT PLAYS OUT

Let's have a look at a few examples. If you have Chiron in Cancer, you are carrying a wound (or, if you like, a vulnerability) in the area of family relationships or your sense of security. You must work to heal your sensitivity, insecurity and family issues. You see, 'gone wrong', Chiron in Cancer is reactive and determined to do whatever it takes to find security in your unstable world. 'Gone right', you are a creative being who remains kind, sincere and giving, no matter what life presents you with.

If you have Chiron in Aries your wound lies in the area of assertion. I have one client with a rotten temper and he has Chiron in Aries in the fourth house, so it is usually unleashed on his family (fourth house is about family) and those he classes as family. I have another client with the same placement but she is famous for her passive-aggression so, as ever, it works in different ways.

Chiron in the tenth house means there is a wound in the commitment and career area, and in my experience, those who have Chiron in the seventh house, of relationships, are vulnerable in that arena. They need to heal the relationship they have with themselves before they can embark on a serious union with anyone else.

HERE'S YOUR SPACE

Chiron's sign and house placements are full of lessons on how to heal your deepest wounds and relieve your worst pain. By doing this work – which can be very challenging – you not only heal yourself but transform yourself into a healer who can bring relief to others suffering from similar problems.

So, first, identify Chiron in your chart and the sign it falls in, then flip to the appropriate section in 'The Signs' (pages 97–285) and study the 'gone wrong' and 'gone right' traits. Have a look at its house associations too, if you can. Make a note of anything that seems especially significant. You're looking out for things that resonate with your life's most wounding events and deepest pains, so this can be hard going but really worthwhile. You'll find it especially liberating when you're done.

CHIRON GONE WRONG	CHIRON GONE RIGHT

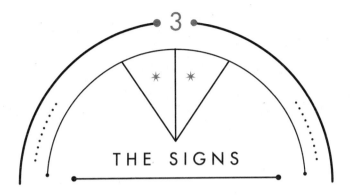

THE SIGNS

This chapter is where you'll find everything you need to know about all twelve signs of the zodiac (and perhaps even a little more). You may have arrived here straight from the Introduction, ready to scan your own star sign and intending to leave it at that. If that's you then hello, and welcome! I always hoped you'd be able to use this book on whichever level you wanted, and I've no doubt that you will learn a lot about your own star sign or the star signs of people you are interested in knowing more about.

Having said that, if you want to delve a little deeper there is a whole lot more to uncover. Remember that, as well as the Sun, which indicates our star (or Sun) sign, you have a host of other planets to discover in your full chart, all with interesting clues to uncover. So, if you have a planet other than the Sun in a particular sign, everything you read about that sign's characteristics will apply to the areas of your personality indicated by that planet.

The signs are presented in their natural order, beginning with Aries, the first, and finishing with Pisces, the twelfth. Each section is a mini portrait of the sign: the good, the bad and the ugly! The focus is on each sign's 'gone wrong' and 'gone right' characteristics, and how they impact on your life. As well as sections on love, career and health, perhaps most useful of all you'll find a summary of tips and practical suggestions for how to turn up the sign's 'gone right' energy and turn down the 'gone wrong'. I call these sections 'The Fix'.

You can either read the whole section on, say, Virgo and make notes on the segments that jump out at you, or flip straight to the end and read 'The Fix' on how best to manage its impact and maximize its potential.

As you will know, if you've arrived here having read the two previous chapters, we all have a little (or a lot!) of each of the twelve signs in our full birth chart so it is worth reading about all the signs to see which ones 'speak' to you most. Surprisingly, it may not actually be your star sign. If that's the case for you, it means that another sign is playing a more prominent role in your full chart. You might, for example, have Jupiter (the planet that signifies our skills and talents as well as where we go to the extreme) in intelligent but controlling Virgo. In which case, even if you've never given Virgo a second thought because your star sign is Leo, you will no doubt find that a lot of Virgo's traits chime strongly for you. More often than not, the sign that you love or dislike most in others is one that features prominently in your own full chart. And so the plot thickens.

And if you're flipping to this chapter as you begin to interpret your full birth chart by cross-referencing planets and the signs they fall in for you, then you're going to wind up reading every single sign in the chapter, combing them for clues. It can become highly addictive as you start to find them. If something about a sign speaks to you, either about yourself or someone you know, you can bet your bottom dollar that the sign in question features prominently in your (or their) chart. I used to make bets on that when I lived in the US and I never lost. It will turn out that you're fascinated by Aries because it's your rising sign (which represents your personality), or by Cancer because your boyfriend has the Moon (emotional life) in Cancer (home and family), which explains why he's a comfort- and security-loving homebody.

Whether you're scanning, flipping or delving deeply into this chapter, its main objective is to equip you with information about the 'gone right' and 'gone wrong' traits of the signs. To remind you, the signs represent the 'how' in our chart. As in, 'How does a particular planet play out?' The signs can only really be interpreted in relation to the planet that's operating within them. Only you can answer questions such as 'Am I maximizing Jupiter's awesome power in the most positive way?' And to do so, you need to get to know the sign it falls in for you.

Dynamic Astrology is all about building your understanding of how the planets, signs and houses combine in your full chart, then using that knowledge to tweak your behaviours to bring in more 'gone right' energy and minimize the 'gone wrong'. Here's to accepting, embracing, then reducing the shadow side and beaming out your light!

- ARIES -
THE PIONEER

FIRE SIGN

OPPOSITE OF LIBRA

FIRST SIGN OF THE ZODIAC

FIRST HOUSE

RULED BY MARS

Aries 'gone right' is easily the most dynamic and exciting of all the signs. Those born under Aries readily pioneer uncharted territories, break new ground and generally make original things happen, leaving the rest of us in the haze of dust they merrily kick up behind them.

Billie Holiday, iconic jazz musician and singer-songwriter, was born under the sign of Aries and her life demonstrates plenty of Aries traits and associations. She reached the peak of her fame at a time when segregation was rife and racism largely went unchallenged. Black musicians were asked to use the back door and the service lift in the hotels where they were performing – even as the star of the show. So turning a 'controversial for its time' poem called 'Strange Fruit', about lynching, into a huge mainstream hit was not only an act of creative genius but a brave move. Billie was pioneering and fought against the odds to follow her passion, which is typical of Aries 'gone right'. Aries is often learning about battles (ruled by Mars, the god of war), and finding inner peace is one of their life lessons (one they share with opposite sign, Libra). Billie had very little peace growing up and was constantly facing trouble and adversity until she finally found a passion (which is key for Aries). She joined a band aged fourteen and began channelling her enormous energy into music. She was said to be an 'improvising jazz genius'. She may not have been the best singer of her time but if you have ever heard her sing, you will surely agree that her gripping voice captures your attention and holds it until she is done with you.

The 'gone wrong' side of Aries is that you guys can also be too fast, too furious, too angry, driven by your need for new experiences and even just plain aggressive. Aries folk have much to learn about peace and progress: your energy has the power to 'game-change' when you are at peace with yourselves, attuned to your passion and following your own path. You need to learn ways to channel your powerful energy towards positive change, and you are going to have to cultivate loyalty and integrity to be happy on a soul level.

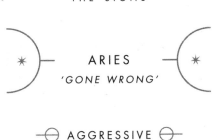

ARIES
'GONE WRONG'

⊖ AGGRESSIVE ⊖

People with terrible anger issues always have a planet in Aries 'going wrong' somewhere in their charts. Aries' anger can be monumentally destructive. You are prone to explosive tantrums: like Tasmanian devils, you unleash absolute chaos, then wonder where everyone has gone, or why the bridges are burning. You regularly attract aggression or passive-aggression, even if you do not display it yourself. The cowardly among you fail to embrace your innate potential for dynamism, and so make everyone else unhappy as you know on a deep level that you are not going to fulfil your potential. This makes you explosive, either inwardly or externally. Aries tends to be reactive and argumentative, if not to others' faces then behind their backs. You will declare war on those you perceive as your enemies. Any war will do so long as it prevents you from having to take a long, hard look at yourself.

THE LEARNING

If you have a strong Aries influence in your chart, you are probably already aware of the damage your temper can release, as you've almost certainly experienced the fallout in relationships, either with your family or at work. One of your biggest overall lessons is about peace, in all senses. How to appreciate it, cultivate it and practise it, for your own sake and everyone else's. The very first step towards living in a state of peace is realizing that it begins within. You need to stop rushing about, sit down and listen to your inner voice. It might help to connect with a spiritual teacher or another source of calm: try meditation or yoga. It won't be easy but, as with everything in Dynamic Astrology, the first step is recognizing that something needs to change. The solutions will soon follow. Anger can be tamed, like everything else, but this requires honesty, hard work and self-acceptance. The first and most fundamental step is to ask yourself what's fuelling your anger. Dynamic Astrology can be really helpful with this because it involves looking honestly at the 'gone wrong' traits that make up your shadow side, whether that's a tendency to anger, guilt, competitiveness, resentment or whatever.

Then you need to learn to manage any pent-up energies. Do not internalize anything as this results in passive-aggression and makes you a little like a pressure cooker ready to explode at any moment. Vigorous physical exercise is very effective as you burn out some of that fire. It could be a spinning class in the gym, five-a-side football or running in the morning, whatever suits you so long as it's really energetic! There are lots of anger-management techniques out there too, and many will give you the tools you need to master the flames that scorch.

One very simple technique for dealing with your temper in the moment is to pause and take some very deep breaths (make sure they are deep: this activates the vagus nerve and stimulates calm). Timeouts, in which you step away from a difficult person or situation, can be helpful. Practising meditation is enormously effective: it trains the mind, though that's a longer-term strategy and requires patience. If you're a beginner, a session with a meditation practitioner might be a good place to start or you could find a local centre to join. There are also some effective apps, if you prefer to explore by yourself. One I particularly like is Headspace. The founder trained with Buddhist monks. The ultimate goal is to be able to meditate alone, anytime, anywhere. There are no quick fixes but every little helps. You also need to practise, every day, thinking before speaking and breathing deeply until your rage begins to pass. Eventually it will become second-nature.

If you live or work with Aries, you may be on the receiving end of some pretty unpleasant and hostile attacks. A woman I know with Mercury in Aries (Mercury indicates the mind and the way we communicate) has a dreadful temper. Although I insist to her that she must accept responsibility and learn to control it (if she doesn't she risks ending up alone), I have also suggested to the people who love her that they should try not to put themselves in her line of fire when the anger flares. It is usually fast and furious but short-lived. When she gets angry they should remove themselves from her until, like a child, she learns how to stop hurting them.

If you are faced with a person like this, do not match fire with fire. There are no winners if anger is allowed to triumph. Speak to them when they are calm and more able to accept responsibility for how their outbursts make you feel. Do not allocate blame. Instead be gentle and firm. Try not to be afraid of them, though if you feel threatened you should remove yourself from them. Then call them, or write them a letter or an email. Keep your motivation clean: do not use their issues to gain advantage over them in any way. Help them to improve with awareness. None of us is perfect.

SELF-CENTRED AND COMPETITIVE

Aries can be extremely selfish and self-centred, never stopping for long enough to realize the impact of your actions. You can be mercenary too, fighting for the highest bidder or aligning with whomever you feel is most likely to win. Driven by your desires and passions, you make moves to satisfy your urges without a thought for anyone you might hurt in the process. Aries is a born leader and for this reason you can fool yourself into thinking you do not need anyone, but humans are pack animals and we all need good people in our lives. Selfish people rarely attract authentic folk who stick around for long. Why would they?

You also need to win at all costs, which only attracts useless battles and alienates all the good people you spent so much energy attracting in the first place. Relentless competitiveness indicates someone who is never able to enjoy success even when they do win. It's always on to the next thing with Aries 'gone wrong', and to hell with anyone who gets hurt along the way.

THE LEARNING

If you have a strong Aries influence in your chart, you need to slow down for long enough to begin to grasp how harmful your rapid pace can be to yourself and others. If you are honest, you will know you have the capacity to be self-centred and self-serving so wake up and do something about it. Make a concerted effort to listen to those around you; do not dismiss others' issues as trivial. You must learn to progress in life because progress aligns you with your true soul purpose. Put the needs of others before your own without the expectation of recognition. Try doing one small selfless thing each day: let someone else win or have the last word; give a homeless person a meal; stop rushing for long enough to help someone who may need support, a kind word or just some precious time. Your reward is the sense of satisfaction and the joy that comes from serving as part of the greater community.

You need to put your competitive streak to good use: compete with who you were yesterday and be a better person today. Keep it light and laugh at yourself – the minute you get too serious it's all over, and 'gone wrong' wins the day! You must give others credit for their part in your success, too. To ignore their role is very bad form and a real no-no if you wish to develop your character. Any rewards you win will be superficial and short-lived.

If you are dealing with this type of Aries 'gone wrong' behaviour at work, it is probably coming from a boss or a very competitive colleague snapping at your heels. There are several ways you can handle this, depending on what results you are aiming for and how much risk you are prepared to take. You must not engage in battle, just remain confident in your own skills. Try to appeal to the person's higher mind (we all have one!), respond gently and avoid getting annoyed or switching to victim-like tactics. You can also try asking them probing questions, with the aim of triggering awareness. Above all, have compassion for them: you are obviously a person they wish to emulate.

I have a friend who resorts to Aries 'gone wrong' behaviours and I often use humour to defuse things. I say something like, 'Okay, enough about you, back to me!' She laughs and apologies flow. Or, if that's not appropriate, keep the goal of triggering awareness in mind and, when a selfish decision is made, ask, 'Okay, so what does that look like for the team?' or 'Shall I notify So-and-so about that?' Never be aggressive or bring in other team members to back you up: to an Aries 'gone wrong' this kind of intervention is like an open declaration of war – they will start building an army and lining up the bombs before you have even finished your lunch. You may lose your job if the perpetrator is senior but it may be good to handle this head on, for your own growth, integrity and life lessons.

Whether you work, live or love with Aries, always begin with 'I'm sure you don't mean to come across like this but . . .' Aries just keeps moving and they often have no idea they are impacting you so negatively. You must help make them aware with love and kindness if you wish to prevent it happening.

Try your best to tackle any issues openly and calmly, without using the actual labels we're discussing: Aries is likely to explode at their mere mention. Ask them to take your needs into consideration, then explain how you are left feeling when they do not act upon your requests. Check that your motivation is pure, and that your actions are based on helping the person in question to grow. Then you can be assertive and stand your ground.

⊖ RESTLESS ⊖

Aries has enormous energy, and they like to get things done. They can grow bored easily, though, so may often begin things, then leave them for others to complete. Aries is great at motivating people and getting things started – in fact they are truly dedicated at the beginning – but when the sign goes wrong they are rarely there for the end of anything.

THE LEARNING

If you have a strong Aries influence in your chart, you need to learn to complete what you begin and to learn the lessons about peace and quiet, as we've already seen. In this context, I find it helpful to compare Aries with its opposite sign of Libra. Libra also needs to learn about peace and quiet, but from the opposite perspective: Libra will often compromise too much to keep the peace, then become resentful that their needs are not being met or are ignored. Aries often fails to think about their actions for long enough to bring about any kind of peace: they either blow up in a temper tantrum or wander off in search of the next project, person or challenge.

If this is you, you can benefit from anything that burns off your Aries-driven high-octane energy. Sport is often the answer, and intense workouts can solve plenty of problems. Physical exercise has been demonstrated to bring about a feeling of calm energy afterwards, so it's a positive double whammy for Aries that will help to make you less reactive and explosive.

You will also find it helpful to build your ability to stay in a situation or work on a task even after your Aries desire to move on has kicked in. You are not always one of life's natural completers, but sometimes we all need to force ourselves to work at something until completion for our own sense of achievement. The key thing is to build your awareness of these traits, then slowly work on your resolve to see things through.

If you live or work with a restless Aries, try to help them slow down for long enough to understand what they're doing. Help them by going for a run with them, then making them conscious of how relaxed they feel afterwards. It is wise to help them to discover ways to relax, and you could explore various methods together, such as exercise, meditation, playing or making music, cooking a meal and so forth. If you work with Aries, help them to form the habit of ticking off a checklist, which will encourage them to complete tasks. If they are truly brilliant and productive in other areas, perhaps allocate someone to support them. Try a colleague with plenty of Taurus in their chart.

ARIES
'GONE RIGHT'

DYNAMIC

Aries 'gone right' is passionate, committed, exciting and inspirational. You guys are self-motivated and super-dynamic, *über*-attractive and enticingly passionate, filled with zest and pizzazz, absolutely irresistible! Fast and furious, dynamic and effective: the aware among you know that when you slow down for long enough to observe the big picture, great things can happen . . . and happen they do!

THE LEARNING

You need to learn that, though speed and agility are sometimes crucial, slowing down enough to let inspiration hit, and to take care of the details, is just as important. And watch out for being accident-prone. Your tendency to rush around from place to place at high speed can land you in hospital if you're not careful!

INNOVATIVE

You have the skill to get projects and companies off the ground and are usually comfortable starting something from scratch, or backing something new and innovative. Your ideas are plentiful and you work with a naturally progressive vibe that can motivate people to join you. And you are usually pretty good at getting them to do exactly what you want!

THE LEARNING

Aries people are here to innovate and pioneer, but you must work on projects of value and focus on sustaining them and healthy relationships with others for longer periods of time. The most valuable lesson for you is to learn how to direct your enormous drive towards pursuits that help others as well as yourself.

⊖ COURAGEOUS ⊖

Unafraid to stand up for the underdog, Aries has courage and is feisty. You make fearsome allies, and are strong, brave and courageous friends, partners and leaders. You are usually comfortable with risk, not afraid to buck convention, and will fight dated regimes or silly rules with a smile, a team and a plan.

THE LEARNING

Aries can make great leaders but only when you have mastered the art of 'leading by example', so building your awareness of the needs and opinions of others is a lifelong learning that will allow you to achieve even greater things.

Let's take Facebook founder Mark Zuckerberg as an example. He has Mercury (the mind and how he communicates) in Aries and a seriously competitive streak. He never rests on his gold-leafed laurels. He is constantly pushing the boundaries in the digital arena and always striving to improve Facebook. He is also known for putting his team first, the sign of a person who leads from the front. On the not so good side, Aries can be prone to go to war and fight for the position of top dog. Ever since Facebook's conception Zuckerberg has been caught up in legal battles with the Winklevoss twins, who claim it was their idea. When Eduardo Saverin, Facebook's co-founder and original investor, failed to find more investment, he was booted out and decided to sue. Saverin's Moon is in Scorpio, and Scorpio is unlikely to go down without a fight. He is now a billionaire who renounced his US citizenship in what was seen as a move to avoid paying taxes, an accusation he denies. Zuckerberg is not known for sharing the position of top dog readily. You could say that Aries is super-competitive and loves to fight but Aries also attracts competition and fights from others.

IN LOVE

Aries in love 'gone right' is simply fabulous. You make your partner feel like number one, put their needs above all else and see off any competition with relish. You are exciting and spontaneous, always ready to fly off at the drop of a hat to explore the jungle or dive in the oceans. You are generous and like to shower your partner with plenty of affection and gifts that delight them.

Aries people typically have a high sex drive and are very physical. You make fantastic and adventurous lovers, and when your partner matches your energy you are sure to be loyal and faithful. It may be good for you to slow down in this area too, though. Try to introduce patience and sensuality if you are the fast and passionate type.

Aries tends to pursue ardently at first, but 'gone wrong' you can become high-maintenance because you get bored so quickly. You have a tendency to value the new and discard the old once it's outlived its initial attraction. You either flee as soon as any kind of hard work is required, or act in such a way that your partner leaves you, thereby diminishing your feeling of personal blame. The way to tackle this is to attract a multifaceted partner with depth and try where you can to deepen the bonds you have formed, rather than let them get stale. It's wise to know that in life we have lessons to learn and to remember that, if you get bored or restless, the grass is not necessarily always greener on the other side of the fence. Try watering the grass you've got. Talk to your partner and try to find solutions, rather than skipping off.

A client of mine, with Sun, Mercury and Venus in Aries, married a Gemini and she certainly keeps him on his toes (which is needed!), with her intelligence and wit. He is faithful and committed to her and his passion keeps her interest, too. You see, both signs have the curse of boredom to contend with so the combination works.

If you are in a relationship with an Aries, you need to be sure you can keep up with them, on all levels. They love to feel like the hunter winning a great prize, so don't be too easy or they may lose interest. If someone seems worth it they will stick with them and fight for the relationship: if a person seems one-dimensional they won't bother or will quickly get bored and shut down, or even be unfaithful. You can counteract this by keeping lines of communication open, planning high-energy activities to do together and focusing on keeping the passion alive between you.

CAREER

Aries 'gone right' at work is super-dynamic and powerfully persuasive. You guys can make the kinds of things happen that others only dream of. The happiest Aries are usually working for themselves or, at the very least, within a progressive environment. You're often drawn to project management. You like to set new trends and hit targets. Ambitious and driven, you want to win and are willing to take the sort of calculated risks that ensure you 'win big'. Your motto might be 'You've got to be in it to win it' or 'Fortune favours the brave.'

In general, Aries needs independence and autonomy and, being such a great self-starter, you are usually best suited to work that allows you freedom, the opportunity to innovate and the potential to lead by example. If life circumstances prevent this career path and you find this frustrating, set something up on the side and build your new project slowly, whether it's a company, a brand or an idea.

Talking of leadership, you are always searching for new challenges and projects, inspiring and motivating other people along the way. You are usually fearless leaders, preferring a free rein to do what you feel is necessary to make progress personally and for the company.

On the other hand, your aggressive drive can be disastrous for your own career and a nightmare for everyone you work with. 'Gone wrong', you are a very bad loser, who steps on people's toes without a thought. You are always ready to battle with supposed enemies and are not interested in peace, which is ultimately not productive. If you are unable to lead, you may become passive-aggressive.

A client I used to work with is always waging war on someone. When I started working with him I picked up on his internal battles and suggested he bring some peace into his life. His issues stemmed from feeling powerless as a child, due to an overbearing father, so now, using his status and money, he sues anyone who gets in his way and is as aggressive as can be: single, childless and lacking in the sincere-friend department, his unhappiness continues. I tried to help him to see that these kinds of battles always begin within and that sometimes you need to let go, trust the universe and move on. He cut my final retainer in half and stopped talking to me. I let it go. That is Aries 'gone wrong'.

Another Aries client and good friend of mine is a real superstar: an award-winning TV director and filmmaker, he is never afraid of risk. He uses his own money to find, create and fund projects, then tries to sell his eye-opening films to the people in suits with the money. After many years of closed doors the timing was finally right and he is winning awards right, left and centre. We both laugh when folk tell him how lucky he is. Luck? I call it tenacity, the courage to follow his passion, vision, and enough gumption to take risks, make sacrifices and gently refuse to accept the word 'no'. He is pure Aries 'gone right' and his work embodies that.

HEALTH

Aries 'gone wrong' needs to slow down. You are always pushing yourself to the limits, mentally and physically, and you run the risk that one day you'll overstep the mark – with serious consequences. If you are fortunate not to have experienced health problems so far, that's usually an indication that you have plenty of Earth- or water-sign activity in your full chart, which calms the ship, so to speak. But don't rely on this to work for ever.

You can be rash and rather accident-prone. Again, this means that you need to slow down and think before you act. Being rash disconnects you from the voice of reason and strategy and ensures you are solely tuning into reactive behaviour, which serves nobody in the long run.

'Gone right' you like activities that keep your fitness at peak level but you also know that you need help to slow down so engage in strategic games, like chess, and mind games, such as Sudoku. Competitive sport appeals to you, of course, but Aries 'gone right' is a good sport, and enjoys the thrill of any competition, game or tournament.

Meditation is good for everyone but is especially important for fire signs such as Aries, who need more Earth, via calm, stability and consistency, in their lives.

THE FIX FOR ARIES

1. **Slow down.** You need to make space in your schedule and brain to think about the moves you are making. Beware the shallowness of a busy life!

2. **Exercise regularly** and engage in high-octane or competitive sports such as spinning, tennis, five-a-side football, netball or martial arts.

3. **Learn how to relax.** Study meditation and practise chilling out without having to be exhausted. Be kinder to yourself: if you are always rushing around you miss the magic that can be found in the moment.

4. **Find your passion** and follow it, but don't turn it into another competition. You don't have to be the next Billie Holiday, but doing something positive that excites you will help you channel your energy in ways that help you.

5. **Focus on finishing things.** This will strengthen your aura (the protective energetic field around you) and make you feel more accomplished.

6. **Manage your energy.** If you have a temper, do something about it before it ruins your experience of life and repels gentle people. There are many ways to do this but being honest about it is the first step. Also, do not keep going to the point of exhaustion as this forms a very bad habit and can be detrimental to your health in the long run.

– TAURUS –
THE ARCHITECT

FIXED EARTH SIGN

OPPOSITE OF SCORPIO

SECOND SIGN OF THE ZODIAC

SECOND HOUSE

RULED BY VENUS

Taurus 'gone right' is gracious, tenacious, grounded, and among the most talented beings here on Earth. You guys have a tremendous ability to find solutions, fix and make things, and attract resources. All the people I know who are multi-talented have Taurus featuring prominently in their charts.

There can be no better example of this than Leonardo da Vinci, who is famous for being one of the most diversely skilled and multi-talented beings who ever lived. His recognition rests principally on his paintings, such as the *Mona Lisa* and *The Last Supper*, but his notebooks contain exquisite, intricate scientific drawings that were way ahead of their time, and he is credited with 'inventing' the tank, helicopter and parachute. Da Vinci also helped to train many students throughout his life, which is typical of Taurus 'gone right'. You tend to sit comfortably with your own talents and also support and nurture those of others. All very Taurus traits!

On the other hand you can be stubborn, materialistic, greedy, possessive, and so out of touch with yourselves that you fail to notice your deep soul-longing for real experiences and sincere, authentic people.

Taurus has a deep connection with nature, and some astrologers believe that their role is to act as guardians and custodians of the Earth. Whatever your personal belief about that, in my experience Taurus people usually find nature a great source of healing. Mother Earth is one of the keys for Taurus to find authentic happiness. And authenticity in everything is essential for Taurus to grow.

Some believe that the Buddha was Taurus. He left behind worldly attachments to find solutions to suffering and search for the meaning of life. Buddha became so disillusioned by the superficial pomp surrounding him at his parents' royal palace that he left it behind and began to search for the cause of human suffering. He came to the conclusion that enlightenment was the only way to transcend suffering, so he sat stubbornly under a tree and meditated until the answers finally came to him.

Before we launch into looking at the 'gone wrong' and 'gone right' traits of Taurus, here's a quick reminder of how to interpret them. You may not be acting out all of the 'gone wrong' yourself, (or all of the 'gone right' either, though people are usually much quicker to own those traits!). Perhaps it's more that you are attracting these issues from others. Either way, the 'gone wrong' characteristics are your shadow, and recognizing that will help you to advance towards 'gone right'. As I often say, don't fear the shadow. Everyone has one. Show it the light!

TAURUS
'GONE WRONG'

—⊖ GREEDY AND MATERIALISTIC ⊖—

Taurus people delight in pleasurable experiences and enjoy the finer things in life. You may be thinking there's nothing wrong with that, and really there isn't, but if a Taurus person is lacking in perspective, it can have a couple of unfortunate consequences. The first is quite mild but can still be problematic: you don't much like to share, so would prefer people did not use your gadgets, borrow your clothes or pick at your food. Taurus often gets attached to their stuff and, more seriously, their relationships. (Your generous nature usually prevails, and you often end up buying someone their own gadget just so you don't have to share yours.)

The problem gets a little more serious when your need for more of everything drives you to associate worth (your own and other people's) with possessions. Taurus 'gone wrong' is greedy in general and you wrongly expect that an excess of food, drink and material stuff will make you happy. This attitude can prevent you from accessing your true selves and reduces your potential to bring good people and happy experiences into your lives. Simple is best for Taurus. This pull can also make you one-dimensional, to the point of being bland or boring. In the worst-case scenario you run the risk of living an empty life driven by materialism and jealousy of others. Needless to say, this can alienate others.

If you have a strong Taurus influence in your chart, rather than giving in to your craving for the latest gadgets and the most expensive clothes and shoes, you would do better to go walking barefoot in your garden or the local park. A much healthier way to make your heart sing! Remember that your greatest lessons are connected to authentic experience and the power of nature to align you with your highest energy. Get outside and move away from concrete. Go into the countryside, the wilder the better. Even the local park in your lunchbreak will make you feel much better.

If you live or work with Taurus, their penchant to be a tad greedy, not to share and to prioritize material gain over all else may get on your nerves or bore you to tears, depending on your own astrological background. But there's a lot you can do here to help yourself and the Taurus person you care about.

Most Taureans feel a strong attraction to Mother Earth. Sometimes they just need a reminder that there's a whole beautiful, natural (and free!) world out there to explore beyond the food, fast cars or one-click internet purchase. Go with them on those country walks.

I once worked with a man who was very materialistic. He had Jupiter in Taurus (Jupiter shows which sign we tend to push to the extreme). He was a really nice chap, but very driven by his love for gadgets and gas-guzzling cars. I used to show him the statistics for climate change and he always ignored me. Then, after the birth of his first child, I showed him the latest statistics on climate change. His wife told me, years later, that he changed the family cars to hybrids. 'We have to do our bit,' he told her. It took a few years but he got there in the end! This is often the way with Taurus folk: you have to plant seeds and be patient. Don't push!

If the full-blown 'gone wrong' has already kicked in and turned into envy of other people's lives and possessions, you'll have to exercise some serious patience and a whole lot of smart. Taurus is stubborn but they do love to solve problems, so your first step is to get them to recognize the issue as a problem, then work with them to find the fix. From there on it's a question of harnessing their realistic sensibilities to find solutions that work for them.

SELFISH AND UNGRACIOUS

Taurus appreciates comfort, pleasure, beauty and fine things, as you would expect from the sign ruled by Venus, but this can lead them astray. Those of you who value only skin-deep beauty or plenty of assets in your romantic and sexual partners, for example, usually end up attracting total superficiality, thus failing to connect with the authentic and nourishing potential of the Taurus path. You struggle with self-worth, misunderstanding what is truly valuable, and can be extremely ungracious. Those who believe that the more they have the happier they will be often end up missing small acts of kindness and trampling on others' hopes and dreams. Taurus can be like a raging bull in a china shop in the selfish pursuit of its own short-sighted desire. Driven by an unconscious need to build your own assets to compensate for no sense of worth, you often get it very wrong indeed.

THE LEARNING

If you have a strong Taurus influence in your chart, you need to practise keeping your desires in check to free up space for deeper and more meaningful experiences in life. An endless pursuit of assets and pleasure is something that you will need to tame wherever you notice it, either in yourself, your loved ones or your business associations. Try to focus on finding pleasure in simple things, in good people's humanity and kindness. Support others and leave yourself second, like the house your sign is associated with.

If you live or work with Taurus, try to respect their boundaries but explain to them that sharing and helping others will make them feel good too. Be sure to recognize when they manage it and remind them how good it makes you, the family or team and themselves feel.

UNFORGIVING AND STUBBORN

Taurus can hold a grudge for many lifetimes, becoming rigid when opposed and blaming others for any adversity or challenge they may face. As with people influenced strongly by Scorpio (Taurus's opposite sign), you guys can get hung up on how others have wronged you. This is dangerous because it leads to a build-up of resentment, which can make Taureans unattractive to be around. Even more fundamentally, it can seriously stunt your own happiness and ability to grow.

THE LEARNING
If you have a strong Taurus influence in your chart, you would do well to remember that transformation is a key word for Taurus (as well as Scorpio). Scorpio triggers it and Taurus needs to embrace it. Being unaware can leave Taurus stewing in a lifetime's worth of grudges built upon resentment, envy and jealousy, all driven by your lack of self-esteem and the fact that you are valuing the wrong things. Those who hold on to limited perceptions and judgements, who have fixed their minds, run the risk of becoming fixed in their bodies, too. Stiff necks and shoulders are common ailments of Taurus people who do this.

I know one man with Saturn in Taurus (Saturn, and the sign it falls in, shows which sign's energy we need to work hard to master, see 'The Signs', pages 97–285) who used to blame the whole world for everything that went wrong in his life. He yelled at other drivers on the road and spent his life clocking up lists of complaints. He also had terrible problems with his neck and back. One day his five-year-old granddaughter came to visit, and when he told her that he had missed her, she innocently said, 'But you're always so cross with everyone that I'd rather play with my dolls.' She woke him up. Nobody likes to be around negativity, and blame is a loser's game that alienates the ones we love.

You must learn to let go of grudges and accept responsibility for your own faults. Far better to have compassion for those who have wronged you and to remember that every bad deed or unkind word generates unhelpful karma from which there is no escape. (That applies to your own stubborn grudge-holding just as much as the behaviours of others!) Forgiveness of self and others will liberate you to work on self-improvement through honesty and increase your happiness.

Your stubbornness needs to transform into tenacity, which is a hugely valuable trait in any situation and is especially rewarding if you are working towards challenging yet positive goals, such as a higher vision or a worthy cause.

If you live or work with Taurus, the main thing is to understand that they do not operate like this on purpose: it's in their make-up. Not that ignorance is an excuse for bad behaviour, but it should trigger your own compassion and patience. If you're dealing with a Taurus who is unforgiving and holds a grudge, you can help them. Remind them it's not only unattractive but seriously harmful to them. With determination, forgiveness can be achieved in even the most horrific circumstances. I sometimes ask clients who are struggling to forgive to focus on the example of Nelson Mandela. When he was finally set free after twenty-seven years in prison, a reporter said, 'You must feel hatred for those responsible for your incarceration.' He responded, 'No, I do not feel hatred, because if I did then I would still be in prison.'

—⊖ ENVIOUS AND JEALOUS ⊖—

Taurus struggles with both of these afflictions. Like your opposite sign Scorpio, 'gone wrong' Taurus is often persecuted by the green-eyed monster: jealousy. But unfortunately you also have envy to contend with. You Taureans are not only prone to feeling jealous in your relationships and possessive of your partners' time, affection and attention, you tend to envy other people what they've achieved or acquired.

Remember, even if envy and jealousy are not manifesting through your own behaviours, you might be attracting them from others. You will almost certainly have to deal with them at some point and possibly throughout your life. One of your major life lessons is to learn how to transform them.

THE LEARNING

If you have a strong Taurus influence in your chart, you may be presented with many opportunities to learn how to transform envy and jealousy through the power of acceptance, self-love and love for others.

If you suffer from envy you must step away from the person or situation who triggers it and then do some serious work on yourself. A few of the signs get jealous (Leo and your opposite sign, Scorpio) but for you it manifests as resentment. You need to start by being honest with yourself and taking responsibility for your life. Do not compare your lot with those of others. There will always be more successful, more beautiful and more blessed people: this is their good karma, and even if they seem not to deserve it, it is not for you to judge. Better to clean up your attitude by being happy for them, and grateful for what you already have.

If you live or work with a Taurus in the grip of envy or resentment, it can be very difficult to deal with. A jealous and possessive partner is particularly challenging. In my experience this either stems from the fact that they are themselves untrustworthy and so accuse you to throw the blame elsewhere, or that they are deeply insecure. In either case, do not be tempted to become their therapist. Instead encourage them to address their behaviour and get independent professional help. These two afflictions destroy lives so take them seriously. The major key in overcoming them is honesty.

Some other situations are less serious, though still annoying. Try to be patient. It is almost always worth it! Try to encourage your Taurus person to wake up by giving them opportunities to talk honestly and without judgement.

I once had a Taurus friend who was secretly very jealous of me and I used to poke the green-eyed monster within him because I was young, fed up with his behaviour and mischievous. But this is not the way to do it! Better to ask them directly if they want what you have, and try to encourage them to find something similar (obviously this won't work if they want your partner!). Either way, do not accept their behaviour: tackle it gently with love.

TAURUS
'GONE RIGHT'

⊖ TALENTED AND SUPPORTIVE ⊖

Taurus is all about talent. You can turn your hand to most things and are particularly skilled at problem-solving and fixing things that have been broken. The most successful among you seem to have a knack for recognizing talent in others, which you generously nurture, often providing valuable direction, structure, support and resources.

Taurus's combination of practicality, reliability, patience and resourcefulness makes you guys the most tremendous source of support to friends, family, lovers and colleagues. Taurus is the friend for life of our dreams: genuinely motivated to help, and loyal to a fault. You will listen to others patiently for hours, then deliver a genius and practical solution.

I am always attracted to folk with Moon in Taurus as they are the very best at nurturing me and they are usually amazing cooks! I also have a friend with Jupiter in Taurus and he is one of the most skilled people I know: he writes music, makes the videos to go with it, and is the best hair stylist I have ever met. My friends and I have to lure him over to our places with home-cooked food and beg him to cut our hair.

THE LEARNING

It's important for you to cultivate your talents as it is a guaranteed boost for your satisfaction in life. If you are not fortunate enough to use them at work, try to make them a reality in some other way. If you are a great cook, have dinner parties and invite good friends; if you make music, put it online and share it for free. Nurturing other people's talents makes you feel good on many levels and it deposits large amounts of karmic credit into your personal bank, so keep up the good work.

⊖ RESOURCEFUL AND PRACTICAL ⊖

Taurus people are natural producers, who thrive on actualizing dreams and concepts, their own or other people's. You are usually more comfortable around practical endeavours than lofty ideas: if you can't see the value in something you tend to refuse to get behind it. But when you do get on board, you will stay until the bitter end, braving all weathers to complete the task in hand or to keep your promises. (That famous Taurus stubbornness really has its uses when it transforms into tenacity!) Seriously skilled in practical matters, Taurus people also have a highly developed sense of aesthetics, so what you construct you make beautiful. You are at your best when you build things slowly but with enjoyment firmly in mind: hence the title 'the architect'.

THE LEARNING

You need a solid plan before you can make anything into a reality. Explain this to people and ask them to deliver. When you create or build something it will usually last as it's always built on firm foundations. Things that take time usually work well for you: a flash in the pan doesn't satisfy your needs.

NURTURERS OF LIFE, ENERGY AND THE ENVIRONMENT

When Taurus people are conscious of how they are using their energy, they are among the great nurturers of the Zodiac. Many of you spend time patiently cultivating seeds to fruition, often in a literal sense because gardening is a very Taurus activity. Soil in your hands is like manna from Heaven to you, while the patience and love required to build and maintain a garden speaks of Taurus 'gone right'. Even if you don't have much outside space, you can have indoor plants or grow herbs on a windowsill.

THE LEARNING

Taurus is here on Earth to defend Nature, to cherish and harness her power. Taurus people, or those with plenty of Taurus in their charts, need to be outside regularly to reset and lift their earthly energy. Many mistakenly surround themselves with concrete or bombard themselves with electrical currents from the most expensive devices and gadgets, which will always fail to provide them with any real comfort, eventually making them resentful, irritable and sorely unhappy.

Those of you who aren't attracted to gardening need to find another activity that allows you to build something from scratch. It could be anything from a sculpture to beats for music tracks, an outstanding piece of architecture or the finest meal. The old saying 'From little acorns, mighty oak trees grow' describes Taurus at its best. Those who help nourish the planet, and other beings, radiate energy that has the power to attract everything that they need.

IN LOVE

Taurus 'gone right' is a dependable, loyal, generous and committed partner, who stands by his or her love through good times and bad. You value your other half's needs above your own and are the most supportive of all of the signs. You bring all the ingredients required to form a long-lasting union based on respect and trust. Taureans are fantastic, tactile lovers, who ooze and appreciate sensuality. Attentive, sensual and gentle, you relish pleasure, your own and your lover's.

You Taurus folk prefer to resolve relationship issues rather than admit defeat. Taurus 'gone right' will usually be the last man or woman standing, such is their determination to get to grips with the problem and move on. Taurus appreciates tradition and sound moral values. Flighty associations do not motivate them and most thrive as dedicated partners, lovers and parents.

In fact, instant relationships are not particularly good news for Taurus. You need to build unions slowly and surely upon solid ground. For this reason you do best when you get to know a potential partner before making any long-lasting commitments or promises that may be broken: you hate breaking promises.

Problems can arise as a result of your tendency to become fixed. When your expectations are not met you can become obstinate, difficult and resentful of your other halves. And the worst-case scenario is ugly indeed. Taureans can make the most jealous and possessive of partners, who are simply dreadful at sharing. You envy the friendships of your partners and will even drive a wedge between them and their friends if you feel threatened. This all stems from your lack of self-esteem.

A client of mine and her former partner are both Taurus. They loved and fought with passion. She was from a very wealthy family and he grew up in poverty. She had many friends and he had few. They stayed together in love for years and she tried repeatedly to support him, until his lack of self-worth and insecurity over her vast social circle and their differing backgrounds made him so aggressive, jealous and possessive that it killed their love and eventually drove her away. Had he worked on his jealousy, they might have stood a chance. He was a quintessential example of Taurus 'gone wrong' in love.

The lesson is to build your own self-worth: you must work on whatever you do not like about yourself to create sets of solid values. Learn to take things slowly in relationships and make sure that you do not become possessive. If you remain confident and trust others, all will be well. If someone betrays that trust, it may simply mean that there is someone much better for you out there: keep an open heart at all times and listen to your gentle intuition as opposed to paranoia. Explain to your partner if he or she is triggering feelings of possessiveness and give them the chance to explain, then to alter their behaviour (assuming that your request is reasonable, made with sincere motivation and not out of unhelpful jealousy).

If you are in a relationship with Taurus, you need to give them plenty of affection. They need physical contact and sensuality from their partner, especially if they have Venus or Mars in Taurus.

If they become stubborn, gently use your humour and reason to lift them out of this habit. The worst thing you can do is push them, which is only likely to make them dig in their heels. Instead you should plant seeds, then leave them alone and let things develop at their own pace. Talking of pace, Taurus people need time to acclimatize to change, so it's best for everyone to respect that.

Finally, when in doubt, feed them! They need good food and nourishment. If you manage all of this, you will be rewarded with loyalty that stands the test of time.

CAREER

Taurus is the most talented, supportive and resourceful of the signs, and 'gone right', you Taureans can usually ensure that any idea becomes a reality. You are patient, dedicated and extremely resourceful, and good at recruiting the right experts for the job if you do not possess the skill to get it done. You break things down into ministeps and are so practical that you can virtually see problems before they arise. You are not happy until you have fixed a problem, which makes you shine in any arena that requires focus and sheer tenacity.

A client of mine is a gifted and humble music producer, who has many platinum records under his belt. He works with bands and artists alike who require development, beats and arrangements. I have seen him work on one good record until it's absolutely mind-blowing.

He never wastes anything: still drives a ten-year-old car, preferring to use his assets to develop artists and perfect existing tracks. This is Taurus 'gone right': they use their talents and resources to the best of their ability and never waste anything, thus respecting the planet.

'Gone wrong' at work, Taurus is a nightmare. You lack patience and are irritable and irritating. Many of you suffer from the green-eyed monster and fight any new idea or change stubbornly. You can make life difficult if you feel threatened by someone who seems more talented than you. You can also be bullies.

If you are behaving like this, you need to accept responsibility and try to change. Before you dig in your heels, ask yourself what your motivation is: is it for the project? Is it to protect your client or company? Or is it driven by your own needs? Awareness is always the first step, but whatever the causes, you need to look to your 'gone right' traits to use different energies.

HEALTH

Taurus needs to work with the body and must watch out for neck, back and shoulder issues. You carry the weight of the world on your shoulders and often become so weighted down with stress that the body fights back.

You love food but should eat little and often. Keep the ingredients as nutritious and natural as possible so that you're feeding your sensitive beings with plenty of healthy sustenance. Your energy levels and moods are a direct manifestation of what you have consumed.

Comfort is something you crave and Taurus needs beauty to refuel. However, the kind of fuel you require can be found only outside man-made construction. Exercise is important to all of the signs, but Taurus needs to make sure that they connect with the great outdoors: they should walk, run and, of course, meditate like the Buddha. Preferably under a tree!

THE FIX FOR TAURUS

1. **Go outside.** Step out of houses, offices, cars, trains, buses and planes and spend time walking instead. Sit in the park for lunch and tune in to Mother Nature, who will heal your heart and rejuvenate your energy.

2. **Forgive and accept.** Forgiveness doesn't mean you need to allow the perpetrators back into your life, but it will allow you to move on and release both them and yourself from a lifelong entanglement with negativity and bad feeling, which serves no one. Accept what has been and embrace what is to come. Move on with grace!

3. **Build things.** You don't have to be an architect to do this: anything you can make from scratch will heal you in wondrous ways. Cook fresh food and cultivate seeds.

4. **Tackle jealousy.** If you are jealous, face it and try to look at the cause, then raise your vibration by adopting a positive attitude and know that on some level the other people deserve their good fortune. If you are a jealous partner, look at your fears, work on them, and get help. If you face jealousy, be gracious but direct them to get help if you can.

5. **Eat good food.** You need to eat little and often and nourish yourself with food that hasn't been processed. Heavy meals and harsh ingredients mess with your health and drain your energy, making you irritable and impatient.

6. **Check your values.** Do not place too much importance on things that do not matter. What really matters? Love, health, family and friends, not inanimate objects and material nonsense.

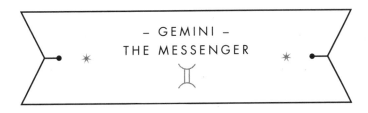

– GEMINI –
THE MESSENGER

AIR SIGN

OPPOSITE OF SAGITTARIUS

THIRD SIGN OF THE ZODIAC

RESIDENT IN THE THIRD HOUSE

RULED BY MERCURY

Gemini 'gone right' folk are easily the most interesting people of the Zodiac. You are constantly on the search for experience and knowledge, and are real thinkers and philosophers but also fun and light to be around. You have razor–sharp minds and mad skills in the communications arena. You're also born strategists and negotiators, who can convince people to buy more sand when they already own a desert. Being around Gemini people can feel like a shot of pure pizzazz for us duller mortals, and it's no surprise that Geminis are often surrounded by adoring fans. They are multi-taskers, warp-speed smart, and kings and queens of the witty remark and lively debate. All in all, they're pretty dazzling.

There can be no better example of Gemini brilliance and popularity than John F. Kennedy, whose charisma is legendary. People loved him at the time and he remains one of the most popular US presidents even now, more than fifty years after his untimely and tragic death. JFK spent most of his short time in office in negotiations with the Soviet Union to contain the threat of nuclear war; and also debated and battled with Congress to enact the Civil Rights Act, which was finally passed in 1964, the year after his death.

Unfortunately, Gemini 'gone wrong' tends to get bored quickly and is prone to flightiness and telling lies. JFK's example is illuminating on this score too: even the FBI director had to get involved when the president's extramarital affairs become a serious public issue, in particular his alleged affair with Marilyn Monroe (who, by the way, was also born under the sign of Gemini).

GEMINI
'GONE WRONG'

◯ IGNORANT, SCATTERBRAINED AND SHALLOW ◯

Gemini's shadow side is the opposite of sparkling wit and well-informed debate or skilful negotiation. Gemini 'gone wrong' is a gossip, downright ignorant and even bigoted. It sounds really harsh, but I've seen it play out too many times not to bring it up: when you Gemini folk aren't working with the 'gone right' side of your sign, you close yourselves off to all that potential for brilliance and settle for lazy opinions and convenient prejudice.

Gemini 'gone wrong' is flighty, with no ability to concentrate. You don't lack for great ideas but you quickly get bored. You have a tendency to start endless projects, though you usually fail to finish them. When your ideas don't become reality, you can be malicious and hostile to anyone who is successful and gets things done.

I know a woman who works for an advertising agency. She has Mars (energy and drive) in Gemini and was never short of ideas for clients' brands but her greatest desire was to write a book. Years later she still hasn't managed it. I try to encourage her but she has a different idea for the book every few months and only ever manages to write a few chapters before running out of steam. Luckily she hasn't become the malicious type of 'gone wrong' Gemini but her lack of focus prevents her from accomplishing her dream, which is a shame.

Gemini will do anything to avoid an inconvenient truth. (Think of the property salesperson who will say whatever it takes to clinch the deal, never mind the dry rot!) You refuse to educate yourself and consume nothing but glossy magazines, reality TV and chat shows. You don't care about facts or humanity. You do as little research as possible, skim the surface of any reasoning and deliver a jumbled assessment based on trivia and personal opinion. Then you surround yourself with people who operate on the same shallow level. As a consequence you regularly miss things, including any kind of subtlety or depth. It's as if you're stubbornly refusing to embrace any sort of meaning in your life for fear that it might challenge you to go deeper than your limited views and short-sighted perceptions. And the tragic thing? This is such a missed opportunity. You are tasked as the communicator of the Zodiac so you need to put in some work to reach your dazzling potential.

THE LEARNING

If you have a strong Gemini influence in your chart and you recognize any of these 'gone wrong' traits, please remember that this is not about a character assassination. You're not a terrible person just because you've got some challenging Gemini traits, and in any case, I'm sure you don't have all of them! But you need to own the ones you do have if you wish to change your experiences here on Earth, primarily for your own sake.

I often think that Gemini 'gone wrong' is frightened of their own intelligence and potential so they take the easy way out. But once you start to dive beneath the surface and educate yourself, you'll discover curiosity and incredible aptitudes for learning that you didn't even know were there.

You thrive on information, so you need to make sure it's the inspiring and factual kind. As US politician and statesman Daniel 'Pat' Moynihan said, 'Everyone is entitled to their own opinions but they are not entitled to their own facts.' (He had the Sun in Pisces with Gemini as his rising sign.) In this day and age of free information anyone can educate him- or herself online, or find a teacher to help unlock their skill. Find something that sparks your curiosity and get started. Before long you'll (re)discover that learning makes your heart sing with joy.

If you live or work with Gemini, and they're driving you mad with their refusal to research facts, read the documents you've sent them for a meeting or to check the fine print on a contract, try to trigger their awareness by mentioning the words 'shallow' and 'trivia'. Explain to them that they are dumbing down their considerable intelligence with a refusal to embrace depth, to learn and grow. If they are open, sit them down and argue your case logically, then offer them a solution.

GOSSIPY AND OPINIONATED

You Gemini folk certainly have the gift of the gab, but in its 'gone wrong' manifestation that translates to a love of gossip, which lowers your energy vibe and the mood of the person unfortunate enough to be listening! If this is you, you're also a chatterbox, who loves the sound of your own voice and never lets anyone else get a word in edgeways. Blah, blah, blah . . . Here come the hot air and high phone bills.

Argue? Oh, boy, does Gemini 'gone wrong' love to argue. Debate is for the intelligent; arguing is for Gemini 'gone wrong'. We all know the type: they devour the chat magazines, then become judge and jury.

Gemini 'gone wrong' needs to count how many times they are left red-faced and do something positive to prevent it.

THE LEARNING

If you have a strong Gemini influence in your chart, you need to learn to leave the arguing and opinion-making until you've actually done enough research not to come across as daft. As I said above, laying off the celebrity gossip magazines and finding something that interests you more than trivia will help to unleash your Gemini 'gone right' mental agility.

You also need to rediscover your ability to listen as well as talk, so practise pausing to think before you speak, and asking the other person questions, rather than talking over them.

You will discover that when you are open to growing, you will attract people who have much to teach you. The smartest person knows that they actually know very little. Smart people also surround themselves with people cleverer and more knowledgeable than they are.

If you live or work with Gemini, and they're the scatty, gossipy, shouty sort, don't get drawn into a row. Even when they're presented with fact, reason or logic you won't be able to change their minds. It's better to say gently, 'We're never going to agree on this as you obviously have your mind made up and I wouldn't wish to change that.' If they push you, share your facts and every time they react, remind them that they asked for your opinion.

If they are gossips, quickly change the subject or just end the conversation. Gossip lowers the energy of the planet so it impacts on us all. I usually say, 'Oh, that's low-vibe stuff. Let's switch it up.' If you are not quite that blunt, just change the subject. When you do it often enough, they get the message. At the end of the day, they are all about messages!

—⊖ DECEITFUL ⊖—

Gemini 'gone wrong' cares little for the truth. There's no nice way to say this: a Gemini person in full-blown 'gone wrong' mode lies easily and is often two-faced and contrary. You guys are the ones who talk to someone at a party until another more interesting or influential person comes along. You are seriously 'bendy' and will align with anyone or anything you think can benefit you. I consider Gemini in its 'gone-wrong' mode as a salesperson who cares little for the planet, humanity or the person they are selling to. It's all about the sale, the deal and, of course, the money. People manifesting Gemini 'gone wrong' fill their lives with superficial nonsense and can be tricksters who lack any sincerity.

THE LEARNING

If you have a strong Gemini influence in your chart and this is chiming with you, that awareness is great news: you can use this wake-up call to grow and improve! It is usually your speed of retort or fear that causes a lie, so slow down and get comfortable with admitting you don't know, rather than fabricating. And if it makes you feel any better, there's a distinction between malicious or damaging lies and the sort of truth-bending that can make life a little more fun. Why spoil a good story with the truth? You just need to confine your (white) lies to outrageous anecdotes rather than total fabrications that damage your credibility and destroy other people's faith and trust in you.

Those bad lies? They are truly toxic. A few years ago I got chatting with an old lady who needed some help with her shopping. She asked my age, and when I told her, she informed me that it had been her favourite age: when she had reached it, she was old enough to know what she was doing and young enough not to care. In return I asked her what had changed since she was my age. I'll never forget what she said: 'These days, lying is commonplace but in my youth, a liar was an outcast and people were genuinely horrified.'

If you live or work with Gemini and you're fed up with their tendency to avoid the truth, sit down and ask them for an honest talk. Ask them why they feel the need to fabricate or avoid the truth. Tell them you find them interesting enough as they are, and be ready with some examples to back this up. If you do not wish to tackle things head on, leave them clues to let them know that you are aware of their untruths and exaggerations.

If it's your partner, stress that you love them and are willing to work on things if they at least meet you in the middle. Most Gemini folk will accept this suggestion if it's made in good faith. If they do not and they ramp up their lying until it reaches malicious levels, you will have done your bit for humanity karmically by trying to help them change. And in that situation, if it were me, and if it was my friend or partner, I would have to distance myself from the relationship if they couldn't make a sincere effort to change. There are some relationships in which trust is so fundamental that a sustained breach is impossible to resolve. Trust is hard to build, and if it's destroyed there will always be cracks. If someone is unwilling to be truthful and they have your heart, maybe take it back.

The current US president, Donald Trump, has the Sun in Gemini, Moon in Sagittarius and Leo rising. It makes for an interesting combination. Now, President Trump is an avid climate-change denier, even though the world's leading scientists have confirmed time and again that the problem is man-made and the threat is real. Does the fact that he has multiple investments in fossil-fuel companies have anything to do with that? Gemini 'gone wrong' is the salesperson who cares little for the truth. Its opposite sign is Sagittarius, the great truth-teller, and the president's Moon in that sign suggests he has a big lesson to learn there. And Leo 'gone wrong' is inclined to egotistical behaviour that in extreme cases borders on narcissism. Trump has Leo as his rising sign, which is strongly associated with personality.

GEMINI
'GONE RIGHT'

QUICK-WITTED, AGILE AND ANALYTICAL

Gemini's strengths stem from traits associated with its ruling planet: you're bright, smart, seriously quick thinkers (Mercury being the planet of all things mental and intellectual) and absolutely fantastic communicators (Mercury again, the messenger of the gods).

Objective and thoughtful, you Gemini people think about things deeply and move from subject to subject with ease, capturing the attention of anyone you want. You are usually able to see both sides of an argument and can bring to the table logic and rationale laced with lightness and wit. Super-interesting and interested in other people and many subjects, you are thoughtful, clever, funny and charming, with simply brilliant minds. You are also the strategists of the Zodiac and are tasked with bringing the messages of the universe into the open.

Enthusiastic and optimistic, you refuse to be dragged down by detail and always look at the bigger picture. Your analytical skills are only ever rivalled by the analytical sign Virgo and inventive Aquarius, a fellow air sign, with mental agility and ideas. One of my dear friends is Gemini 'gone right' and she is a real thinker, cool-headed, well-educated and smart, who isn't afraid to debate a bigot or campaign for the truth. I have seen her in action and she runs rings round ignorant folk who upset others.

THE LEARNING

If you have a strong Gemini influence in your chart, you need to remember that your thirst for knowledge, your vivid memory and natural capacity for learning can make you intimidating to others. Remember to bring thoughtful consideration to bear on your interactions with other people. In my experience, this issue can be a particular concern with Gemini children, whose teachers sometimes struggle to support them as much as they need. Gemini kids must be fed with the right knowledge and educated from a young age for them to reach their highest potential. So, parents, if you have a Gemini child, be alert to this.

─⊖ IMAGINATIVE, ORIGINAL, ARTICULATE ⊖─

Geminis have incredibly fertile imaginations. 'Gone wrong', that can lead to lying, but in 'gone right' mode, you are brimming with originality and eclectic ideas. You are the very best kind of storytellers. I know a lot of creative people, but the ones with the real wow factor always have a strong Gemini influence. Gemini, alongside Aquarius, has the ability to think of things that nobody else has.

'Gone right', you're also intellectually curious and have taken the time to strengthen your innate gifts through study and the under-valued art of listening! You're skilled in the arts of debate, logic and reason, and frequently seem to have thoughtful answers for any question put to you.

Skilled communicators, Gemini 'gone right' listens as much as they speak, as they absorb, process, then make a plan of action to execute the ideas brought to them. Gemini is the messenger of the Zodiac, here to send out messages that will inspire, encourage or heal the planet and the rest of us mere mortals.

Two of my dear friends are classic Gemini 'gone right'. They are the best strategists I know and they always give me stellar advice. They think about everything deeply, then deliver a well-thought-out opinion. I love to sit with one in particular from dusk till dawn as we dance around so many fascinating topics. She shares knowledge and tells me incredible stories that stimulate and inspire me!

THE LEARNING

If you have a strong Gemini influence in your chart, polish your communication skills and use them where they will be of most value. You Gemini folk have the job of communicating messages to the rest of us, and it would be better for your soul to find the most positive avenue for this task. Look for causes that inspire you and opportunities to communicate a message you truly believe in.

Even the most articulate communicators can benefit from talking less and listening more. When I work with clients to interpret their chart and I'm tackling a tricky issue, I always pause and ask myself, 'Should I say that?' I call it 'going up the stairs' for advice from my intuition. I suggest making a concerted effort to listen more and not be tempted to fill gaps with mindless or nervous chatter. I work with an actress who used to do this after auditions. It took away the power of the performance. Stop, listen, and wait until the time is right to speak. The key is to slow down your responses and train your own intuition.

IN LOVE

Gemini at its best makes for the most interesting and exciting friends and lovers. You are genuinely fascinated by your partner and highly motivated to figure out how to communicate effectively with them. You are also a complete delight to be around and bring a light, fabulous and fun energy to the relationship. One of your great strengths is that you don't take yourself too seriously, and even those of you who would admit to being a tad shallow are so witty and funny that it's easy to forgive you.

Gemini needs someone multi-faceted and lively to ignite their passion, a partner who stimulates their mind and excites them on an intellectual level. Otherwise their flighty side may kick in. For you to stay faithful and committed, you need someone who can hold your attention for longer than a strawberry season! But remember that, as a Gemini, you have a tendency to bore easily. If you're thinking that the grass is greener somewhere else, remind yourself that this possibly says more about you than it does about the other person or your relationship. It might be wise to reconnect with your curiosity about your lover before you ditch things too hastily. Otherwise you may find yourself flitting from one disastrous union to another, hurting people along the way.

Gemini 'gone wrong' acts out their shallow side in all sorts of ways. You are often more interested in how a prospective partner presents to the outside world, or in what they can do to help you get on, than in any kind of deep or meaningful union. You fail to focus on anyone other than yourself for long enough to get to know them properly. Then you think you're bored and move on to the next unsatisfying and short-lived relationship.

I have a Gemini client who refuses to date anyone unless they're very rich. She is honest about it and is so funny that you just have to forgive her shallowness. Of course, she has never had a long-term partner (her average is a year) and soon scoots from the scene when the private jets and Jimmy Choo shoes stop coming.

It doesn't have to be like that, though. One of the most inspiring couples I know are a fabulously well-matched pair. She is Gemini and he is Aquarius. He spent years trying to get her attention and now he has it he keeps her interested with his smarts and sense of fun. For Gemini to stay, they need regular injections of intelligence and humour. He also has Jupiter in Gemini, which connects brilliantly to her star sign. They excite each other and are both hilariously witty, intelligent and multi-faceted enough to keep the interest and passion alive. They have just added another Aquarian to their lives: even their little boy is hilarious.

If you are in a relationship with a Gemini and things are going well, they make you feel like the most important person in the world, which can become addictive. Keeping them interested can be tough, though, unless you have as many layers as an onion. They appreciate lightness and don't like intensity: if you are prone to taking life too seriously, it would be wise to kick up your heels and lighten up (so long as it feels good to you and doesn't entail any loss of integrity).

CAREER

Gemini needs variety in their career or they go to sleep, become bored and seek trivia to fill in the gaps. Variety is the key word for Gemini in all areas of their life so it's a good idea for you Gemini people to choose professions that allow you plenty of eclectic tasks and situations, and where you can share your love of communication. You make fantastic writers as your storytelling skills are second to none.

Gemini folk are excellent people-people, too. You are charming, congenial and so truthful that you shine like beacons. Not truthful like your opposite sign, Sagittarius, by the way. Those guys hit you over the head with blunt truth as an object. No, no. Gemini is much more thoughtful than that. You care about how you deliver information. You study and research your subject and are often expert in more than one field. You also make the very best legal-eagles as you miss absolutely nothing. You tend to breeze through investments and make money, serious money, as numbers are friends to Gemini.

I know several hairdressers born under this sign and they love to chat and share stories, which can be refreshing – or annoying if you want some peace! As I've mentioned, you guys usually love people, the more the merrier; but some of you show the other face of Gemini, which is quieter, pensive even, like the writer who spends too much time alone with deadlines and cold coffee. Gemini influences anything to do with messages and communications. You have the ability to break down complex information or concepts and make everything simple enough for everyone to understand.

One of my dearest friends is a superstar art agent based in the US. She is Gemini and has had a long career within which she has successfully juggled many projects, clients and artists. Her sense of timing is second to none (another trait of Gemini 'gone right') and she moves effortlessly between countries, clients and different art forms. What an eye she has! Gemini 'gone right' can juggle and never make you feel that you are anything other than their top priority.

Gemini 'gone wrong' at work cuts corners, skims the surface and tells white lies to clinch a deal or get what they want. I would advise anyone dealing with Gemini in a work context to tune in to whether they are displaying any Gemini 'gone wrong' traits and check the finer details of any agreements personally. Gemini 'gone wrong' would sell his or her grandmother down the river to close a deal.

HEALTH

'Gone right', Gemini is calm, centred and grounded, with fast minds housed in steady bodies. You take care of the mind, which takes care of your whole being.

But often Gemini spends way too much time rushing around. You have a tendency to work too hard and need to get better at switching off from all activity. You're also prone to get stuck in your head, just like your fellow air sign Aquarius. You guys over-analyse things to such a point that you can drive yourselves crazy with the constant replay of events. You have a highly developed nervous system so you really must find natural ways of combating stress and lessening anxiety, which can plague you (along with Virgo, which is also ruled by Mercury). You need to spend time away from gadgets that facilitate communication *en masse*. Get outside into nature and stare at the sky!

You, even more than most people, are really not designed to be overweight. You need to stay lean and agile or you risk putting a real strain on your vital organs. You need to feed yourself with information and knowledge rather than overindulging in food and wine, irritating chatter and senseless TV.

THE FIX FOR GEMINI

1. **Feed your mind.** Read books that quench your thirst for knowledge. Study subjects that challenge your opinions, offer you facts and stimulate your curiosity. Try to focus on one at a time to help ground you.

2. **Tell the truth.** If you skirt the truth to save someone's feelings or prevent World War Three, that's one thing, but try to avoid it becoming a habit. Better to speak the truth or say nothing, which will strengthen your character.

3. **Avoid shallow people.** They take your optimism and often leave you with feelings of despair. Try not to get too entrenched in other people's arguments or politics as they might seek out your reasoning and communication skills to help them win.

4. **Let your light shine.** Your lightness and wit are dazzling and help to bring joy and comfort to those around you. Appreciate that side of you but match it with sincerity.

5. **Relax your mind.** You are prone to over-stimulation, which can mentally exhaust you and drain your vitality. Try meditation or practise Qigong.

6. **Stop rushing around.** Try to have days when you stay at home and chill out. Your energy needs to be protected and too many distractions prevent you from tuning in to the bigger picture.

– CANCER –
THE GUARDIAN

WATER SIGN

OPPOSITE OF CAPRICORN

FOURTH SIGN OF THE ZODIAC

FOURTH HOUSE

RULED BY THE MOON

Cancer is the kindest, most sensitive and nurturing of all the signs, with a real gift for creativity and intuition. It is a water sign and given that it's ruled by the Moon, it's all about emotions – even more so than fellow water signs Pisces and Scorpio. Cancer folk are extremely attuned to emotions, both their own and other people's. You guys are also genuine, sincere and generous to a fault. Most of you have sass and good-natured humour that is largely due to influence from your neighbouring signs (Gemini and Leo). You know how to nurture people and usually love to do so. Cancer people are also big homebodies and you view your home as a retreat from the world. Cancer men and women alike are very family-oriented. Most of you usually have or want children of your own. You are driven to make sure there are children in your life and lavish them with attention and affection.

Cancer 'gone wrong' can manifest in insecurity and over-sensitivity. Cancer people can be easily swayed, so their big lessons concern self-mastery, inner security and how to balance their own and other people's emotions.

There can be no better example of Cancer traits in action than the late Diana, Princess of Wales, who famously said, 'I don't go by the rule book . . . I lead from the heart, not the head.' She was adored by millions for her huge heart, her charity work and total dedication to her sons. Her life epitomized Cancer's 'family first' attitude and its instinctive genius at helping others. She took the princes to school herself and tailored her public engagements around their schedules, which was unheard of in the Royal Household at the time. Her work with AIDS sufferers was hugely influential: she would hug people who were affected, breaking down stigma and increasing awareness.

On the other hand, you didn't have to know her well to understand that she was driven by her emotions (to a perhaps unhealthy degree). This can go right or wrong but, in my opinion, when emotions are in the driving seat and far removed from logic, things can go very wrong indeed. The lesson for Cancer people is to try to fuse the two. It helps to pause and think before making any irreversible moves.

CANCER
'GONE WRONG'

⊝ OVER-SENSITIVE AND INSECURE ⊝

Ruled by the Moon, Cancer's moods are changeable. Cancer is the mirror of the Zodiac and Cancer people reflect the energies and moods of those around them. The problem is that you feel things so intensely that you must guard against being around negative people. Otherwise your moods will dip and it's hard to dig yourself out of the black hole you find yourself in. People with strong Cancer influence often suffer with low moods because they fail to protect themselves from harmful energies and negativity.

You are typically riddled with insecurity and generally feel that you should be doing better than you are, which is not helpful. Self-acceptance is a far more positive way to live your life! You are also prone to take everything personally and become defensive far too quickly. You often need constant reassurance and can be reactive, explosive and, taken to the extreme, even mean or bitter, which means you wear yourself out and exhaust everyone around you.

You can be very fearful. We all suffer from fear to some extent, but for Cancer it can be life-ruining. It could stem from any number of things, but often presents as fear of not feeling secure, not having enough money or not having a trusted network around you to back you up.

THE LEARNING

If you have a strong Cancer influence in your chart, you are so attuned to the suffering of others that you can sense when they feel bad and will do whatever you can to make them feel better, often at great sacrifice to yourself. You tend to take things too seriously and personally. You guys will internalize things too quickly and allow one negative situation or comment to ruin your entire day. Try to remind yourself that life is not out to get you. Neither is it all about you. I always say that Cancer must learn to treat life more like a game of tennis because it's all about interactions. It's not a solo sport! Ask people what they mean before feeling hurt or getting defensive: bounce the ball back into their court.

A lot of Cancer people I talk to wish they were less sensitive but I tell them it's a beautiful thing. You just need to learn how to pause and take a deep breath before you internalize or respond, as opposed to overreacting.

It's essential that you learn how to live without fear in order to embrace true happiness. Security is crucial to your well-being and there's nothing wrong with building up a bit of money in the bank or nurturing your family ties. But the bigger lesson here is that, no matter how hard you try, you cannot create a perfectly secure environment. Life isn't like that. In fact, everyday life is a long series of risks, and trying to micro-manage them all will only make you fearful, anxious and hard to be around. All the opposite of what you want to achieve. So practise letting go and accepting what is. Try to lighten up and not take yourself quite so seriously: it makes life much easier.

If you live or work with Cancer, try not to take their snappy, crabby or defensive behaviour personally. As the saying (kind of) goes, it's not you, it's them. Besides, their mood will soon shift and sunshine will return. They do not usually mean to be reactive, it's just in their nature, especially if you catch them off guard. Classic Cancer behaviour is to overreact, then spend the next few days making calls to apologize and generally feeling terrible about it, which is pretty endearing.

It's true that having a Cancer colleague can be draining. Their mood swings and need for reassurance are time-consuming and productivity-sapping. Behaviours that you might put up with in a loved one are just too much effort in a work context. I once worked with a CEO who told me he had decided to promote a person of lesser ability over a better-suited (on paper) candidate because of the latter's emotional reactivity. He told me that the person was simply too emotional. The guy took everything too personally, which slowed progress and cost the CEO resources, time and money. Out of interest I looked at both candidates' charts. The CEO had chosen a Capricorn over a Cancer.

SLOW TO TRUST AND UNFORGIVING

Cancer is protective of others and also of themselves, which ties in with the need for security. Cancer people can be strong and tough, enduring anything life throws at them. At other times, if your vulnerabilities are exposed, you can be as soft as the underside of a crustacean. It all depends on how you feel at any given moment. You are seriously complex characters who take a long time to award people your trust. If (or when) you do, you expect total loyalty and protection from the other person. If they let you down or leave you exposed, especially in the face of danger or adversity, you will rarely forgive them. Grudge-holding is a trait shared with fellow water sign, Scorpio. You Cancer people hold grudges for a long, long time. If things reach an extreme level you may become hard and determined never to let anyone get close again. You can be vengeful, too, which is terrifying to the recipient. If someone crosses you, or your 'family', you will wage a bitter and emotion-led war on them.

THE LEARNING

If you have a strong Cancer influence in your chart, try to keep your emotions in check. Understand that other people are not always as sensitive as you are. Often they are bumbling through life, unaware of how their actions hurt you. You need to take responsibility and talk honestly to them, rather than bottling things up, which only prevents them from being able to change their ways. Remember, internalizing leads to illness manifesting. Forgive, and trust. If people let you down, that's their karma, but at least you tried, and as long as you communicate with them, all sides can grow and progress.

A particularly powerful technique that helps to externalize your worries is to wait for a full moon, make a list of everything that's bothering you and burn it. This can be a great tool for all of us, but given that you are so influenced by the Moon, it's especially powerful for Cancer.

If you live or work with Cancer, try to be compassionate but let them know that it can be exhausting for them (and you) to be so defensive and untrusting. Have open conversations with the Cancer person and make sure that these conversations come directly from the heart. Do not react in the moment after some drama. Better to choose the right time to suggest that they find healthy ways to channel their emotions. Communication is key.

OVER-AMBITIOUS

Cancer, like its opposite sign, Capricorn, is ambitious and driven to work too hard, to the point at which it is difficult to switch off and relax. This ambition is not driven by a need for status (that would be Capricorn). Cancer needs success for security. Your ambition is driven by your fear. You need the security of money, property and steady incomes. You also need to feel that you have done everything in your power to ensure that you and your family will be safe and secure. For this reason you are not always very comfortable with risk, unless the risk is backed by someone else.

As we've already seen, any behaviour driven by fear will rebound on you and manifest in negative ways. If you let your needs drive you to invest too much energy in the 'success' of any project, you will never be available to all the other joys this life can offer. You might also end up unwell from overwork, and it's likely you'll become closed off and ruthless.

THE LEARNING

If you have a strong Cancer influence in your chart, you need to remind yourself that your happiness and peace are worth more than a huge house and a large bank balance. Ask yourself when enough will be enough. Am I using my life productively? Will I have any regrets if I carry on as I am? If the answer to the latter is yes, please make assertive efforts to change your life, one day at a time. Remember that awareness is the very first step. Dynamic Astrology can be a powerful tool in helping you to understand where your fears and strong need for security come from but it takes work to overcome them.

Start by assessing which parts of your life make you happy and which don't. Make lists. You need to write down everything that occurs to you, however silly or serious. Don't self-censor. Take a few days over this as it's a creative process. When you have your lists, conjure up strategies to change the areas you don't like and give more emphasis to those you do. For example, if it's your job that's making you miserable, try to identify whether the problem is the company, your boss or the work itself. It may be that the same job in a less corporate setting would make you happy, or it may be that you just want to get out of the sector. Let yourself dream about what you really want to do and be prepared to make sacrifices to get there. I've known people retrain at night, or work for years on a passion project that eventually became their job. 'Fortune favours the brave': life's too short to settle for 'okay'. Reach for the stars!

If you live or work with Cancer, try to be patient. Cancer people need security like bees need pollen. If they trample over you in pursuit of their own ambitions, you are well within your rights to insist on an open conversation with them. Choose your timing well, never in reaction to an issue, and be prepared with a logical argument. Try to guide them to recognize their behaviour, and help them to lighten up about it. If things are going well, you can ask them what their goals are and explore healthier ways to achieve them.

CANCER
'GONE RIGHT'

─⊖ PROTECTIVE AND NURTURING ⊖─

Cancer is a protective sign and they defend people steadfastly. Caring, gentle, generous to a fault and extremely nurturing, you guys are the very best parents and make wonderful friends and partners. 'Gone right', you are simply fabulous. My favourite person on Earth, who makes me laugh like no other, is my son Kam: he was born under the sign of Cancer. When he was growing up I nurtured and protected him. Now it seems our roles have reversed. He is very protective of me, ever watchful of any new people in my life and even those close to me. It's quite endearing. As well as Sun in Cancer he has Scorpio as his rising sign, and Scorpio is deeply intuitive. His 'spidey sense', as he used to call it when he was a little boy, is always spot on!

Cancer 'gone right's motto would be: '*Mi casa es su casa*'. But don't turn up unannounced unless it's life-threatening! Cancer likes to be prepared for guests. Creative, nurturing, warm and giving, you take care of people properly and delight in doing so, which is why you are known as the guardians. Intuitive, sensitive and at times sassy, a confident Cancer is seriously cool and brilliant to hang around with. Many Cancer folk are ardent in their passion for the planet and they treat Mother Earth as she ought to be treated, as a mother who provides a home: with respect!

THE LEARNING

You are the great caregivers of the Zodiac but really must ensure that you care for yourselves, too. Otherwise your life can be unbalanced and you allow unhappiness to step in. Learn how to protect yourself without becoming closed. My advice is to remain open-hearted as this is the best protection of all. You may get hurt, but life is all about experience: if you close your heart, life becomes robotic. You may not cry all your tears but neither will you love with all your heart or laugh until you cry. Balance!

EMPATHETIC AND CREATIVE

Cancer people have an almost uncanny ability to attune to emotions. Your emotional intelligence is second to none and this means you are highly empathetic. You understand other people's feelings intuitively and your gut instincts are strong. You have an ability almost to 'feel' the truth.

The benefits of well-developed emotional intelligence are countless and range from more rewarding daily interactions and happy love relationships to higher levels of life satisfaction. But one of the key strengths for Cancer is the way you guys use your empathy to fuel creativity. Cancer people are typically *über*-creative. You make fantastic artists and interior designers and are highly creative with your homes, but you also channel your ability to tap into another point of view to tell stories with meaning, create art and found companies.

THE LEARNING

Your emotional intelligence and your sensitivity are wonderful gifts but it's worth trying to build enough awareness to notice when you're tired, depleted of energy or cranky, and rein yourself in. Retreat! At those times your gut instincts and your ability to read the emotional content of situations are likely to be compromised. You can see only the shadow side of the truth – which helps nobody.

To attune with your emotional intelligence you need to begin by trying to empathize more with others. If it's new to you, be patient: it will take practice. With every word you speak or decision you take, ask yourself, 'How would I feel if I was the other person in this scenario?' Rather than walking past a homeless man or woman without acknowledging them, ask, 'How would I feel if that were me?' Before you say something cutting to your boy- or girlfriend because they failed to tidy up, ask yourself that same question. This will ramp up your emotional intelligence and the rest will follow.

IN LOVE

Cancer is brilliant at ensuring their loved ones feel safe, secure and adored. Cancer people generally make wonderful partners and excellent parents. You are so intuitive that you know what someone needs before they do, which is super-attractive to the rest of us. As lovers you are usually sensual (like Taurus) and gentle (like Pisces), generous and keen to please. Cancer in love will stay faithful and remain in a relationship as long as they are shown kindness.

I have a client whose rising sign is Cancer and whose husband has Venus in Cancer. (Venus indicates love and what we are looking to attract in our romantic partner.) And, boy, did he attract exactly what he needed! She displays many of the 'gone right' traits of Cancer: she is dedicated to her family, and their house is like something straight from a magazine – she designed and decorated it herself. Both she and her husband are all about family. Typical of Cancer.

'Gone wrong', you are so self-protective that you don't allow a relationship the space it needs to blossom. You are terrified of rejection, which is true for most human beings on some level but for Cancer it's a real issue that holds you back from experiencing deeper connections. When you allow fear to rule your interactions, you risk either shutting down emotionally or leaving a relationship prematurely before giving yourself and your partner the chance to try to make things work.

Years ago I met a very wealthy man with Venus and Mars in Cancer. He was in a long-term relationship with a woman he loved but his refusal to commit to her after several years (remember that Venus attracts a person displaying the traits of the sign it falls in for you, and Cancer needs commitment) ensured she left. It turned out that he was working with Cancer 'gone wrong': he was putting his own (financial) security first. He was worried that she was only with him for his money and just itching to take it away from him. He is now even more ridiculously rich and still terrified that every woman he meets is going to take him for a ride. I recently told him that he is living in a self-imposed prison and that nothing will change unless he changes. I hope he can.

When you open up you are often surprised by the affection, care, support and love you receive in return, so try to do it more often, even if it feels uncomfortable! Own your moods and try to communicate more honestly. Your emotional intelligence makes you one of the very best partners, and when you allow this to bloom without fearing that your other half will take advantage of you, you will attract someone equally worthy.

I know a couple who shine in this respect. He has Chiron in Cancer and she has Cancer rising. He heals her emotionally (Chiron is the wounded healer and Cancer is anything to do with emotions) and he appreciates her sensitive, intuitive personality (Cancer rising). They have an emotional connection that seems almost telepathic when it comes to knowing how the other is feeling.

On an extreme level, your Cancer defensiveness and insecurity can, if you have very masculine energy, make you chronically reactive, even explosive. If pushed to the very limits by a destructive kind of chemistry, you may even resort to violence. If this is something you have experienced personally or through someone else, professional help is at hand: you just have to be brave enough to ask for it.

If you are in a relationship with Cancer and can see past their mood swings, you are tipped for the very best kind of commitment. Try to let them know how their moods erode the magic of your union and work together to find ways to overcome them or reduce their impact. Remember that they do not respond well to being pushed, and try to be understanding about your partner's need to take regular time out. Encourage them to go for a walk or listen to music – whatever it takes for them to release their worries and mitigate their moods. Nurture your partner's goodness and match their love at every opportunity.

CAREER

You Cancer people are naturally creative and are particularly well suited to careers in design (especially interior design since it taps into your love of home). You are also natural caregivers and are very well suited to the caring professions and any work that serves others. A lot of Cancer people I know work in hospitality. Their predisposition to take everything personally is a great quality in this context. The company's reputation, the venue's lighting, the ambience, the food and the service need to be second to none, as if they were entertaining someone in their own gorgeous home.

Whichever sector you work in, 'gone right' you bring your emotional intelligence to the office with you and put it to work. You are intuitive, kind and sensitive to the needs of the brand, the team, the projects and clients. You care deeply about everything you do and make the best co-workers and bosses. In short, you are an asset that every business needs.

Many of the very driven businessmen and -women I know were born under the sign of Cancer or have plenty in their charts. They almost always surround themselves with family whom they trust to create what are essentially family businesses, even on a gigantic scale. Think of Rupert Murdoch, who built the Sky empire and owns Fox. He has the Sun in Pisces, which gives him vision and probably a passion for film, but Pluto (strongly associated with power), Jupiter (skill, talent and extreme behaviours) and Mars (drive, energy and motivation) in Cancer. Pluto shows where he is motivated and where his power lies. Since it is in Cancer, this speaks to family and his need for security. Jupiter shows where his skills lie, and Cancer, along with Capricorn, its opposite sign, is known for building empires to leave a family legacy (all Cancer traits).

I have a dear friend who runs a multimillion-pound family business. She was offered a large sum to sell out to a competitor but decided not to do so because she was concerned that some of the people working for her wouldn't be able to find other work and that they each had families to support. All very true to the sign of Cancer!

HEALTH

Cancer, like all water signs, needs to monitor its energy. You need regular space and time alone to gather your thoughts, to cleanse and restore your energy. (Remember, you have a tendency to take on other people's vibes.) One of my dear Cancer friends calls it 'needing a moment': 'I need a moment,' she says, and we all know that we should give her time to be alone, usually to immerse herself in a fragrant bath, lit only by candles. By the way, the bath is one of the places that Cancer loves to retreat to, and anything with water usually soothes you. Time at the beach dipping your toes in the ocean is guaranteed to rejuvenate you.

Cancer needs to be on guard against low moods. 'Gone wrong', you are inclined to turn into hermits who stay under the duvet with the curtains closed rather than allowing the healing powers of nature to soothe you. You become sad and choose to be lonely, feeling that you are misunderstood by a harsh society. The sooner you can work on your reactivity and learn not to take things so personally, the better equipped you will be to handle life and enjoy well-being on all levels.

Exercise and meditation are good for everyone but they are particularly vital for Cancer because they are proven to combat depression. If Cancer doesn't take steps to nurture and heal itself, your low moods can tip into full-blown depression. Mindfulness is especially congenial to Cancer types and is a powerful weapon against low moods, anxiety, stress and all forms of mental illness.

The pioneering work of Ruby Wax (Aries, the pioneer) is helping to bring mindfulness to the masses in an honest and cool way. Ruby, who suffers with depression, has Uranus (associated with awakenings) and the Moon (strongly associated with emotion and the need to take care of yourself) in Cancer. In fact, many of my clients and friends who suffer from the 'curse of creatives' (depression) are Cancer or have plenty of the sign featuring prominently in their full charts. Whatever industry you work in, it's worth taking seriously the issue of your mind and soul's well-being. The risks are too high for you not to.

I know a woman with Sun and Moon in Cancer in the eleventh house (house of Aquarius, which does not know when to stop). She is amazing but she uses her Moon in ways that are not helpful. She allows herself to feel absolutely everything with no self-protective limits whatsoever. I have tried to explain to her that she needs to learn how to tune out or she will burn out (she often does: I have had a few calls from her while she was checked into a clinic). So if you are highly sensitive you need to learn when the glass is scarily close to being empty. In my experience everyone has their own red flags that signal when they are close to burnout. The trick is to get good at spotting yours before you get to the point where there is nothing left. You do not have to get to that stage. Stop, replenish, relax. Turn off the phone and laptop – in fact, lock them away. Only be around folk who lift you and love you until you feel strong again. I am not a medical professional but I know that these little tips have helped plenty of people.

THE FIX FOR CANCER

1. **Play tennis with life.** Instead of internalizing everything and thinking you have to do things on your own, tap the ball back and ask people what they actually mean rather than assuming you already know. We all think and act differently, so ascertain the facts before you react.

2. **Communicate** your feelings honestly. Stop blaming people for hurting you and instead be proactive. Give them the chance to explain themselves and change how they operate, or at least how they deal with you.

3. **Take moments out** to heal from the constant bombardment of life's responsibilities. Have candle-lit baths to rid you of toxic baggage collected throughout your day. When you take the plug out, stay in the bath and visualize your worries draining away with the water.

4. *Feng shui* **your home and office space regularly.** You do not need to pay thousands to a consultant: check online where your furniture should be and use frankincense and purifying rituals. Just as you wash your clothes, clear your space.

5. **Declutter** your physical environment and your mind, which reflect each other. In my experience, depression and anxiety hide behind clutter so tackle one room at a time and get a friend or partner to assist you.

6. **Lighten up.** Try not to take things too seriously. This is only one life in a sea of many. Life is very short and oh-so-precious, and while sincerity is key to authenticity, taking everything (including yourself) too seriously is a heavy burden. Watch funny films, tune into your own humour and surround yourself with people who make you laugh.

– LEO –
THE HEART

FIRE SIGN

OPPOSITE OF AQUARIUS

FIFTH SIGN OF THE ZODIAC

FIFTH HOUSE

RULED BY THE SUN

Leo 'gone right' is one of the most impressive, loving and generous of all the signs. Leo people are hard to miss. You shine like your ruling planet, the Sun, lighting up a room with your charisma and sense of fun. Leo folk usually love to entertain and are often very funny – not even just funny, Leo 'gone right' is hilarious, and you bring such joy to everyone. You're also loyal, courageous and fiercely driven by a sense of integrity. You are great lovers of life. It's no wonder Leo has a reputation for being rather fabulous. On occasion, Leo shies away from the spotlight but you are still the most loving, loyal and humorous of the signs.

The 'gone wrong' version is rather less attractive. You can be utterly egocentric, competitive to the point of aggressive, and prone to drama. Try to become more aware of your own humanity, as opposed to following your own pursuits, and to honour the humanity of everyone else as much as your own.

American actress, comedienne, model, producer and film-studio tycoon Lucille Ball was typical of Leo. She spent most of her career entertaining people with hilarity, followed her heart and eloped with a Cuban bandleader, married him and then collaborated with him to produce *I Love Lucy*, one of the best-loved comedy programmes in television history. She went on to become the first woman to run a major film studio.

LEO
'GONE WRONG'

EGOCENTRIC AND ATTENTION-SEEKING

When Leo 'goes wrong' it's a bit of a bore. You guys have an ego the size of a planet. You're proud, self-centred and, at worst, narcissistic. Your ego can get in the way of literally any relationship you have, even with your children. (Leo 'gone wrong' has a really unfortunate tendency to see their kids as an extension of themselves rather than their own people.) You lack self-awareness and talk about yourself and your life incessantly. You care little for what anyone else has to say unless it's about you, and constantly interrupt to bring the conversation back to yourself. It really is boring.

Leo 'gone wrong' can't survive without attention. My friends and I were at an airport once, after a long flight, and a woman was singing loudly and dancing around trying to gain attention. We all looked at each other and said, 'Leo "gone wrong".' At its most favourable this is merely annoying, but at worst it can make life (for you and your loved ones) really hard work. You need recognition for everything. If you give someone something, or do a favour, you need everyone else to know. You are desperate for adoration and can be downright aggressive or out of control in your attention-seeking – and then you wonder why you've lost so many friends.

I know a woman with Jupiter (associated with extreme behaviour in relation to the sign) and Moon (emotions) in Leo who throws angry tantrums if the opposite sex doesn't show her enough attention when she goes out. It can be extremely uncomfortable. She has the typical Leo gift for being hilarious, so everyone forgives her in the moment, but she lacks self-awareness and it's hard to be around her for long. I also know a wonderful man with Moon in Leo and Leo rising: he is extremely funny and sunny in his nature (Leo rising) and very loving and generous, but he is also proud, and prone to dramatic emotional outbursts (Moon in Leo) if his lion pride is wounded, all Leo traits.

I have seen Leo's huge ego, craving for validation and hyper-competitiveness sink relationships and cause massive unhappiness. In the most narcissistic version of this behaviour you are copycats who take, take, take: ideas, recognition, inspiration, credit, anything that makes you look and feel better. You are quite prepared to use people to get what you want in life and will respond aggressively to anyone who pricks your huge ego.

I knew one woman with the Sun (associated with ego and self-identity) in Leo ('gone wrong', inclined to be egocentric and self-obsessed) in the fifth house (associated with self-expression but also drama and ego), all three default settings, which makes them extra powerful. She was a narcissist, but so deeply undercover that we all missed it! She was so charming and magnetic. She was also profoundly jealous and competitive, and almost destroyed one of my gentle, artistic, successful clients by using love to manipulate him (among other tactics). She slowly distanced him from his music, his friends and his support network, chipping away at his self-worth and confidence until he broke and she had him where she wanted him: vulnerable. It was awful and it took a whole heap of energy, love and healing to bring him back from the brink. Leo 'gone wrong' becomes the egomaniac who needs to be top dog, or top lioness!

THE LEARNING

If you have a strong Leo influence in your chart, always give credit where it's due and strive not to be the copycat. Acknowledge where your ideas came from and do not compete with your friend, lover or colleague. There will always be people more successful, creative, beautiful or handsome than you! This is their own good fortune, and everyone's lives can seem better than ours if our eyes are trained in that direction. Don't be jealous. Confidence is the most attractive trait on earth so work with it and shine in your own right. Your super-power is the power of love. Self-love and love for others.

If you live or work with Leo 'gone wrong', I feel for you! It is possible to manage their behaviour, but it isn't easy. For a start, don't challenge them in front of anyone else. That will only trigger their ego and they will tear your head off. The aim is to make them purr like a pussy cat not roar like a lion. Use humour where you can. Leo loves to laugh, and jokes are a good way to make them aware of their behaviour. A light touch, along the lines of 'Okay, so can we talk about me and my day now?' may help them to relax and actually hear you.

─⊖─ MELODRAMATIC ─⊖─

Leo 'gone wrong' loves drama, and I'm not talking about the kind you watch on TV. Every tiny setback, perceived insult or inconvenience is turned into a major drama and you like to drag in as many people as possible. 'He said *this* to me and I am devastated!' 'She did *this* to me and I am so sad!' It can start to feel relentless to the unwilling audience of your little show, and make you really hard work to be around.

The drama thing is all related to your need for constant attention and validation, and your inability to tolerate even a passing bad mood. You need sunlight and happiness in your life, and the moment you don't have it, you resort to drama to mask your unhappiness or selfish behaviour: anything to distract yourself from even a squeak of misery.

THE LEARNING

If you have a strong Leo influence in your chart, it would be wise to remember that not everyone finds every tiny detail of your life as fascinating as you do! Remember, generating melodrama takes a lot of energy, which is a finite resource, so this behaviour can have a really draining effect on you and the people around you. The most useful work you can do to dial down your tendency to indulge in it is to strengthen your tolerance of your own negative emotions. Nobody is immune to occasional sadness, disappointment, irritation or frustration. Not even Leo! You need to learn to contain energy and situations, not magnify them.

If you live or work with Leo, first, remind yourself of all the joy this Leo 'gone wrong' also brings! Try to have compassion and remember that Leo fears being left behind; they fear not being noticed, which is why they create drama. The best thing you can do is explain kindly that it is not helpful for them or you. In my experience, Leo's drama is often frustrated creativity, so encourage them to find a creative outlet and release all their dramatic instincts. Depending on their interests, it could be as literal as the local amateur dramatic society, a salsa club or a scriptwriting class. The point is, they need to channel creative energy 'gone right' and stop the histrionics, which are creative energy 'gone wrong'.

GRANDIOSE AND OSTENTATIOUS

Leo 'gone wrong' is inclined to show off in every area of life. You can be highly materialistic, and extravagant spendthrifts. I often think that perhaps you have past-life soul-memories of being royal! Leo is the lion, the king, and you need to be perceived as the best. Capricorn likes the finer things in life, as does Taurus, but without the need for any labels showing. Leo will have the brand name ostentatiously emblazoned for all to see! You guys want the biggest diamond rings and the most expensive cars to show the world how successful you are.

It all comes down to your concern with how you are seen in the world. Status is very important to you. Your huge ego demands not only that you have a lot and achieve a lot, but that everyone notices and acknowledges it. Even your generosity can have a dark side. All is well as long as you feel appreciated for what you do for others, but if not, you are inclined to lose your temper and unleash the roaring lion, which is not pretty. Your ego combined with your love of status and attention can make you impatient, greedy, selfish and superficial. This needs to be looked at with honest eyes and worked on every single day.

THE LEARNING

If you have a strong Leo influence in your chart, know that this attention-seeking behaviour boils down to (lack of) confidence, which is one of your lessons in life. The aware among you are humble and quietly funny. You know that the beauty of the soul is the ultimate attraction, not the plunging neckline or hundred-thousand-pound watch. Work on your self-love and confidence, and know that if someone is attracted to you for what you have as opposed to who you are, the union will not last. And you want more, right?

If you live or work with Leo displaying this behaviour, you may want to try allocating them an alter-ego. (Many of the most successful artists of all time had one, and most had Leo going on in their charts, too. I have checked!) Then, before you interact with them, ask which persona they're working with at that moment so you can adjust accordingly. On a more serious note, you need to remind them of what is truly valuable in life. Attachment to status symbols can seem like a bit of a joke, but, actually, it can really get in the way of soul happiness. None of these things can be taken with us. Try to help your Leo see, with humour if it helps, that working with the soul, which never dies, will bring them far more contentment than any amount of bling ever could.

LEO
'GONE RIGHT'

─⊖ LOVING AND GENEROUS ⊖─

Leo 'gone right' uses a huge heart to shower their partner, friends and family with love. You Leo types make others feel important, and such is the enormity and depth of your love, you can extend it far and wide. For those of us on the receiving end, it's magical: when Leo hugs you, their warmth envelops your whole being and makes your soul sing.

You Leo folk are so generous, too, with your time, your money, your attention and your love. Your first instinct is to give. Leo is like the polar opposite of stingy! One of my Leo best friends brings me the loveliest gifts whenever she visits.

I went to meet a few clients for drinks last Christmas, and my Leo client not only brought me a rather extravagant gift but insisted on paying for everything. That is Leo all over: they want everyone to be as happy as they are and will do whatever it takes to ensure your comfort and happiness without thinking twice.

THE LEARNING

If this is your nature, know that we appreciate it but we all love you for you and do not need expensive gifts! If you can afford it, then great, please continue. If not, please know that we just want your company. It beams like sunshine and brings us such joy!

─⊖ FULL OF INTEGRITY, BRAVE, LOYAL ⊖─

Leo is noble, honest and has a deeply ingrained sense of integrity. Your moral compass is very strong (a trait you share with your opposite sign, Aquarius) and, 'gone right', you are deeply concerned to live in alignment with your values. You are disappointed by other people who lack these qualities.

You are as brave as you are honourable and will fight for anyone you see as being part of your 'pack'. Loyalty is a mantra to live by, as far as Leo is concerned. The lionesses in my life are the most loyal friends I have and, when put to the test, have never let me down. Leo would rather die than be seen as flaky or disloyal.

THE LEARNING

Leo 'gone right' is loyal to a fault: just make sure that the objects of your loyalty warrant it. You have such huge hearts, and can be disappointed if your gusto for life is not matched. It's hard to live up to, too, so please accept us lesser humans! Know that your kindness and generosity are never missed. When we do things for others and expect nothing in return, these good deeds fill our hearts with happiness, which in itself can be the reward. Imagine that karma is a watchful being that never sleeps or misses anything: good deeds are always recognized in this respect and encourage more positive energy into our lives.

FUNNY AND ENTERTAINING

'Gone right', you are hilarious. You are as sunny as Los Angeles: jolly, happy and zinging with positive energy. I know a few Leos who are successful comedy writers and easily among the funniest people I know. Two of my oldest friends are Leo and they make me laugh like nobody else can. Mind you, Leos know how powerful their brilliant gift for humour can be, and aren't shy about using it. Even when you guys know you're being a tad self-centred, you turn it into a joke and are instantly forgiven. You use your humour to get away with blue murder.

At best you are theatrical, fun-loving and throw the very best parties with no expense spared. There can be an ego-driven side to this kind of behaviour, as we've already seen, but 'gone right', Leo lives to bring sunshine and joy into the lives of others and is simply irresistible.

THE LEARNING

Try not to exhaust yourself in the process of being the life and soul of the party. Make sure you take time out to relax and just 'be'. You have a tendency to shine, shine, shine, but even the Sun takes a rest and gives the Moon her time to shine.

IN LOVE

Leo is all about love and you frequently make the most fabulous partners. You are attentive and affectionate lovers, who give generously and constantly to your partners, showering them with an abundance of time, love, affection, attention and gifts. Let's not forget the gifts! Leo is all about heart, and you have huge ones. Your warmth, humour and charisma make you hugely desirable to other people.

As a Leo 'gone right', you delight in supporting and boosting your partner in any way you can. You are proud of them, and though some of you need to be adored, many of you just need respect. Plus, you are only too willing to do some adoring back. When things go right, Leo is happy to sign up 'till death us do part'.

But there is a flipside to all this fairy-tale stuff. When you're channelling Leo's 'gone wrong' energy, you are proud, selfish, ego-driven, difficult and demanding. You can be an absolute nightmare to be involved with. Naturally, some people simply won't hang around if you're dishing out this kind of energy, which leaves you in a quandary. You need love like other signs need oxygen, but you often end up driving away the love of some very good people.

To avoid this scenario, it's vital you try your best to put others first and make an effort to listen and be interested in what your partner is saying and doing. The only time a person can really say that they are ready to commit is when they're prepared to put the other person's needs before their own, and they yours, so everyone is taken care of!

If you are in a relationship with a Leo and things are going well, you probably already know how wonderful life with them can feel. They offer such an abundance of everything that they become addictive, like a drug. Leo in love needs you to pledge your allegiance and your heart to them, and gone right they will give, give and give some more in return, making you feel so loved and appreciated that anyone else's love will fall short.

Having said all that, you need to be aware that they can be demanding and exhausting for more chilled-out partners, so be sure you have the energy to take on a Leo in the love arena. You need to give them plenty of attention, affection, love and buckets of laughter. They need love like they need food, and if you don't give it to them, they become demanding and dramatic.

Many have voracious sexual appetites, which you would do best to match if you wish to keep them, and they like the finer things in life: if you are buying them gifts, get the most expensive thing you can afford or something that was made for them and given from the very depths of your heart.

If you fail to live up to their ideals, give them insufficient attention and affection, or wrong them, they will make your life hell before leaving you for someone better. 'Gone wrong', their egos can cause untold drama and chaos, which can be so exhausting and unreasonable that you simply have to wean yourself off the drug and walk away. But if they are working with Leo 'gone right' energy, and feel appreciated and happy, you will have the best kind of union another person can offer.

CAREER

Leo is brilliantly suited to working in areas that involve healthy competition or in the entertainment industries. You need to feel that what you are doing is important and are not usually happy unless you're in a leadership position. You like to be in charge and you take your career very seriously. Winning is essential to Leo: a trait shared with fellow fire sign Aries.

I have three Leo clients who work in the legal profession. In my experience, Leo is often attracted to the law. I know one barrister who wows judges and creates elaborate scenarios to put his clients' points across. The element of showmanship involved in being a barrister, combined with the clear win (or not!) at the end of a court case, makes this a very Leo profession.

I have a Leo friend who works in law in the US. He is forever helping people pro-bono, especially artists who cannot afford legal advice. He only takes on people and cases if he knows he will win and then, slowly but surely, goes about changing the game for them. He is funny, yet also reserved at times, noble, humble and as honest a man as ever I met. He has all the traits of Leo 'gone right'.

'Gone wrong', you can be a total pain to your colleagues. At your absolute worst you are prone to taking others' ideas and resources, then refusing to give them credit. Unsurprisingly, this can make fellow team members feel unappreciated and resentful.

I had a rather well-known client who was desperate to change career. She set about copying everyone else's ideas and ended up alienating many good folk in her selfish bid for success (which she gained in the end, as Leo on target often does). She was too proud to admit that she had had plenty of help along the way, and consequently lost all the genuine people that she had had around her, replacing them with sycophants. Leo 'gone wrong' just wants their ego to be fed. They don't care about sincerity or truth.

I also have a Leo client who works in TV, and he is so funny, warm and kind. He loves the spotlight and in his arena he shines like the Sun! He loves to make people laugh and cares about everyone, including the people who support him behind the scenes, even though he has never met most of them. Family-oriented and generous to a fault, he is pure Leo 'gone right'.

HEALTH

Leo is all about the heart so you must do all you can to protect yours. On a physical level, keeping fit, eating a healthy diet and not smoking are particularly important for you. You need to avoid putting too much strain on your heart.

On a more soul-based level, because you give your heart so fully, you tend to wind up heartbroken, which can be devastating as you struggle to bring balance to your own negative emotions. When you Leos are low, you can sink to the very depths of darkness. There is a burden that comes with the expectation that Leo is always happy and jolly, the life and soul of the party. In my experience you can suffer with immense sadness that you lack the resources to process.

Sunshine is important to you to keep your spirits high. You usually gravitate towards sunnier climes and don't do so well in dark places. I know several Leos who suffer from seasonal affective disorder. You also need to undertake regular exercise to keep your serotonin levels balanced, as well as look after your heart. Even better if you exercise outside under the Sun!

You won't be surprised to hear that you will probably need to work on ego issues throughout your life. Remember, it may not be your ego that's creating the issues: it may be that you're attracting them from others. Either way, they're going to come up as this is one of your fundamental life lessons. If your ego gets too inflated, something will usually happen to burst it for you. And, again, you lack resilience to deal with this, other blows and inevitable lows so your health can suffer as a consequence.

Children are a source of healing for Leo. You are soothed and inspired by their innocence and their unbridled enthusiasm for life, but it's important to remember, especially if you have your own children, to honour them as their own beings rather than extensions of yourself.

THE FIX FOR LEO

1. **Build confidence.** Even if you are one of the few shy Leos (they do exist), stand in your light and be the best version of yourself that you can possibly be. Don't feel inferior if you're not the classic extrovert Leo. We are all shiny stars. Know that.

2. **Express yourself in positive ways.** Be creative; find an avenue of self-expression to avoid attracting high drama into your life. Buy a colouring book!

3. **Let others shine.** Try to listen more to others and talk about yourself and your own life less: you'll become more interesting and interested in the wider world.

4. **Avoid selfishness.** If you are attracting it from others, look at your own behaviour to see how you can alter it. If it's you being selfish, take an honest look at whether this is actually serving you, and change. Do things without expectation.

5. **Stay humble.** Trust that the universe will reward you for good deeds and generosity. Tone down your need for recognition and constant validation as it rarely comes until you let go of that drive and validate yourself.

6. **Turn up the humour.** Your sense of fun brings light to us all and serves to get you the attention you desire in a more balanced way.

– VIRGO –
THE PERFECTIONIST

EARTH SIGN

OPPOSITE OF PISCES

SIXTH SIGN OF THE ZODIAC

SIXTH HOUSE

RULED BY MERCURY/CHIRON

Virgo 'gone right' is frank, trustworthy, innocent and kind, with a gift for making other people feel special, wanted and deserving. You have razor-sharp minds and are the undisputed healers of the Zodiac. You are also the most cool-headed of the signs: logical, analytical and hard-working. Virgo people tend to be clever, with a penetrating intelligence that cuts straight to the point. You are easily able to detach from your emotions, too, and are good at taking tough decisions that nobody else wants to make. I often say that if you had to undergo brain surgery you would prefer a meticulous Virgo to be carrying it out rather than a sensitive Cancer. Virgo would just say, 'Cut here. Remove that. Make an incision there.' Cancer would worry that they were hurting you and balk at the sight of blood. It's very Virgo to concentrate on the job in hand and get on with making it a success, no fuss required. You people are seriously cool and mostly unflappable. There's a kind of purity to Virgo that is so attractive. Integrity and honesty are paramount, and you have extremely high standards in every area of your life. (Sometimes those expectations are hard for us mere mortals to meet.)

Of course there's a shadow side to all this pure, clean energy. Virgo is one of those signs with a bit of a reputation. In my experience, everyone has known at least one difficult Virgo who over-analyses, criticizes and tries to control every situation and person they come across. It's true that Virgo 'gone wrong' can be hard work on many levels. Your inability to tolerate change or anything with even a hint of chaos stems from anxiety: your near-constant companion. You try and fail to get a handle on that by insisting on detail, order and routine from everyone and everything.

Many people judge Virgo folk harshly, but I always defend you by explaining that you only behave like this because you are terrified of being vulnerable. You fear being taken advantage of or dropping a ball. All my experience of Virgo suggests that when you channel your 'gone right' energy there is nobody more honest, kind or decent, or more likely to achieve great things. Your ability to identify what needs to be done, create optimum conditions, then dedicate yourself to the task until a project is finished means that you are one of the Zodiac's great achievers.

One of my dear friends and clients is Virgo: she is honest, kind and thoughtful, and a seriously successful photographer. She has a knack for making you feel better about everything. (And, as an aside, her work seems to me to encapsulate Virgo 'gone-right' qualities.) She always seems to know where her clients' insecurities lie and moves to soothe them; her work is heavily cutting edge yet clean, and her timing is always on point. She makes everything look pure yet edgy. Many Virgo clients I work with are like that: they work best when everything is clear and upfront; they do not respond well if they have to wing it.)

Your life's big lessons concern boundaries and control – just like your opposite sign, Pisces but from a differing perspective. Where Pisces needs more boundaries and to develop more discipline and self-control, you need to learn to let go and allow a little more spontaneity into your life. Virgo should put down their need for everything to be perfect and embrace the magic that life has to offer in the moment. Those who over-control things miss out on spectacular opportunities to live life.

A great example of Virgo traits 'gone right' and 'gone wrong' is the singer, songwriter, record producer and philanthropist Michael Jackson. His need for perfection was well known and his sense of timing made him nothing short of a musical genius. As well as the Sun in Virgo, he had the Moon in Pisces (Virgo's opposite sign), so his major life lessons were all to do with boundaries! In a nutshell, Virgo has too many; Pisces often has too few. In terms of his appearance, he became obsessed with his version of perfection and almost destroyed his nose in his misguided attempts to make everything 'perfect'.

VIRGO

'GONE WRONG'

CONTROLLING AND CRITICAL

There's no denying that Virgo's 'gone wrong' energy can make some of you guys difficult, controlling and critical, to the point where the person on the receiving end would rather jump off a cliff than hear any more. (You witter on too. I've known Virgos who talked until I felt as if a pneumatic drill was using my ears to break into my brain. Which, come to think of it, would have been less painful than having to listen any longer.)

You can be cutting and sharp. You literally pick everything apart, the most beautiful rainbow, the sunset, and let's not forget people, even those you love and who love you. When you unleash the Virgo tongue your poor victim may feel as if they have been sliced down the middle by a samurai sword. I'm not going to mince my words: you are capable of real cruelty.

An older member of my family whom I absolutely adore has Virgo as her rising sign, which is the resident sign in the first house and strongly associated with personality. Lots of other people in the family find her critical and difficult. I see through this to her true heart, which is pure gold. But it isn't always easy. I have been a creative freelancer for many years, which as those in similar professional situations will know means I go through feast and famine periods. She told me one day that she felt it very unlikely I was ever going to be successful or make enough money to create any real stability for myself and my son. Some would take offence and allow all sorts of ill feeling to arise from that cutting statement, but I knew she was just fearful for me. My refusal to join the nine-to-five brigade unsettled her Virgo sensibilities. I am Aquarius so I showed her love, then continued to ignore her in this respect.

There's a general fog of negativity that sometimes seems to come down over Virgo, an inability to see the good or the potential in anything. For example, you can be extreme penny-pinchers: the type that calculates the bill to the last penny and refuses to contribute any more than you feel you owe. 'Service charge? What service?' you complain, then proceed to ruin the night by picking apart everything that supposedly went wrong.

I call Virgo 'gone wrong' Victor Meldrew, from *One Foot in the Grave*. The main character has to have been based on a Virgo! Moan? Oh, wow! The glass is not even half empty, it's in negative equity!

THE LEARNING

If you have a strong Virgo influence in your chart and any of this is chiming with you, you may be feeling quite uncomfortable. Please remember that even if you sometimes behave like this, nobody is saying that you're not a good person. You can overcome this negative behaviour, and in fact it's urgent that you do, because at the moment your free spirit is imprisoned in a deeply fearful place ruled by your offensiveness towards yourself and others. It doesn't have to be like that. Recognizing your tendency to be critical is the first step. We'll work through the plan of action as we progress.

As I always say to your critics, Virgo goes on the attack out of fear. Fear of being out of control. Fear of being hurt. So the first and most important thing for you to do is admit that you're vulnerable and imperfect. You make mistakes. Everyone does. You are not immune to the universal law that says we all screw up from time to time. This is your biggest life challenge, and you need to do anything and everything you can to be okay with not being perfect. Remember, when you admit to your vulnerabilities people will perceive you differently and treat you better. Life gets easier in every sense.

If you live or work with Virgo, you surely know just how challenging life with them can be. Trust me, it's worse for them! It's easy to react to criticism negatively but try not to fight back. Don't take things too personally. This really is a classic example of the issue being far more about the Virgo person than it is about you. Look to the root cause of Virgo 'gone wrong's fear and all will be revealed. Their real drive and motivation is usually as pure as freshly fallen snow. The fastest way to cut through their fears is to ask them what they are afraid of. Yes, they'll probably snipe that they aren't afraid of anything, but stand your ground and eventually they'll come round and open up to you. Dig deep into your stores of compassion. If you can muster any humour, that's also helpful.

─○ OVER-ANALYTICAL ○─

'Gone right' Virgo is brilliant at analysing situations, problems and people, but 'gone wrong', you can get seriously bogged down in trying to assess every single factor, test it for risks, evaluate, measure and generally grind the life force out of it. This can be draining, anxiety-provoking and make it impossible for you to reach a decision.

I've known Virgos procrastinate so much when asked to do something that I could have completed the mission, gone home, had a shower and put my pyjamas on in the time they've spent weighing up the pros and cons and dissecting everything that could go wrong. (Did I mention you tend to lean towards the negative side of life?)

THE LEARNING

If you have a strong Virgo influence in your chart, you should find better ways to manage your anxiety. I suggest a two-step process. First, you need to be rational and ask what the potential risks and issues are. Then I suggest flooding yourself with feel-good juices: list to yourself all the things that are going well! 'I am safe, I am healthy, my family is safe, I have a roof over my head,' etc., etc. The simple (important) things.

It doesn't hurt to be as prepared as you possibly can be for the eventualities you're worrying about, but after that, let it all go!

One of the simplest and most powerful things you can do is admit to your ways, own them and explain to others how you operate. If you tell them you're working on your issues as nobody is perfect, you'll create allies, not opposition.

If you live or work with Virgo, try to be patient with their need for meticulous analysis and step-by-step planning. Give them as much detail as you can without driving yourself crazy, and remember that they rely on logic for the most part – so appeal to that. If you have a Virgo boss, respect their need for perfection. Be honest at all times but use the words 'expectations' and 'realistic' rather than over-committing and causing upset for both sides.

⊖ UPTIGHT AND ANXIOUS ⊖

Here we are getting to the root of all Virgo 'gone wrong's struggles. At best you are a bit stressy and in need of lightening up. More often you are chronically anxious. Your need to analyse and control is about fear. And when Virgo 'gone wrong' is full blown it can lead to a person becoming seriously uptight and way too clinical, which all stems from anxiety and the deep fear of not being in control – which is not good for them at all. Even a Virgo who's working hard on their 'gone right' energy finds it hard not to worry. At its most damaging this can tip into stress, psychiatric disorders, and even obsessive-compulsive disorder. Every single person I've ever worked with who exhibited OCD-like symptoms had Virgo prominent in their chart. My Virgo musician friend's house is immaculate: you could eat off his Virgo floor. *Slightly* veering towards OCD!

One of the most anxious people I know is a Venus in Virgo, especially in her relationships (Venus governs our intimate relationships). I have been working with her for some time and have seen her partners come and go: they find her too uptight and controlling and her anxiety keeps her up at night. I am trying to help her see that she needs to control less and open up to people without fear that they will take advantage of her (this is usually what Virgo folk fear): in expressing her fears she will give her partner the opportunity to support her and to vanquish them. I suggested that she writes down all her fears before she sleeps and puts them in a 'worry box': that way she isn't taking them to bed with her.

THE LEARNING

If you have a strong Virgo influence in your chart you need to lighten up. Humour is a great medicine for us all. Try to focus on the magic of the moment. Practising gratitude is a powerful way to push back against worry and negativity. Anxious people make endless mental lists of issues that scare them, but not of the things that are wonderful, secure, healthy and positive. Try counting all the things you're grateful for.

If you live or work with Virgo, try to make them laugh. Tell them funny stories and remind them not to take everything so seriously. Meditation can be an enormous help so suggest that they download an app or join a meditation group. This helps to tame and train the mind: living in the past often creates depression and living in the future can create anxiety. Encourage them to be in the moment, which is all we ever really have.

VIRGO
'GONE RIGHT'

HEALERS

I believe that Virgo is the most powerful and natural healer in the Zodiac: Virgos know intuitively what to say, and when, and can make you feel like the most valued person on the planet.

A friend of mine had a breakdown when her partner left her. She spent months in hospital where they tried to rebuild her with prescription drugs and talking therapy, but she only really healed when her Virgo godmother stepped in. She took my friend to stay with her, then confiscated her phone and held her in a bubble, giving her a pure, safe space in which to work through her pain. It took a few months but that woman did what all the most expensive doctors and medications could not. She allowed my friend to heal. My friend is now happily married and living her life. Virgo 'gone right' heals, protects and fixes us when we break – and, due to the unreasonable expectations and pressures of today's society, more and more of us do break.

THE LEARNING

There is nothing more rewarding than fixing a bird's broken wing, then setting it free to live again. Our society is so manic: we are asked to work until we drop, expected to look ever-youthful and always be happy. This world needs Virgo, desperately. If you are

Virgo, please know that the service you provide to the rest of the planet far outweighs the hard work you can be. One of your roles in life is to be of service and this feeds and nourishes your soul.

HONEST, CANDID, TRUSTWORTHY

Virgo is the purest sign of the Zodiac and often referred to as 'the virgin'. You are often a little naive (which can be annoying or endearing, depending on who's doing the evaluating!) and you have a certain childlike quality, which ensures that you never really age. I think it has something to do with the fact that you are sincerely pure at heart. Your honesty shines through, like the moonlight, and when you decide that someone is worthy of your affection, you are always there for them, attentive, forthright and candid. You are usually frugal with compliments but when you do give them, the recipient can be sure that they're sincere. Virgo is like the antidote to poppycock. You never suffer fools gladly. From the Virgo point of view, flattery, truth-bending and lies are wrong. You are seriously honest, not in the blunt Sagittarius way. It's more clinical, more logical.

THE LEARNING
You may feel that you stand alone when you are truthful, then beat yourself up over it afterwards, which is typical of Virgo. As long as you take care not to hurt people unnecessarily or speak the truth out of revenge, we need more of you.

ASTUTE

Virgo people displaying 'gone right' traits are intelligent, penetrating and astute. You are the most analytical of all the signs and seem to have a knack for distinguishing quickly between what will work and what will not. You also have an uncanny sense of timing that ensures you deliver helpful information from your knowledgeable brain at the right moment. If a friend or colleague needs a spot-on diagnosis or someone to cut through the chaos and tell them what really needs doing, Virgo is the solution.

THE LEARNING

Recognize your skills and own them. Make more of them. Do not shy away from them. One small suggestion: it is always better to wait until you are asked before offering your advice or opinion. That way you are working with a receptive audience and will encounter little resistance.

—⊖— HELPFUL AND SUPPORTIVE —⊖—

You like to put all this mental precision to good use and love to be helpful. You are great at sitting patiently with a problem or listening to someone pouring their heart out until you have found the fix, or at least made the person feel better. You particularly like to support people who are trying to make a go of something: Virgo loves a trier. You don't usually make moves to help people who are not trying to help themselves.

You can be extremely self-sacrificing and many of you experience joy mainly through service to others. This obviously has a positive side but also drawbacks – primarily for you. You are usually very generous with time, service and money to charity. In fact, some of the world's most prominent philanthropists, including Warren Buffett, have a strong Virgo influence in their charts.

THE LEARNING

Being of service is fantastic but make sure that you create a balanced life and have fun in the process. Lighten up and be frivolous from time to time! Get involved in a cause that you care about but make it fun. Enlist your friends and dance for twelve hours straight for charity (not in heels, of course!). Run a marathon in a silly costume or get sponsored to criticize nothing and no one for a whole twenty-four hours.

IN LOVE

Virgo shines with a purity and certain innocence that makes them instantly attractive, and you are faithful, dedicated lovers and partners. I know a Virgo man who stopped talking to his married friend because that friend had had an affair. This is typical of Virgo: they do not appreciate betrayal, lies or dishonesty. The funny thing is that this guy didn't even like his friend's wife, but as far as he was concerned, if his friend could lie and cheat on his 'life partner' he wasn't the man he'd thought he was. Virgo can be a puritan, but you are often seriously decent human beings.

The problem is, you have such high expectations that it's often difficult for anyone to live up to them. You are the perfectionists of the Zodiac and must be careful not to be too critical of others or you risk being lonely. The issue is that you see someone's potential so have trouble accepting who they are in that moment. You try to improve them to make them beyond compare, but it's unrealistic. Virgo 'gone wrong' puts their lovers on a pedestal for a moment, then spends months or years picking them apart in a bid to improve them. This can be highly destructive of everyone's happiness. The other person begins to unravel and usually has to leave the relationship to rebuild their confidence. Virgo folk must accept the reality of their partner from the start and learn how to celebrate the imperfections that make us all unique.

I knew a couple who were madly in love but my Virgo client was controlling, even critical at times. I knew that this was due to her Virgo fear of vulnerability but her Aries partner was angry with her because he felt that she was infringing on his independence. Virgo tried to micro-manage Aries (good luck with that!), learning in the process that the only person she could control was herself. The way to an Aries heart is to give them plenty of freedom and to encourage their energy and passion for life. The way to Virgo's heart is to help them push through their fears, give them plenty of reassurance and help them to laugh.

CAREER

Virgo is a high achiever, excelling at anything that requires dedication, focus and high levels of concentration. Your innate sense of (typically clean and precise) style makes you fantastic designers, especially in fashion, and you are strong stylists. The other vocation that draws Virgos is medicine and anything connected to healing. You make brilliant surgeons, doctors, nurses, scientists and IT people, with your attention to detail, patience and level of concentration.

As a Virgo, you need structure and order to perform to the best of your abilities: you do not do well in chaotic environments. Your unrivalled organizational skills typically make you a huge asset to any employer, and when you're channelling 'gone right' energy, you're not only methodical but almost Zen-like in your ability to clear a space for your best work to shine through. I know several Virgo freelancers who are fantastic at setting their own rules: they get up at the same time every day and go through their routines to get into the work zone with calm and precision.

Your other great strength when it comes to your career is your incredible work ethic. Nobody works like Virgo. Beyoncé Knowles, for example, was born with the Sun in Virgo and, although her talent is globally respected and recognized, she will openly testify that it is hard work and focus over many years that have helped shape her into the superstar she is today. Apparently, even at an age when most kids were playing with their dolls and riding bikes, she preferred to practise running and singing at the same time.

HEALTH

Virgo's health problems typically stem from their inability to let go of stress. You internalize way too much so suffer with your stomach (everything from IBS to ulcers), not to mention high blood pressure, a host of anxiety disorders and OCD.

It's absolutely essential, for the sake of your long-term health, that you learn how to manage stress. A simple but effective technique that helps Virgos is, as I mentioned earlier, to write down everything that concerns you. You are not the kind of person who finds it easy to share your worries so anything that encourages release is a good idea. And if you think you may have an anxiety disorder, a phobia or OCD, then do seek professional help.

While it is true that Virgo tends to suffer with more ailments than the other signs (it governs health and healing in general), you are also prone to hypochondria.

My friend with plenty of Virgo in his chart (the musician with the immaculate floor) suffers with various health problems, and while many are certainly real, a few are undoubtedly psychosomatic. It can be a bit tricky to handle, to the point that we, his friends, are often reluctant to ask him how he is! His music, by the way, is nothing short of perfect and he is known to 'spend three days on one snare' for a tune, which can make him rather challenging to work with, but everybody loves him: he truly is one of the most honest people on the planet and the very best kind of friend a person could wish for.

THE FIX FOR VIRGO

1. **Admit to your vulnerabilities.** Be more open, make sure that your boundaries are not too rigid and try not to control everything so much. Let people know when you are struggling and give them opportunities to step up.

2. **Take time to heal your energy.** Clear your space and play beautiful music to relax you and heal your soul. Try using a mantra that reminds you that all is well a few times a day.

3. **Lighten up.** Easier said than done, I know, but try not to take everything too seriously. Tune into the innocence and childlike sense of wonder that's naturally inside you. Life is easier when you go with the flow and appreciate its magic.

4. **Think before you speak.** Every time you feel yourself ready to criticize or pick something or someone apart, stop yourself and say something nice instead. Hold your tongue until you've cooled down.

5. **Have more fun.** Try not to make life all about work. Relax more and spend time using your healing skills to assist your friends and loved ones. Life is too short to be negative: it dampens your spirits and kills your potential for joy.

6. **Face your fears.** Make a concerted effort to tackle your anxiety and break the habit of worry. Learn new skills to do this – meditate, run, do yoga and try flooding yourself with feel-good juices (see page 182), until anxiety subsides. At the very least try it! I promise you it works!

– LIBRA –
THE BALANCE

AIR SIGN

OPPOSITE OF ARIES

SEVENTH SIGN OF THE ZODIAC

SEVENTH HOUSE

RULED BY VENUS

Libra 'gone right' is the most refined, civilized, diplomatic and graceful of all the signs. More often than not you are also admirable, and you're always charming and persuasive. You are the natural mediators and diplomats of the Zodiac and you bring peace to situations that sorely need intervention. Your symbol looks like a bridge and you move between people and situations building bridges and bringing an element of harmony where it was previously lacking. You have a fundamental need for peace and balance in your lives, and for that reason you are usually skilled in the art of compromise, which is why you are happiest as a 'we', rather than walking Earth alone. Partnerships and unions (above all romantic, but also friendship-based and at work) are of paramount importance to Libra. Relationships make you tick.

You are brilliant strategists and are able to see all sides of a situation or argument before making judgements. You are fair, just and easy-going, making you such a pleasure to be around.

Did I mention pleasure? Ah, yes. You love pleasure of all kinds, as well as beauty, art and culture. You have an incredible eye for what will look good. I know a few artists and they all have plenty of Libra in their full charts. The Italian artist Caravaggio had the Sun in Libra, and his work, particularly with the 'Goddess', is utterly exquisite. One of his most famous paintings is *Death of the Virgin*, painted between 1601 and 1605. It was highly controversial at the time because he used a well-known lady with a rather colourful reputation as the model. This taste for irony is not typical of Libra but more likely due to his Moon and Chiron in Aquarius. (Aquarius loves to shock and often rebels for the sake of causing outrage.)

Libra's ruling planet is Venus, which is strongly associated with love, beauty and pleasure, as well as art and culture. (In Roman mythology the goddess Venus was also the patron of the arts.) You are the great romantics of the Zodiac, fabulously seductive (unless you have a lot of neighbouring sign Virgo in your full chart, which puts the kibosh on that!), and know how to make people feel physical and emotional pleasure.

You are often pleasing to the aesthetic eye, although the real beauties in my experience are not necessarily those with the Sun in Libra but those who have Libra featuring prominently in their full charts, particularly Venus, their rising sign or Mars.

There can be no better example of Libra 'gone right' (and 'gone wrong') in action than Brigitte Bardot, the French actress, singer and animal-rights activist, who has been called one of the most beautiful women ever to have lived. She has the Sun, Mercury and Jupiter in Libra and also has planets in the humanitarian sign of Aquarius. She has dedicated her life to helping animals. The way the planets combined in Bardot's chart seemed to result in a beautiful woman with a need for justice. You see, Libra is all about justice and equality, especially for those with no voice, such as animals. But this is where the contradictions set in.

Unfortunately, Bardot also seems to work with Libra 'gone wrong', which is judgemental and even bigoted. She does not hide her dislike for anyone who isn't Caucasian French, is anti-immigration and has a string of convictions for inciting racial hatred. Libra can be full of contradictions but one thing is certain: their judgemental side is the worst and they can wage war on anyone they see as different. This need for hate campaigns is driven by deep unhappiness and is the opposite of equality, which Libra needs to embrace to be at peace.

Libra 'gone wrong' can be shallow, vain, extravagant and terribly needy. You can't survive without validation from others and are very often people-pleasers, sacrificing your sense of self to keep someone else happy only to become resentful later. Libra must learn to be independent and less needy. You should take a tip from your opposite sign, Aries, who needs no one's approval and therefore seems to attract it readily.

LIBRA
'GONE WRONG'

—⊖ VAIN, SUPERFICIAL AND MATERIALISTIC ⊖—

Libra 'gone wrong' is vain and even a tad lazy (think of the goddess lying on a chaise longue while men adore her and women feed her grapes or fill her cup). You care only what others see. You can be insincere and shallow so you fill your life with trivia and pastimes that will attract the adoration you crave. You are obsessed with your personal appearance and overindulge in anything that brings you pleasure, regardless of how it may affect anyone or anything else. Although Marie Antoinette was born under the sign of Scorpio, her lack of restraint and her excessive, ostentatious lifestyle can be accredited to Libra 'gone wrong'. She had both the Moon (emotions) and Jupiter (planet of excess) in Libra.

Libra gone wrong always judges a book by its cover, never bothering to dive beneath the surface, which can make you both ignorant and bigoted.

You do not like anything or anyone that could be classed as 'ugly' so you tend to manipulate other people into handling anything unpleasant. This is not only morally questionable, it also cuts you off from experiences that expose you to depth and might trigger emotional learning.

THE LEARNING

If you have a strong Libra influence in your chart, try to recognize when you are being superficial. If you do not, you run the risk of attracting relationships that are only skin deep. The first sign that hard work is needed will see them disintegrate. Libra is rarely alone, but if you do not embrace your depths, you will attract partners who love you so long as you look good, then find a younger model at the first sign of ageing. Harsh but true. Do not judge or avoid others who look different or less attractive: you may miss out on someone who has plenty to offer you and depths with which to enrich your experience of life. Remember that this life is just one of many and, if you carry on you, may be reborn as a gargoyle.

If you live or work with Libra, you need to know that their unrealistic expectations are the fastest route to their own disappointment. If they are single, they will be assessing every single (and at worst married!) person as a potential mate, which can be utterly exhausting and rather boring for you. If you have the energy, try to encourage them to seek inside themselves for deeper meaning. This can be tiring but ultimately rewarding when you see them open like the beautiful flowers they are.

NEEDY, UNABLE TO BE ALONE

You are often so scared of your own company that anyone will do to distract you. You have a driving need to be in relationships, and are so desperate for validation from others that you often attract people who will end up making you make you feel awful (and even more alone). Some of you can't bear to be alone because you fear your subtle inner voice, the one that encourages you to wake up and walk your true path.

THE LEARNING
If you have a strong Libra influence in your chart, it's imperative that you learn how to validate yourself. You must be brave and face yourself. Try to quiet your mind for long enough to hear your inner

voice. It is nothing to be scared of. (I know one Libra lady who sleeps with the television on in a bid to drown her thoughts.) Once you are comfortable with listening to yourself, you can try talking to yourself. Remind yourself of all the reasons you are a likeable and good person, and the things that make you beautiful. Be alone rather than in the company of people who make you feel anything other than wonderful. The lesson here is to stop asking for others' opinions and looking to them to tell you how much they need you. Stand tall and be comfortable in your own skin.

If you live or work with a Libra who is needy, it can be draining and totally time-consuming. You might well find yourself praying that they find an 'other half' fast, to take the flak. I had a Libra boyfriend once who hated being alone; *that* went well when I booked myself (solo) into silent retreats and he booked romantic trips for us both. If you work with a needy Libra this can drain time and resources as they want constant reassurance that their work is good enough and they do not like to do things alone. You can either suggest (kindly) that they work on their confidence, or find them a more suitable role. One word of warning: do not use the word 'needy'. It will trigger a strong reaction from Libra because, as we all know, the truth hurts!

─⊖ JUDGEMENTAL AND CRITICAL ⊖─

In an extreme manifestation of Libra 'gone wrong', you combine your role as the judge of the Zodiac with your unfortunate tendency to superficiality and make harsh, shallow judgements of others. You complain that others misjudge you but you are always seeking their imperfections and faults before you see anything else. Sometimes these judgements are based on people's looks, clothes or status. Sometimes, as we saw with Brigitte Bardot, they are even more prejudiced and are based on race, class, gender, or any point of difference you decide is 'unacceptable'. If this sounds like you, I urge you to change your behaviour quickly. It really is never too late!

THE LEARNING

If you have a strong Libra influence in your chart, hold back on making rash judgements until you are armed with facts. Try to see the good in all people and situations. You have heard the saying 'Those living in glass houses shouldn't throw stones.' This might have been written for you. Change the habit and, before you speak, ask yourself, 'Will this cause disharmony for me or anyone else? Every time you judge someone, you lower your vibration, which limits your potential. In my opinion, whatever we dish out we attract back, so be mindful and change your behaviour.

If you live or work with a judgemental Libra, call them out whenever you can, with love and kindness, of course. Do not attempt to embarrass them in front of anyone else, just quietly remind them that what goes around comes around, and this type of behaviour always boomerangs: it may not be immediate but it is on track.

INDECISIVE AND PASSIVE

Libra 'gone right' loves to take everything into account so you can achieve a balanced judgement. But 'gone wrong', this can cause a crisis of indecision. You are so accustomed to weighing up the pros and cons of a situation that you can very often miss out on opportunities, and drive others to distraction. I know one Libra man who got so sick of his own indecisiveness that he now flips a coin to make decisions, then sticks to them rigidly. This is, perhaps, extreme but it solved the problem. Avoiding making decisions is weak and reduces your potential to embrace life.

You can also be seriously passive, so determined to keep the peace that you sacrifice your own needs and desires in the name of compromise. Your desire to avoid confrontation makes you unhappy as life sends you people who will push you to the limits. This makes you more unhappy and results in anything other than peace! Your ultimate goal.

THE LEARNING

If you have a strong Libra influence in your chart, you need to make decisions, then stick to them. If people are pushing your boundaries, learn to assert yourself and stand your ground, like your opposite sign, Aries. (You have much to learn from each other!) Your need to be liked can lead you to sacrifice who you are, so stand your ground peacefully and assertively.

    If you live or work with a Libra who is annoyingly indecisive, try to help them. If it drives you insane, can you imagine how hard it must be for them? Encourage them to tune into their inner voice, which always has the answers. If they need to be liked, remind them that they are setting themselves up for failure. Even one of the most compassionate men in the public arena, the Dalai Lama, has antagonists and critics. It is impossible to please everyone: remind them of this.

LIBRA
'GONE RIGHT'

─⊖ FAIR, JUST AND BALANCED ⊖─

You listen to everyone and give people fair chances to he heard. You are constantly moving between friends and family groups, making peace and acting as the diplomat. You are such a pleasure to be around that everyone seeks out your wise, fair and non-judgemental counsel. You bring a balanced approach to all that you do and always look at the big picture.

THE LEARNING

Try to take your own needs into account as well as everyone else's. You are often so busy acting as peacemaker that you leave your own feelings and preferences at the door of the war zone. You could apply for a role with the United Nations (a very Libran organization!). But when does it stop? We appreciate your fairness so much: please understand that, even when we don't show it, it is always gratefully received.

I have a client who gets really upset when her friends or family squabble. She spends all her time and energy trying to keep the peace. I tell her that sometimes you need to let people get on with it and stay outside the ring, but she allows it to impact on her whole life. I have suggested that she tries to let them know how much it hurts her when they fight and ask to be left out entirely or, even better, ask them to stop.

CHARMING, SWEET AND GRACEFUL

Libra is the most charming of all signs. You can charm the venom out of snakes and still get them to thank you afterwards. You are smooth and silky in your approach, with such congenial natures that everyone takes pleasure in being around you. You have an inner grace that inspires the rest of us to be more like you. 'Gone right' you are sweetness itself, oozing with grace.

THE LEARNING

Please be sure not to use your superpower of charm to manipulate people into doing what you want or giving you what you think you need. This isn't wise and usually backfires.

GENEROUS

You are usually as generous as saints and enjoy helping others. Your need for company has its benefits as you love the finer things in life and don't mind footing a bill for the sake of good company, if your friends or loved ones have fewer resources than you. You are generous with your time, your heart and your money, which is appreciated by the good people you are prone to attract.

THE LEARNING_

Please do not fear being taken advantage of as this restricts your goodness. Watch for red warning flags by all means, but remember that the eye of karma sees all: no good deeds or behaviours go unnoticed by the law of cause and effect. And, in the end, what is the point in making dinner for one or drinking fine wine alone? If you can share with others, do so. Just make sure that all 'transactions' are balanced and equal. If you have more money than your friends or partner, it's okay to share. Before my feast-and-famine freelancing days, I was very well paid. One of our group, a wonderful Libra, didn't earn as much as the rest of us but we all wanted her with us so we insisted on paying for her when we could. She in return would buy us small gifts and carry out acts of kindness, which we all appreciated. A balanced friendship or romance doesn't have to mean always splitting the bill fifty-fifty.

—⊖ PEACEFUL WARRIORS ⊖—

Libra 'gone right' fights against injustice and champions what is fair for all like no other sign, without sacrificing their innate sense of peace. An international symbol for peace and equal rights has to be Mahatma Gandhi, who was born under the sign of Libra. His tireless work towards non-violent activism is an example of this sign personified.

Jimmy Carter, the former US president, was also born under Libra. He won the Nobel Peace Prize in 2002, for his work in trying to end the Israeli–Palestinian conflict and his decades-long championing of human rights. Peace, equality and equal rights for all are Libran policies.

THE LEARNING

Libra must stand up for equality and justice and actively campaign for what is right. Not only is that a great end in itself, it will also appease your soul's need to do this work. This is your role in the Zodiac. Some Librans will choose the superficial route and hop on and off private jets looking pretty, but the authentic ones among you will get your delicate hands dirty. This is ultimately even more beneficial for you than those you campaign for. It might mean standing up for someone who is being bullied on the Tube or aiming for the next Nobel Peace Prize: either option is equally powerful for your inner contentment.

IN LOVE

'It takes two to make life go right' is essentially Libra's motto. Love and relationships are everything to you guys: you are literally in love with the idea of love. On the plus side, you are romantic, seductive and sensual. 'Gone right', you are utterly devoted to your partner and will do anything you can to fulfil their needs. You're also utterly loyal. Libran men and women enjoy some of the longest and most successful marriages that I know of: they do not like to quit, no matter what.

Your famed inner peace and grace typically help you to maintain a positive perspective even when the relationship breaks down: Gwyneth Paltrow, the American actress and founder of Goop, is a Libra and her 'conscious uncoupling' method of divorce is a fine example of the famed Libran grace, even under extreme circumstances.

'Gone wrong', you are materialistic, shallow and so vain that even your own mirrors get tired of your reflection. You also attract one-dimensional people and shallow situations, and will use anything other than your authentic selves in seduction: diamonds, designer clothes, expensive cars and homes. You strive for beauty, and beauty alone, and will discount nothing in its pursuit, including invasive cosmetic surgery. You also expect your partners to look good and really don't mind if they are vacuous with it.

But, like Virgo, Libra 'gone wrong' can also manifest in over-the-top expectations of your partners (and yourself). You really do need to chill on this front and just accept what really is.

You hate to be alone and can be excessively needy, which will often drive away even good and patient people. 'Gone wrong', you either hop endlessly from one relationship to another or are unfaith-ful: if one relationship is seemingly failing, you will line up the next to hop straight into without necessarily ending the first! You can be materialistic, shallow and so dull and one-dimensional that you push all the authentic people away from you, and are left with sycophants and superficiality.

If you're in a relationship with Libra, you need to be adept in the art of total seduction. They're highly seductive themselves and expect to be treated in the same way. Libra wants to be wooed! If they need expensive gifts, they are working with 'gone wrong' and you should exit as fast as you can. 'Gone right', they will appreciate attention, affection and small kindnesses. They love sensual romance, candles, home-cooked food and beautiful music, and when you see your Libran partner appreciating these things you can take it that they are using the sign's 'gone right' energy.

CAREER

Libra is usually so fair of face that any profession where looks can be used to advantage is a good bet. Models, actors and politicians are often born under the sign of Libra or have plenty of it in their full charts. You also make incredible artists, photographers, paint-ers, musicians and, of course, human-rights advocates, lawyers and diplomats.

Libra 'gone right' in the workplace is a joy to work for and with. You are thoughtful and genuinely seek harmony, so you don't back-stab or gossip. You will do everything you can to bring balance to the workplace.

Many moons ago, I worked for several years as a creative for an entertainment company and had the best boss ever. He was Libran, so fair and just that he made working for the company an absolute joy. He made sure the freelance team were paid on time, he took into account extra work and awarded hefty bonuses. You never had to ask him for anything as he was always one step ahead. He was no pushover, though, and when I asked him if he had ever been indecisive (one of the plagues of Libra) he said that he had made a conscious decision not to let this define him so, no, not any more: he made decisions and stuck to them.

'Gone right', you Librans take the whole team into consideration and strive to create harmonious environments for all concerned. You are not motivated by money and success alone, being at least as interested in the purpose of the work you do and a peaceful and calm working environment in which to do it.

But you like to be liked and this can be a good or bad thing, depending on the levels to which you take it. If you want to be liked so much that you avoid making difficult decisions, this is often detrimental to your project or company. I often say to clients who struggle with this that the aim at work is to take the overall needs of the company or project into consideration, removing the ego-led need to be liked by everybody. It's impossible to please everyone and Libra has to accept this.

HEALTH

Libra needs peace and balance to function properly. Peace of mind and a calm environment are absolutely vital for your overall well-being. If you are surrounded by chaos, discord and folk who disturb you, your physical and mental health will suffer. You Librans are vulnerable to stress and anxiety, which you are not well equipped to deal with. You need love and harmony to function properly, but real love begins with acceptance.

Oh, and, of course, you need people. Even more so if you have the Moon in Libra (Moon often indicates what we 'need' to sustain us emotionally and Libra is all about relationships). Some signs are happier when they have their own space; Libra is not usually happy alone unless you have worked hard on that aspect of yourself.

Music is soothing for you. Play it regularly to promote inner calm and inspiration (perhaps avoid gangsta rap). Create your own playlists to achieve different aims – upbeat, soothing and so on. Getting lost in music is a form of therapy for you.

An organized environment also plays a crucial part in your well-being, as does the art of decluttering (and it really is an art). When I need to declutter I pull everything out, then slowly discard what I no longer need and put the rest away in an orderly fashion. It works wonders.

Your love of art is definitely innate and a passion to cultivate. Find your medium: take art classes, life drawing or watercolour painting, make the most of the galleries around you – look into modern art if Renaissance isn't your thing.

You must be careful not to sacrifice your heart and dreams to keep others happy: you will risk making their lives (and yours) unbalanced, and Libra, above all else, requires a balanced lifestyle to be healthy and happy on all levels.

THE FIX FOR LIBRA

1. **Compromise** is an art form that you need to master. It means taking a balanced approach. Before you sacrifice your own needs, stop and think about the long-term consequences.

2. **Spend time alone.** If you are already doing this, great! If you struggle without company, know that your soul (or mind) is your best friend and become reacquainted with it to find inner calm. Go for walks, appreciate scenery and nature, and take time for you. Be comfortable in your own skin.

3. **Learn not to be needy.** This is probably Libra's most unattractive trait and one of the most unhelpful: it repels good, drawing the wrong people and experiences towards you. Remember, you are worth more. Take a deep breath before acting needy and actively try to be more independent.

4. **Stop judging.** The first person you need to stop judging is you. Nobody can live up to the kind of standards you set, including you. Every time you start to judge, stop yourself and dig out something positive to say instead. You will feel much better about yourself every time you manage it.

5. **Practice sincerity.** If you make a concerted effort to be sincere in all your interactions you will attract this behaviour from everyone else, deepening and enriching

your experiences. If you have planets in neighbouring sign Scorpio, this issue probably won't apply to you, but if you attract or practise insincerity, crank up the sincerity in your life.

6. **Boost decisiveness** by learning how to trust your inner voice. The first thought is usually the best, before all the weighing up steps in. Take deep breaths and ask for the answer. Then wait for it to come. It takes time and practice but is well worth doing. Stop calling all the people in your phone book and listen to your best friend: your intuition. Failing that, flip a coin!

– SCORPIO –
THE POWER

WATER SIGN

OPPOSITE OF TAURUS

EIGHTH SIGN OF THE ZODIAC

EIGHTH HOUSE

RULED BY PLUTO/MARS

Scorpio 'gone right' is extremely intuitive, like fellow water signs Cancer and Pisces, and is one of the most instinctual of all the signs. Scorpio folk are determined and focused. You have serious emotional depths, and a magnetic air of mystery that is simply irresistible to the rest of us. You absolutely refuse to be controlled or dominated by anyone or anything. You hate superficiality and like to dig deep in every area of life, probing and investigating until you get to the bottom of an issue or have demolished the façade and seen to the very core of a person's character.

Scorpio is all about power. You are here on Earth to learn how to handle it wisely. This is not to say that you are all automatically powerful, but you will have experienced some power-plays growing up, which offer you incredible opportunities to recognize and use power as a force for good in your own lives.

'Gone right', you use your immense empathy and embrace your insights into the darker side of life. Martin Scorsese was born under the sign of Scorpio and you only have to look at his film history to see that he is seriously deep and has a penchant towards making the darker side of life sexy: crime, the Mafia and bloodshed.

There is no better example of Scorpio in action than the billionaire founder of Microsoft, Bill Gates. He was criticized for his less than pure business techniques at the start of his career but later became a huge philanthropist who never tires of using his power and enormous fortune for good. Through the Bill and Melinda Gates Foundation, he donates to various charities and pioneering scientific research projects. He says that he feels an overwhelming desire (a key word for Scorpio) to address some of the rampant inequality on the planet. If only all other billionaires felt the same: we would wipe out poverty and inequality sharpish.

None of the other signs have your capacity for such good – or such bad. You have tremendous staying power and, along with Taurus, your opposite sign, probably the strongest will of the Zodiac. Jimi Hendrix, for example, had Mars in Scorpio (Mars being the planet of energy and drive) and was determined to be a rock star from a very young age. London, and a few well-connected people there, launched his career, but it might have been over before it began were it not for his unstoppable Scorpio determination. Jimi used a left-handed guitar, which someone (a jealous competitor no doubt!) stole just before a gig. Jimi just flipped a standard guitar behind his back and played it upside-down, dazzling his fans and the critics. That defining moment in his career is the perfect illustration of a classic Scorpio trait: you guys are absolutely unstoppable when you decide to do something.

The skilled Scorpio is artfully persuasive, devastatingly seductive, captivating and irresistibly sexy. You are hotter than a naked flame. You smoulder and smoke and often get burned. Legendary but tragic film star James Dean had the Moon in Scorpio, which gave him sex appeal that has lasted decades, and such a brooding bad-boy image! All very Scorpio. You also have some serious trance-inducing skills that none can escape, and when you decide you want something or someone, it's 'game over'. The rest of us only know we've been Scorpio'd after the spell wears off and the fantastic flashbacks begin.

The best Scorpio is charismatic, kind to a fault and knows when others are suffering and how to comfort and empower them. You are forgiving, generous and often very influential. Scorpio can easily transform the lives of others . . . and you often do! Unstoppable forces with serious focus, you guys get things done. I say that Scorpio energy is pretty much like a bulldozer: it goes in, smashes things down, then rebuilds something much better. Which fits, because this sign's big lessons are all to do with the processes of birth, death, rebirth, transformation and change. Many of you will have been faced with life-transforming situations from a young age. The best Scorpios are constantly shedding a skin and transforming: change is in their DNA.

The 'gone wrong' side of Scorpio is notoriously power-hungry and, in the worst-case scenario, totally vindictive. Scorpio doesn't just hold grudges: you obsess, sometimes for years, over anyone who has wronged you. You seek total dominance and vengeance, and will attack or betray anyone who stands in your way. Terrifying!

SCORPIO
'GONE WRONG'

VINDICTIVE, MANIPULATIVE, CRUEL

There is no easy way to say this: Scorpio 'gone wrong' can be dangerous, to yourselves and others. Your tendency to think of situations as life-threatening means you often take things too personally. And when you feel threatened you go on the attack – not just a snipe, like Virgo; you aim for total destruction. In reality, the threats are often imagined or wildly exaggerated. You see enemies everywhere and don't so much destroy them as annihilate them. Scorpio 'gone wrong' will trample over anyone to get what they want in life . . . more power and total control.

One of your great weapons, other than sheer ruthlessness, is your penetrating intuition, which allows you to home in on other people's weak points and exploit them. If you sense that someone's motivation is insincere, you will either lose interest (lucky escape for them!) or expose them as a fake without a second thought.

Manipulative, controlling and super-secretive, you guard your own secrets closely but will probe and grill others until they share their deepest fears and darkest secrets, then use them for your own purposes – blackmail included, the more emotional the better.

Your will to be the dominant power in any group or situation means you often choose to disempower others and attempt to steal their light rather than find your own. Dangerous and vindictive, you are rarely alone, as the dark seat of power attracts followers, and people are scared to be on the wrong side of you.

THE LEARNING

If you have a strong Scorpio influence in your chart, this may make for uncomfortable reading. Perhaps you recognize some of the above traits in yourself, or perhaps you're thinking that you've been on the receiving end of some of this behaviour. Remember, we can either attract the traits assigned to our sign or use them, but either way they exist to teach us. You may also be thinking, 'I go out of my way to hide my power and try consciously not to be cruel to others!' And that's quite possible. Those of you with integrity and heart are terrified of your 'gone wrong' traits, so much so that you try to deny your power, which often becomes problematic. I always say that Scorpio is most likely to 'go wrong' when you are not comfortable with your own power, so you shouldn't shy away from it but embrace it for good.

If you know that sometimes you behave like Vlad the Impaler (he was reportedly a Scorpio), remind yourself that this darkness is profoundly damaging to others and also to you. It will drive away your allies and the people you love, and expose you to others' vengeful cruelty. It doesn't have to be like this. You, of all people, with your brilliant intuition and powerful drive, have unlimited opportunity to create your own power. There really is no need to turn to the dark side when the potential to achieve great things with integrity is well within your reach.

If you live or work with Scorpio, it's wise to do everything you can to help them to stay in their 'gone right' power: if they're channelling their flip side, the only sensible course of action is to take steps to protect yourself. Remind them that with great power comes great responsibility and ask them to assess how they keep theirs in check.

⊖ WEAK-WILLED, FEARFUL ⊖

Scorpio 'gone wrong' can be the polar opposite of powerful, with absolutely no willpower at all. If you're not out to get everyone and running amok, then you're often cowering away, terrified of your own shadow and of change in general, wrestling with your addictions and inner desires.

Scorpio is heavily associated with transformation. When you don't embrace change, you get stuck in a fearful place. Resentment, anxiety and tension build. Part of the problem lies with the amount of energy you spend on suppressing your desires, trying to resist them, then giving in to and feeling guilty about them. Desire is a huge driving force for Scorpio. Not only sexual desire, though that's part of it. What Scorpio wants, it either goes out to get or it suppresses. 'Gone wrong', you have a habit of denying your intuitive knowledge of what motivates you. You bury your desires and obsess over them until they either burst out and you give in to them, or they start to poison you. Scorpio is inclined to use drink, drugs and sex to excess, and is vulnerable to full-blown addiction.

THE LEARNING

If you have a strong Scorpio influence in your chart, and you're more the anxious than the ruthless type, you need to acknowledge what you want from life and face your desires, or you risk becoming enslaved to them. Far better to be brave with yourself and honest with others than risk falling into a life of endless internal battles to take decisions, fight your demons and give up bad habits. You have huge resources of willpower, determination and inner clarity: you just need to allow them to surface. Scorpio is on Earth to learn many lessons but one that remains constant through his or her life is the need to transform. The potential is there. If you resist shedding your old skin, though, you fight your highest self. Step into your power and leave all that low-vibe stuff behind.

If you live or work with a Scorpio who has a weak-willed and addictive personality, you should do all you can to evoke their strength and empathy. (This is so strong in Scorpio that even if it's buried you'll still be able to get to it if you persevere.) Try to let them know how destructive their actions can be. If they are addicted to power, stand up to them with love. If they are addicted to anything else, suggest a total break from habit with a change of routine, even a job or house move when situations are extreme. And, as always, if someone you love is addicted to alcohol or drugs, do what you can to steer them towards professional help, but know that until they are ready to deal with it, you cannot fix them.

JEALOUS

This is the most common problem with Scorpio and, in my experience, one of the most destructive ways in which Scorpio 'goes wrong'. It is not always easy to spot as some of the worst cases I've come across involve folk with a planet other than the Sun in Scorpio. For example, Jupiter, associated with our skills and talents on the one hand and extreme behaviour on the other, in Scorpio shows a person who is either highly adept in the ways of empathy and kindness or totally consumed by the poison of all poisons – jealousy.

THE LEARNING
If you have a strong Scorpio influence in your chart and you recognize that jealousy is an issue for you, take heart. It's a horrible feeling, but you can learn to dissipate it. You need to work through your darkness by bringing it into the light, face your demons and

tell your loved ones you are working on your issues so they can help and support you.

I say this often: do not be jealous of anyone or anything. We each have our own paths and everyone makes choices that result in good fortune as well as lessons to learn from the not-so-smart choices.

If you live or work with a Scorpio who's jealous, it might be of some comfort to know that however unhappy their jealousy is making you it is nothing compared to how they feel. The trouble with jealousy is that, though it is usually transparently obvious to us, the person suffering it would rather do anything than admit to it. And it's impossible to address until they do. Your best bet is to try saying things like 'You could have this too' or 'Is this something that you feel you want?' That way you are attempting to bring the issues into the open. But until your Scorpio person faces this monster, you would do best to show as much patience and compassion as you can muster. If they don't or won't own up, you will have to protect yourself. I once worked with a Scorpio 'gone wrong' and he was *über*-controlling. He bullied and blackmailed me until I stood up to him. Then he totally changed the way he dealt with me. You must stand up to a jealous Scorpio, but do it with sincere motivation or you will create an enemy for life.

SCORPIO
'GONE RIGHT'

EMPATHETIC AND FORGIVING

Scorpio is highly intuitive and has almost X-ray vision, seeing through the walls we humans put up for protection! This gives you incredible insight, which as we have already seen, can be used for bad as well as good. But when you're using it for good, it results in your superpower: empathy. Your natural warmth combined with your ability to feel others' pain means that you are kind to the core, generous with your attention and sensitive to their needs.

Scorpio has a terrible and often justified reputation for going on the attack but, in my experience, you never hold a grudge once you really understand the other person's motivation. In fact, you have tremendous powers of forgiveness when you look at the root cause of another person's behaviour.

THE LEARNING

You may be using your powers of forgiveness brilliantly already, in which case, fantastic. If it is something you struggle with, though, or if you frequently end up feeling you've been wronged, consider switching your frequency: perhaps life loves you so much that it keeps sending you people who will offer you the opportunity to learn forgiveness, often in the guise of betrayal. Nobody ever escapes the eye of karma, or the law of cause and effect, so if someone hurts you it will not be long before they are suffering, too. Why not forgive them now, and have compassion for the path of personal suffering they have embarked upon?

MAGNETIC, COMPELLING

Scorpio 'gone right' is absolutely fabulous and, oh, so addictive: nobody forgets an encounter with a Scorpio person in a hurry. All that intensity, that enigmatic brooding charm . . . You guys are as magnetic as the poles, literally oozing sex appeal and charisma. You are charming and sincere yet quietly commanding. Scorpio 'gone right' is secure in its power over others and doesn't need to shout to exert its influence. You prefer to persuade, seduce or convince through sheer magnetism.

Scorpio folk are often so terrified of being manipulative that you shy away from your power, but this can become a big problem: you risk causing more harm than good. As my beloved teacher once said, you just need to check your motivation. It really is that simple. Scorpio 'gone right' has the purest motivation and should not be afraid of his or her hypnotic powers. If, for example, you are trying to get someone to do something that is for their greatest good (not yours!), then by all means use your ability to manipulate the situation!

THE LEARNING

To be at your most effective, Scorpio must embrace power and be confident and comfortable enough to use it wisely. 'Gone right', you have an almost otherworldly force behind you when you set your minds to something and are usually high achievers in all areas of your life, from personal relationships to career.

⊖ INSPIRING AND EMPOWERING ⊖

We all know about Scorpio's power games but, actually, when you're in your 'gone right' space, you love to use your considerable abilities to inspire and empower others, just as much as to advance your own agenda. You team up well with others as long as you are given honesty and respect, and will defend them even in the face of death or extreme loss. You are brave and admirable in the face of danger. Scorpio 'gone right' knows that power is not an infinite resource, and that one of the most powerful things you can do is empower somebody else to reach their potential. If Scorpio 'gone wrong' has a lot of enemies, Scorpio 'gone right' has a lot of friends, supporters and allies. Most of all they have respect and admiration.

THE LEARNING

Think about this for a moment: when you serve only yourself you are failing to embrace true power. When you empower others, the karmic clock of cause and effect begins to tick and you feel amazing. It helps to purify the times when you were perhaps not quite as generous.

IN LOVE

Scorpio does not easily fall in love or give their trust and hearts, but when they do, they devote themselves utterly to their loved ones. 'Gone right', Scorpio is loving, loyal, charismatic, magnetic and sensual. They are faithful for all eternity, seeking deep soulmate unions as opposed to superficial relationships.

Sexy! Did I mention sexy? Scorpio people usually radiate sexuality without even trying. I'm not referring to people who over-sexualize their appearance for attention – that is not Scorpio's style. Scorpio is classy and subtle, totally unintentionally arresting. My friends and I laugh when we enter a room and see someone literally smouldering with sex appeal in the corner. We say, in unison, 'Scorchio!' And I have heard plenty of people say, 'He/she isn't my usual type, but there is just something sexy about them.' I smile because I know they're probably talking about the powerful lure of Scorpio. You guys can be quite wild in the bedroom, too: totally passionate and present.

On the 'gone wrong' side, you can be a real nightmare. You would win Olympic medals for playing power games and are the masters of emotional blackmail. If you feel you have been crossed you will declare psychological warfare, to the point of making your partners question their sanity. You can be extremely jealous and have a capacity to be unkind, attacking your partner for no real reason other than that you feel like it. The insecure among you become possessive, paranoid and, at worst, abusive in your relationships.

In a less extreme scenario, if the union lacks intensity and depth you quickly get bored. You either leave, or if you stay, you will almost certainly look elsewhere for someone who ignites your desire. Scorpio is usually very loyal when their emotional and physical needs are met, but if not, they will give in to lust without a backward glance.

If you're in a relationship with Scorpio, you need to be aware that it will fast become all-consuming. It's that Scorpio intensity again – no half-measures. So if you're looking for something breezy, it's best not to get hooked on a Scorpio in the first place. Either you'll leave them and unleash their vengeful fury, or you'll wind up ensnared by their powerful charm. Which can be fabulous, but only if it's something you were fully signed up for. Otherwise it can feel more as if you're being loved to death! I know one couple who got together in their teens. He has Mars in Scorpio and she has Venus in Scorpio: it really is an incredible match. They both tell everyone that they knew from the moment they met that they were soulmates.

Talking of that, it's worth asking yourself in the fairly early days whether you are happy to go to the depths of experience with your Scorpio partner. They demand a lot of commitment, passion and energy. If that sounds good to you, you are in for one hell of a ride and life will never be dull.

But Scorpio 'gone wrong' is a scary encounter. They will obsess over every perceived insult or misdemeanour, and if you let them down or betray them (or, let's be honest, if they so much as *think* you've betrayed them), you may as well extract yourself carefully right away, because they will never let you forget and (openly or subconsciously) will, no doubt, seek revenge. On an extreme level, they become the stalkers who trawl the internet, looking for ways to destroy someone they cannot have. Be careful.

But it's not all scary. Scorpio 'gone right' makes for an intense union and they are usually the most committed partners, just so long as your life together is forever transforming and your sex life is sensual and dynamic.

CAREER

Anything that gets beneath the surface of superficiality and triggers emotion is usually where you will find Scorpio at work. As you would expect, Scorpio is very drawn to positions of leadership. In June 2015, dadaviz.com conducted a survey using data from Wikipedia on the star signs of heads of state and governments. The results showed that Scorpio was the dominant sign. Sagittarius, then Leo followed.

Scorpio 'gone right' make brilliant bosses. You use your sense of 'feel' and gut instincts to make moves: moves that are successful. You have an almost spooky sense of what works and what doesn't and will not be thwarted when you get your teeth into something (or someone!). You know how to motivate people and empower your team. Most of you hold the mantle of power with conscience and are not corrupted by fame, wealth or power because to you it's nothing new.

It's not just about leadership, though. Scorpio is a sign that teams up well with others, as long as you are given honesty and respect. You also have the ability to focus like no other sign, and when you put your minds and formidable wills to something, you are unstoppable. You have serious insight and are avid deal-closers, as you can see beneath what is 'presented' into the core of someone's desires.

I have a friend with the Sun, Mercury and Jupiter in Scorpio who is a very successful film producer. She always knows when an idea will work or if a film will do well and has infallible instincts for when to pitch an idea for funding. And when she moves to close the deal, it's done! She is humble, confident and yet quietly powerful, an irresistible combination. This is Scorpio 'gone right' at work.

You are drawn to powerful professions that result in transformation in some way – politics, journalism, publishing and the media. Anna Wintour, legendary editor of US *Vogue* and arguably the most powerful woman in fashion, has the Sun in Scorpio. I also know the head of a huge US publishing house: she is Scorpio and well known for using her gut instincts to acquire new authors.

Scorpio power can be incredible when used as a force for good. Leonardo DiCaprio is using his by taking on the climate-change-denying establishment in his bid to help the planet and reveal what is being hidden (a classic Scorpio obsession) in terms of facts.

HEALTH

Scorpio, you need to take good care of your energy and your mind. Your sensitivity and highly developed empathy means you're like the psychic sponges of the Zodiac. You take on a lot of negative energy from people around you, and events you perceive as negative can affect you long after the moment has passed. Even watching the news headlines can leave you tired, stressed and depressed. You need to cleanse your personal energy regularly with Epsom salts baths. When you are in the bath and ready to get out, pull the plug out and imagine the vacuum is pulling all the negativity and stress away from you with the water. I am a big fan of full-Moon rituals for letting go of things we've become too attached to, or to release anything you've been worrying over. Try making a list of everything you need to get rid of. The guy or girl you went on a date with and are waiting for a call from, hopes of being promoted at work, the argument you had with your partner, fear of not being successful: let it all go as you burn that piece of paper and watch it disappear with all that negativity. That act of release is very powerful. Try different processes until you find your fix.

You can obsess over things to the point of illness, and this may cause deep psychological issues. Anything that helps to switch focus can be beneficial. That might be exercising to the point of exhaustion or a hobby that requires you to be totally present in your body and in the moment. I know one over-anxious Scorpio who took up tango and found that when she was dancing she had absolutely no energy left for fretting.

Meditation is a powerful tool for all of us and can help you enormously, as can simple daily rituals to let go of worry and fear. Scorpio loves a ritual, so find something that works for you, whether it's prayer, quiet time or writing that list of your anxieties, then burning it. Writing and storytelling are cathartic, as long as you don't write as a way to get your own back on those you feel have wronged you, which is a very Scorpio 'gone wrong' thing to do!

You need to watch out for your tendency to addiction. Anything that controls you is bad for your soul. Alcohol, sex and drugs can be particular problems for Scorpios. You need to leave all addictions and toxins behind: they will pull you towards the darker side of life. If you try to get a grip on your behaviour without success, don't give up. There are supportive communities online for those who are trying to either moderate or abstain from their drug of choice. Professional help is available if you need it.

Scorpio often lives in the past and, whether it's full-on obsession or mild nostalgia, this can be unhealthy. In particular, the way you hold grudges is bad for you: you must develop ways to move on and live in the present without fear. Forgiveness is vital to Scorpio's well-being, and forgiveness of self is just as much an issue for you. You give yourselves such a hard time (not like Virgo!) that (like your opposite sign, Taurus) you must be present in the very moment, cultivate self-love and acceptance.

Scorpio people need more sunshine and lightness in their lives and anything that can help you to stay in the light is good for you.

THE FIX FOR SCORPIO

1. **Do not obsess.** Practise letting-go rituals, such as repeating this simple Tibetan Buddhist daily mantra, which can help to lift your energy: '*Om mani peme hung*'. It means 'Purify my mind, body and speech.' (It helps!)

2. **Cleanse your energy.** Use sage sticks, frankincense resin or essential oils and take regular baths with Epsom salts. You can also try using the salts as a scrub in the shower and imagine washing off everyone else's energy. The ritual holds the power.

3. **Embrace power.** Know the power held in silence and take breaks from your obsessive mind. Become more confident and assert yourself with strength and love if others overstep the mark. True power is incorruptible.

4. **Develop willpower.** Make promises to yourself and keep them no matter what. Make sure they are small, achievable ones at first, then move on to any area of life that needs more discipline.

5. **Forgive yourself and others.** Let go of any grudges that hold you in the dark. Be kinder to yourself, and try, where you can, to forgive those who have wronged you. (Is it possible that you overreacted?) Stand in the light and let it soothe you.

- SAGITTARIUS -
THE INSPIRATION

FIRE SIGN

OPPOSITE OF GEMINI

NINTH SIGN OF THE ZODIAC

NINTH HOUSE

RULED BY JUPITER

Sagittarius 'gone right' is a mind-blowing combination of adventure, dazzling smarts and lots of fun. Being a fire sign and ruled by Jupiter, you Sagittarius folk have heaps of positive energy and an infectious passion for life. You're often gregarious and almost always optimistic, like fellow fire sign Leo, but you also have an intellectual side. You are usually wise and knowledgeable beings, who shed light on complex problems with ease and are gifted at telling stories to get your point across. Sagittarius 'gone right' is the accomplished teacher, imparting their wisdom to anyone who is willing to learn. You rarely suffer fools and you value your time, rightly viewing it as a commodity. Did I mention the word 'right'? You are usually right about everything!

And let's not forget luck. Yours is indeed a lucky sign and you are not shy when it comes to sharing your good fortune. Sagittarius loves to socialize and actively seeks out adventure, usually in foreign lands – all the better if others want to come along for the ride. Bright and breezy, you have suitcases full of stories, most of them true. You are probably the most honest of all the signs (next to Virgo, of course). Sagittarius is open-minded and exciting to be around; you are the kind of people to whom interesting things happen.

Above all, you Sagittarius folk are all about integrity. Other people always know exactly where they stand with Sagittarius 'gone right' because you tell it straight. You don't play games and you're utterly trustworthy and true to yourself. You are inspirational, often philosophical and the most enthusiastic truth-seekers in the Zodiac.

On that note, let's talk about the truth. You are pointedly driven by the need to honour your own and speak it as and when you feel. Now, while this obviously has a hugely beneficial side, 'gone wrong', you guys can be truthful to the point of bluntness, even cruelty. (And the flip side of that behaviour is the other kind of 'gone wrong' Sagittarius, who swerves away from the truth completely to get people to do what he or she wants.) Either way, your biggest life lessons, as with your opposite sign, Gemini, concern truth.

Gemini often needs to be more truthful and Sagittarius is typically truthful to a fault. So you must learn, on one hand, to be honest and, on the other, how not to hurt others in the name of your favourite concept.

You are on a search for the meaning of life, and for this reason many of you study religion and spirituality. You can also be highly prophetic, which is different from intuitive.

I have a friend, based in the US, who works with one of the most successful rappers in modern history. The inspirational rapper in question is known in their private circle as the 'Prophet' and has the Sun in Sagittarius.

Bruce Lee, another man true to his sign, was an American/Hong Kong Chinese actor, philosopher and film producer. His legendary films brought martial arts to the attention of the Western public. He inspired Westerners to learn martial arts and refused to succumb to the Chinese community, when he was pressured to stop. He is even reported to have had to fight another master and the prize was keeping his school open. Lee was not religious but he was very well-read in the key texts of Taoism and Buddhism, and he incorporated philosophy into his own version of martial arts (*jeet kune do*), claiming that mental and spiritual preparation and inner strength were fundamental to success.

Interestingly, Lee also had Mercury, Moon, Mars and Venus in Scorpio (that's a lot of Scorpio!), and before he was famous, he had a reputation for being a ferociously driven street fighter. Scorpio is all about will to power, which is not typical of Sagittarius, who prefer to blow others away with their brains rather than brawn.

SAGITTARIUS
'GONE WRONG'

── TACTLESS, HURTFUL, SANCTIMONIOUS ──

Sagittarius is so totally driven by the pursuit of truth that you guys forget the world does not in fact exist only in black and white. Life and other people are way more complex than that. Sagittarius is a fiercely logical and mentally skilled sign, but 'gone wrong', is seriously lacking in the emotional intelligence department. You can be argumentative, hurtful, impatient and blunt. You lack any diplomacy or tact and hide behind 'the truth', using it as your justification for what amounts to nothing more than aggression. You use the truth as a weapon to wound without any compassion, or any thought as to the possible consequences. You simply don't care if you hurt someone's feelings or damage their reputation.

THE LEARNING

If you have a strong Sagittarius influence in your chart, you need to remember that your habit of telling it absolutely like it is can be very uncomfortable for the sensitive souls among us. Sometimes – and I know you may struggle with this, but read on – the truth, the whole truth and nothing but the truth can be slightly inconvenient. And that doesn't mean the person on the receiving end of your wisdom or advice is a devilish liar who's morally compromised. It just makes them, well, human.

The key here is to work on your ability to empathize. If you don't, you will likely end up lonely or surrounded by harsh folk who lack sensitivity. Try to think about your intention before you say something to, or about, someone. What exactly are you hoping to achieve? If it is to help you or them, go ahead (just make sure you pick the right moment, and the correct setting). Anything else is not good behaviour – simply not cricket.

If you live or work with Sagittarius and you feel you're constantly being told what is wrong with you, being lectured to or preached at, I hear you. It's not easy. Before you let it get to you, take a deep breath and remind yourself that Sagittarius does not usually act with malice. Their delivery and timing may be a little off, but they are mostly sincere.

I suggest looking for ways to help them understand that when they let fly a wounding statement, especially if it's personal, it hurts and upsets you and makes you want to avoid them. Take a deep breath and, before you do anything else, check to see if what they are saying holds a glimmer of truth (it usually does!). Tell them the comment was hurtful, and ask them about their intention in a non-aggressive way. Your aim is to get your Sagittarius to question their motives.

NEGATIVE MUD-SLINGERS

When Sagittarius goes spectacularly wrong, he or she is seriously negative. Fortunately this doesn't affect too many of you but when it does, it's cataclysmic. You make other people feel as if they've just crawled out of bed with a hangover the morning after a huge party at their house. Everyone's gone and now they have to clean up the mess. It's depressing, like being sledgehammered by a black cloud. You also gossip and criticize people behind their backs and bring the vibe to low-level mud-slinging. (Again, it's usually in the name of truth.)

THE LEARNING

If you have a strong Sagittarius influence in your chart and you are prone to negativity, especially if it's manifesting aggressively, then take some responsibility. Engage in healing practices, meditate, light candles, burn incense, play uplifting music and, most important of all, switch your mind elsewhere. Do not succumb to it for a moment longer. Say something positive or say nothing, and that includes what you tell yourself.

If you live or work with Sagittarius exhibiting full-blown negativity, you have my sympathy. Fundamentally there isn't a lot you can do to influence them. They are going to have to do a lot of work themselves to change their mindset. One thing within your control, though, is your own reaction to their black moods or cutting verbal attacks. Try to react as little as possible and, whatever you do, don't fan the flames.

—⊖ IGNORANT AND SELF-RIGHTEOUS ⊖—

Sagittarius 'gone right' is a source of inspiring wisdom, but one of the ways it goes wrong is to manifest as a noisy, uneducated, uncultured and opinionated bore. Like your opposite sign, Gemini, you Sagittarius people really need to educate yourselves before sounding off. An uneducated Sagittarius is likely to be self-righteous and ignorant, with all the bluntness and the lack of emotional intelligence that's typical of your sign and none of its wisdom to redeem you. At your worst, you're bigots who don't bother with facts to back up your strong convictions, and, oh, boy, your convictions are strong. Your sign's obsession with the truth has manifested in a conviction that your own point of view is the only truth there is.

THE LEARNING

If you have a strong Sagittarius influence in your chart, make sure that you are not sounding off about topics without facts to back you up. Try to keep an open mind about learning something new, as this is when you are at your best. If you feel strongly about something, put in the time to research your feelings and opinions.

If you live or work with Sagittarius in its ignorant, self-righteous mode, try to use your instincts rather than your emotions when you respond to them. As always, the best strategy is to try to encourage their 'gone right' rather than 'gone wrong' traits, so if they seem even slightly open to it, you can appeal to their love of learning, however deeply buried, and gently direct them to the holes in their argument. Just try not to criticize as you do so. If they are self-righteous, call them out on their behaviour . . . again, gently. After all, there's nothing Sagittarius values so much as being direct and straightforward.

SELF-INDULGENT FAKES

Mostly you Sagittarius folk are honest and 100 per cent genuine, but there is a strain of Sagittarius 'gone wrong' behaviour that manifests in just the opposite. You can be self-indulgent, living grandiose lives that you often cannot afford (a trait shared with fellow fire sign Leo) and, worse, you are cold to the point of frost. You're indifferent to the truth or to notions of integrity, and the worst of you are blatant liars, 'Fake it till you make it' being your motto.

THE LEARNING

If you have a strong Sagittarius influence in your chart, and this behaviour applies to you, fear not: it is never too late to strive for more authenticity in your life. One useful first step is to live within your means and to be honest about your life circumstances – if not with anyone else then at least with yourself. Work for things rather than having big blow-outs. That way you appreciate everything just a little bit more. The aim is to be more comfortable with the way your life actually is, rather than the fantasy version you've built up with the help of your ego.

If you live or work with Sagittarius displaying this behaviour, and you care about them, get involved. Try to teach them the benefits of living a more grounded and honest life. Remind them that they have a natural connection to nature and a need for adventure, which doesn't have to involve exotic trips or first-class travel. Be compassionate, too: their ruling planet Jupiter is prone to encourage excess and it takes work to resist that energy.

SAGITTARIUS

'GONE RIGHT'

INSPIRATIONAL

Sagittarius 'gone right' is one of the most inspirational of energies and it makes you hugely attractive to be around. You use your bountiful wisdom and positive energy to help others and make them feel on top of the world. You truly are the very highest form of inspiration. And you're generous with it. You help and advise others unreservedly and we love you for it.

I have a client and friend born under this sign who has probably inspired me in more ways than I can count and in too many ways to list. She is a successful woman in business, appearing in the *Sunday Times* Rich List as having made a personal fortune of at least £200 million. She's self-made, smart, well-travelled, spiritual and always optimistic. Mrs Sagittarius was the person who inspired me to sit down and start writing about the code at the foundation of my method for Dynamic Astrology. She also guided me to set up my company and to get all my trademarks sorted. Sagittarius is 'Go large, or go home.'

Walt Disney was born under the sign of Sagittarius and his career demonstrates several of its 'gone right' traits. He allowed simple things to inspire him. It was a field mouse, for example, that gave him his success with Mickey Mouse, after years of setbacks when his honesty was taken advantage of. Ever the optimist, he never lost faith in his vision, compromised his integrity or allowed his sense of fun to be tarnished.

THE LEARNING

You have the power to change people's hearts and minds, and when you do, it's seriously powerful for you too. Not only does it make you feel great when you tune in to it, but the rewards are often there years later when you look at how you have inspired someone to follow their dreams and successfully reach for the stars.

─⊖ WISE, OPEN-MINDED ⊖─

Interesting, intelligent and brilliant at best, you Sagittarius folk have rapid minds, a thirst for knowledge and a penchant for involvement with any deep person or subject. You relish the opportunity to study both. Smart to the point of wizardry, your mental prowess can be dazzling to the rest of us mere mortals. I always say that if we were to bring the sign to life, Sagittarius would be Sherlock Holmes. 'Elementary, my dear Watson. Doesn't everyone know that? It's blindingly obvious.' Except that it's not obvious at all to anyone who doesn't possess the smarts of Sagittarius.

Many academics I know are Sagittarius, or have plenty of this sign in their full charts. I can listen to them talk for hours and, because they have such open, expansive minds, they do not shut down if I start to speak about spirituality or practices such as astrology. They try to rationalize it and figure it all out, which is refreshing. In my experience, Sagittarius 'gone right' is always looking to learn and will listen intently, as long as you are enthusiastic and informed.

Sagittarians also typically have a brilliant sense of humour and a sharp wit, which you are inclined to use at other people's expense, especially if the person is displaying ignorant or egotistical behaviour. There is no escape from your tongue, or any wit sharper than yours as it's always wrapped in caustic truths. A tiny bit cruel but absolutely hilarious. You can engage anyone in riveting chat, flitting from topic to topic with ease, like Gemini, but your conversation has real sub-stance and, usually, a good moral twist at the end to keep us gripped. I have a dear friend born under this sign and I find her conversation utterly addictive, her optimism and smarts completely infectious.

THE LEARNING

One word to Sagittarius: please remember that not everyone has access to the vast resources of information your substantial brain contains, or your ability to weave it into wisdom, powerful debates, arguments and stories. Be patient with us because, in most cases, we really would love to catch up!

─⊖ ADVENTUROUS, BROAD-MINDED ⊖─

There's never a dull moment with Sagittarius. You are adventurous and bold, jumping on a plane, train or into a kayak without a second thought and at less than a moment's notice. Sagittarius loves foreign travel and other cultures, and you guys are often extremely knowledgeable about both. Mind you, the kind of hyper-luxurious travel that cuts you off from the culture of the land is not your thing at all. You are hungry for authentic experience to keep your minds open and your hearts learning on every level.

THE LEARNING

Sagittarius 'gone wrong' has a tendency to flit at the first sign that things are getting tricky, so check your motivation before you hop off on your adventures. If you're hoping to avoid harsher realities, which will still be there when you return, this will subconsciously restrict your freedom. Tie up your loose ends first, then skip off into the sunset – go camping, glamping or trudging around the rainforest. Whatever you do, inspiration is to be found on the path of adventure.

IN LOVE

Sagittarius 'gone right' is honest, adventurous and brimming with integrity (and you expect your partner to be the same). You are the ultimate glass-half-full person, with a knack for making others feel special, and your enthusiasm is totally infectious. You're open-minded and generous lovers and are big into romance, which combines nicely with your love of travel and spontaneity in the form of mini-breaks. You like nothing more than exploring other cultures with your partner. In short, you are a joy to be with and, unsurprisingly, you typically have a lot of suitors.

You are independent-minded in relationships and appreciate a partner who is also their own person. You love spontaneous adventures, romantic gestures, and adore showering your lover with gifts.

On the not-so-fairy-tale side, you can be an overbearing presence. If you convince yourself that you know best (and, let's face it, that's highly likely if you're prone to using 'gone wrong' energies), you can quickly become a bore or, worse, steamroller your partner's concerns and point of view. It's not that you're mean, it's just that sometimes you forget another person's emotions are at stake and that they also have valid points and opinions.

You do not like to be around negative people and will do whatever it takes to avoid them. A needy or negative partner won't last long (and, in fact, even a family member you really can't cut from your life is more likely to receive an extravagant gift than any of your time). You have a tendency to treat the whole planet like your playground and you expect people to either cooperate with your plans or get blacklisted.

If you are in a relationship with a Sagittarius, lucky you! I hope you already know all about their inspiring, supportive energy and their love of romance, and haven't had to listen to too many Sagittarius 'gone wrong'-style lectures. When Sagittarius is channelling 'gone right' energy they are funny, witty and wise, and as honest as the day is long.

A couple of words of warning, though: Sagittarius is independent, the very opposite of needy, and they require the same of their partner. It's not that they aren't supportive – quite the opposite – but they just don't do mutual co-dependence. All the Sagittarius women I've known, for example, quite clearly did not wish to become a mother figure to their partner (that's just not your bag: a Cancer probably wouldn't mind!). In a similar vein, Sagittarius does not like possessive or jealous partners and won't stick around for long if they are forced to deal with this regularly. They need to be in unions that give them plenty of freedom. Oh, and they can be flirtatious, which is often challenging for insecure partners.

While we're on the subject, be aware that they have a tendency to get bored quickly if you dare to be anything other than exciting, and find it hard to say no to other offers: in the worst-case scenario they are unfaithful. They generally lack staying power and, instead of sticking around in bad times, will disappear faster than you can order an Uber.

But so long as you go on adventures with them, and they are given plenty of support and freedom at the same time, they are faithful and committed. They are inspiring to others but equally they need to be inspired by their partners, and given plenty of scope to grow and learn within the relationship. Keep them interested and they will remain focused on being with you.

CAREER

When Sagittarius 'goes right', you guys are successful, lucky, generous and expansive. You take risks and often win big, combining your shrewdness and your taste for bold adventure. Steven Spielberg, for example, was born under the sign of Sagittarius and has become the wealthiest filmmaker in the industry through a series of canny risks. You're all about using your smarts, whether that's in business, the media or academia. Your positive thinking and optimistic outlook serve you well and you often have a clear manifesto and the energy to implement it.

Intellectual work and communications are both strong sectors for you, and you make brilliant writers, academics and consultants, such is your ability to pluck enlightening knowledge seemingly from thin air. You also shine as legal-eagles, and in sales roles if the product inspires you.

You have a gift for communicating messages to the masses in some way. There are many 'prophetic' singer-songwriters and performers born under this sign, including Frank Sinatra, Edith Piaf, Jimi Hendrix, Jim Morrison and, more recently, Jay Z. Most of you will communicate in creative ways that inspire an audience. I know a famous Hollywood actor and film director who is a Sagittarius and his latest films are all about getting across messages with a higher vision. His films are laced with meaning, if you know where to look.

You are happiest when you can work outside in some way or when you have plenty of freedom, so ideally you need an active job with lots of variety.

Talking of variety, watch out for the fact that you get bored quickly. Variety is key for you, so you need a job, or career, that excites you. Otherwise you are prone to flit from one post to another. You can also be extreme know-it-alls. As bosses, you expect everyone to be as smart as you are and can fast become self-righteous, pious and egotistical, preaching to all and practising nothing.

You are prone to gamble and, though you are often lucky, you can easily lose it all if you are not careful with your investments and risks. I have a Scorpio relative who has Venus in Sagittarius: he scooped a bit of a win back in the seventies and used it to build a casino empire. Apparently he has no available money now. At least, that's what he says whenever we ask him to invest in our projects.

HEALTH

Sagittarius needs to prioritize healthy living and spending time outside – we all do, but it is especially true of Sagittarius as you are prone to overindulge in the finest of wine and food. It's your ruling planet Jupiter's influence again: you tend to take things to excess. Find an exercise regime you can stick to and make sure some of it takes place outside rather than in the gym.

Sagittarius needs to take care of their liver, so do give yourself at least two consecutive days a week off alcohol. Avoid extreme detoxes as they put even more pressure on your liver if you go back to the nightly tipple afterwards.

You can also be a tad accident prone, a trait you share with Aries, as you fill your life with so many activities and can be on the move more often than sitting still.

You usually feel optimistic but in extreme cases you are quite the opposite and lack any ability to be positive. You need exercise to stimulate you and fresh air to replenish your inspiration levels. If you do suffer with the blues, you can usually conjure up some form of adventure to excite yourself. You like stimulation and should engage your brains in puzzles, books and foreign languages. You need to study to feel secure, which could come in any form, aside from brain-numbing television programmes.

THE FIX FOR SAGITTARIUS

1. **Check your intentions** before you speak your truth. Put down your bow – you know, the one you use to shoot people with the arrow of truth – and think carefully before you take aim.

2. **Try not to lecture or be self-righteous.** Not everyone has access to the wisdom and information you do, so have patience for the less learned among us and share your knowledge with love and kindness.

3. **Take risks but don't gamble away the house.** Your luck is legendary but you go to extremes and can lose spectacularly. Be prepared for either outcome and make a sensible appraisal before you jump in.

4. **Plan an adventure.** It's one of the best ways you can deal with life's stresses. Learn new skills. Study a language, then travel to a country where it's spoken and use it to connect with new people. Create experiences, preferably shared ones. Go somewhere different; volunteer overseas; go on a road trip and take fun people with you. Enjoy the simple pleasures in life, such as sitting near a river or under a tree listening to the birds.

5. **Do not overindulge in anything** – shopping, wine, lovers. Moderation will make you feel better about yourself, and if you limit your expenditure, it will help you to live more authentically.

6. **Spend more time outside** and let the great outdoors replenish your optimism and provide you with fresh inspiration, the kind only Mother Nature offers. Take a book and read in the park. Organize a picnic with friends and take some games with you (cricket, a Frisbee or a kite). Buy or hire a bicycle and go for a ride: it feels liberating to explore in this way.

– CAPRICORN –
THE MASTER

EARTH SIGN

OPPOSITE OF CANCER

TENTH SIGN OF THE ZODIAC

TENTH HOUSE

RULED BY SATURN

Capricorn 'gone right' is dashingly attractive, seriously intelligent, dignified, practical, discerning and meticulous. You guys make the best partners, both in work and love. You are scrupulously honest, utterly reliable, and you never give up on anyone or anything unless absolutely pushed to, usually by a lack of respect or if someone becomes an embarrassment, in which case you will walk determinedly away. Respect (and self-respect) is as vital as oxygen to Capricorn.

Capricorn has enormous fortitude and the strength to achieve their goals and overcome adversity. The current leader of the Canadian Liberal Party, and prime minister of Canada, Justin Trudeau, is a good example in action. His party held just thirty-six parliamentary seats when he was elected as leader but at the next election they took 136 and won a massive victory. Capricorn shoots to win, and you don't take second best very well. You focus on your goals, break them down, then dedicate yourself to making them happen and wiping out the opposition.

There are almost too many interesting Capricorns in the public arena to mention. Stephen Hawking, the physicist and cosmologist, with one of the world's leading minds, has the Sun in Capricorn. His intellect, dignity, absolute dedication and persistence in the face of adversity are beyond compare. Given his scientific background, I find it interesting that he has never ruled out the possibility of the existence of a universal creator. Hawking wrote, 'If we discover a complete theory, it would be the ultimate triumph of human reason – for then we should know the mind of God.' I often refer to his views on political and environmental subjects when I need a learned opinion. Capricorn is all about fact and reality over concept or blind belief.

Muhammad Ali, legendary boxer and one of the greatest sportsmen of all time, was also born under the sign of Capricorn. Even as a child he was seriously ambitious and absolutely dedicated to the sport he loved. Ali began training at twelve and started to win titles at eighteen. He was always stating, 'I am the greatest,' and although this may sound arrogant (Capricorns are often perceived as arrogant), he made it reality. Muhammad Ali is still regarded as the greatest fighter the world has ever known.

He also had three planets in Leo, which gave him a love of the spotlight and dazzling charisma, which he later put to good use when he became an activist for African Americans as a civil-rights campaigner. His drive to fight for equality I attribute to his Moon, Mercury and Venus in Aquarius, the anti-establishment sign devoted to humanitarian causes.

Like your opposite sign, Cancer, you Capricorn folk are extremely family-oriented and you do your utmost to create a stable and steady environment for your partner and children. You are also unendingly supportive of those you love. (My mother is Capricorn and without her support I would never have been able to follow my creative path.)

Unlike Cancer, though, Capricorn 'gone wrong' struggles with accessing his or her own emotions and understanding other people's.

Emotional intelligence is not your forte. You are liable to be embarrassed by any emotional display and can appear cold as a consequence. You are also just a little bit earnest and tend to take life rather too seriously – unless you have plenty of your neighbouring signs, Sagittarius or Aquarius, in your birth chart, in which case fun is also high on the agenda.

You appreciate the finer side of life, though unlike showy Leo you would rather own one fine diamond than a large collection of bling. This figures, because Capricorn is reserved in everything he or she does. 'Gone wrong', you are materialistic and worldly, obsessed with status, recognition and success, and ruthless in your pursuit of it.

I call Capricorn 'the master' (partly because you can be somewhat authoritarian – the influence of your ruling planet Queen Saturn is strong with you guys!) but, more significantly, because your deepest lessons, as with Cancer, concern emotions and security. Your experience is directly opposite, though. Capricorn is comfortable with commitment but terrified of emotions and failure. Yes, this is true for plenty of people but most are not afraid, like Capricorn, of failing: social standing is everything to you. This means that you can become very rigid and a hard taskmaster. You are tough critics who are hardest of all on yourselves. You must learn how to master yourselves before you turn your attention elsewhere. In your case, mastery also requires compassion, first for yourself and then for those around you. If you cannot be easier with the prospect of failure, and with your emotional existence in general, you risk being miserable.

I always say that whenever you meet someone who is discerning, reserved, authoritarian and just a little magnificent, you can bet they have strong Capricorn in their charts. The famous New York artist Jean-Michel Basquiat was born under the sign of Capricorn (Venus, Moon and Chiron in Aquarius, so a rebel too). Even as a struggling street artist, coming into contact with the already infamous Andy Warhol, he demanded a token price for his art. That is Capricorn all over: they are skilled negotiators who value their work, and tough business people who refuse to sell themselves, or their work, short.

Basquiat had his Moon in Pisces, which usually indicates either an extremely spiritual or artistic mother (Moon) or one who is absent. Basquiat's beloved mother, who was a major source of inspiration and encouragement for his art, was committed to a psychiatric institution when he was still a teenager. I believe his lack of emotional support and steady mothering during these years and his devastation at her frequent committals eventually drove him to drugs (classic Pisces 'gone wrong') and killed him.

CAPRICORN

'GONE WRONG'

— COLD, RUTHLESSLY AMBITIOUS —

'Gone wrong', you Capricorn people can be pig-headed and utterly ruthless. You climb the ladder to success and trample over anyone who gets in your way. You are cold, materialistic and overambitious: power is your number-one goal and you will do whatever you must to get it.

Scorpio 'gone wrong' is also motivated by power and capable of ruthlessness but Scorpio is all about passion and an emotional need for power. Capricorn 'gone wrong', by contrast, is so icy cold he or she borders on psychopathic. If someone makes you look bad you will eradicate them from your life and your pulse rate will hardly rise by a beat.

I once worked for a Capricorn tyrant who used to have his secretary call people on a Friday afternoon at five o'clock and send them into his office so he could fire them. By the time they returned to get their coats, their desks had been cleared and they were locked out of their computers, just like that!

Think of Chairman Mao, who was born under the sign of Capricorn. It is thought that between two and five million people died under his rule. When he exceeded his own execution quotas, he said the killings were necessary in the name of securing power.

THE LEARNING

If you have a strong Capricorn influence in your chart, keep your need for status in check or risk alienating good people. You have much to gain from learning about emotions, which may often seem ugly to you, as well as combating your fear of failure. Know that failure is not necessarily the end of everything. It can be used to keep us humble and grounded. It is what you do afterwards that counts, and where some people rebuild, others go after the achievements of others. It is a good trait to be able to detach emotions from tough decisions but you must also learn how to channel compassion to become the very best version of you.

If you live or work with Capricorn, it's helpful to bear in mind that their reputation means everything to them. If you embarrass them or mess with their career or do anything that might harm their reputations, they will not forgive you easily. They often give the impression that life is one big business transaction to them, so be professional at work and earn their respect. If you're in a relationship with a Capricorn, try to limit your emotional outbursts. They tend to take an efficient approach to relationships, though this may be diminished by the other signs they have playing out in their full charts.

⊖ RESTRICTIVE AND CONTROLLING ⊖

Capricorn 'gone wrong' is inclined to throw cold water on other people's plans and goals, bringing inconvenient truths to the equation and a dose of reality to dampen their enthusiasm. This can make you seem highly restrictive and controlling. For example, if you have Saturn (the ruler of Capricorn) sitting on your rising sign, your personality may be restricted in some way. People with this placement were often restricted by authoritarian parents in their formative years and later become controlling themselves. I know a gay man with this exact placement in his chart: he is very uncomfortable with his sexuality, having grown up with a highly disapproving father. This has led to him being very controlling in his personal life, which prevents him finding real love. He is now working with a psychologist to help him break free from this self-imposed prison.

THE LEARNING

If you have a strong Capricorn influence in your chart, try to avoid the need to be seen as conventional. Most of the successful folk I know born under this sign are also self-confessed 'control freaks'. You should ask yourself why you operate like this. Does it stem from controlling parents, or some other authority figure whose influence is still (too) strong? You may not see your control-freakery as an issue but it drives people away and restricts you in experiencing the magic of life and the delight that spontaneous, free-spirited people can bring into your world – which can veer towards dull if you are not careful. We all need rules and structure but they need to be flexible enough to change with differing circumstances.

If you live or work with Capricorn and they are controlling, call them out on it (if you dare!). I have found that controlling behaviour restricts real love and the free flow of creativity, an energy we sorely need. From a more worldly perspective, solutions are often born from creativity: if you control too tightly you will stifle your own and other people's ability to generate them. If you live with a Capricorn, try to help them embrace the more spontaneous side of life. Stand up to them and openly question their motives as many are operating out of sheer habit.

⊖ EARNEST AND OVER-SERIOUS ⊖

Capricorn folk take things seriously, which can be either advantageous or the reverse, depending on the situation. When you decide on a certain course of action you pursue it earnestly and never allow anything or anyone to dissuade you. This can be problematic as it means you are ill-equipped to adapt to new situations quickly – and life is increasingly uncertain and unstable. You need to learn how to adapt in the face of change and how to embrace a new course of action if yours is no longer tenable.

I have a really successful Capricorn client who founded his company years ago and now holds a vast market share. He has really worked on being able to let go of his fixed perceptions of how things 'should' be, and there's no doubt his flexibility has been fundamental to his success. When one of his directors was headhunted by the competition, instead of being arrogant or emotional about it he reacted calmly and swiftly. He knew what a loss this person would be, so he restructured the whole company and brought in that director and the others he valued as shareholding partners. Smart move: they blew the competition away and floated the company a few years later on the stock market. Now they are all raking in millions. This is also a good example of Capricorn's ability to detach from emotions and make the right decisions, no matter how they feel personally.

THE LEARNING

If you have a strong Capricorn influence in your chart, it may be hard to lighten up but you enjoy a challenge, so make this one a priority. Stephen Hawking, who has suffered with chronically disabling motor neurone disease for more than forty years, once said, 'Life would be tragic if it were not funny.' If you have neighbouring signs featuring in your chart (Sagittarius and Aquarius), this will not apply to you but if you are mostly Capricorn, you need more love, light and humour in your life. Sing, dance and do something frivolous at least a few times a month. Learn how to let go and do not fear what others think, or how things will look to the neighbours! That is living half a life. Do not wait until the end of yours to realize that.

When you are dealing with serious decisions and professional situations it is wise to detach emotions. I am not talking about empathy and compassion: they should never leave your side. I am talking about taking things personally. My client could easily have taken his director's threat to leave as a personal slight, let him go and suffered great losses as a consequence. This is a good example of how detaching emotionally and not taking yourself too seriously works well.

If you live or work with Capricorn, try your best to help them lighten up and adapt to change by presenting a practical argument for it. For example, show them the reasons why the current course of action is failing and offer a few alternatives. If you live with a serious Capricorn, tell them you need to have more fun and assure them that you would rather explore ways to do this with them.

CAPRICORN
'GONE RIGHT'

—⊖— COOL AND COMMANDING —⊖—

Capricorn 'gone right' is often cool and always wise – often way beyond their years – strong-minded and moral, super-smart, steadfastly reliable and totally trustworthy. Your deeply ingrained values, natural authority and unflappable nature make you instantly attractive to the rest of us. Your name 'Capricornus' comes from the Latin for 'mountain goat' and, just like the animal, you have the ability to survive in tough terrain. You are extremely tenacious and never lose your cool (in public anyway!). Rather than moan about your circumstances you get on with running up the mountain. This can be comforting to the rest of us as your steadiness and innate good sense mean that you are incredible in a crisis. You're often like the capable superhero who comes to save the day!

THE LEARNING

Unless you are already in a position of authority, in which case it is expected of you, it is usually better to bide your time before stepping in and saving the day. Wait until you are asked or you may seem arrogant and upset everyone. It's not that you mean to – you are super-capable, usually know what needs to be done and are simply itching to get on and do it – but some people work with too much ego and will resent you for it. Wait until the time is right, then go for it!

—⊖ STEADFAST AND SUPPORTIVE ⊖—

You Capricorns will stand by the people you love and respect through thick and thin, as long as you consider their paths are honourable, their goals and dreams practical and viable. (If you don't, you will soon share your opinions!) Once you've decided you're on board with an idea, a project or a person you are endlessly generous with your highly practical support and investment (in every sense). You do not suffer fools, though, or stand on ceremony for anyone; you are after all ruled by Queen Saturn, and she bows to nobody.

THE LEARNING

We so appreciate your support but you need to accept that you are not always right: keep an open mind before making any serious decisions. You are best when you know all the facts and figures so extract them first, then use your skills to execute. As with most things, be prepared to change tactics if presented with unknown factors. Accept that the best-laid plans may go astray and something even better may arise.

—⊖ PRACTICAL AND HIGH-ACHIEVING ⊖—

If someone's in trouble, or needs help to solve a problem, you Capricorns are the go-to sign. We can relax, safe in the knowledge that, no matter how challenging it may be, you will figure it out and get it done. You are supremely practical and can side-step emotion when it comes to making decisions that are often tough for the more emotional and sensitive among us. Your ability to see through flawed plans and identify potential pitfalls makes you the very best kind of adviser, both personally and professionally. When you decide to do something you will work persistently until it is done, and although you honour your obligations, you usually have a fixed attitude to work and will switch off when you need to. This means you are simply brilliant in the business arena: you do things properly, always remaining calm in the face of chaos, never cutting corners. Your motto is 'Do something properly or not at all.' Unsurprisingly, you tend to be high achievers.

THE LEARNING

It may seem to you that you are forever helping the less-organized out of pickles and jams. I know it can sometimes be a struggle to stay patient, but try to understand that other signs are simply not as fabulously practical as you. They're not trying to be annoying: it just isn't their forte. (And remember, they will definitely have their compensatory good qualities!) It can help to offer others practical tips so that in future they can help themselves. Try to enjoy the opportunities life presents to play to your considerable strengths and please know that you are appreciated!

IN LOVE

Capricorn people take relationships very seriously and sincerely. You are utterly trustworthy, dedicated and committed and, generally speaking, wouldn't dream of being unfaithful. You can be so serious in other parts of your lives that you often unleash your naughty side in the bedroom, which can go well or not, depending on your partners' reactions. Some of you like to keep this side of yourself secret and, instead of giving your partners the opportunity to embrace it, you look elsewhere. This tends to lead to big problems because serious Capricorn can't handle the 'failure' or the 'shame' of being unfaithful so you dissolve into guilt and hurt a lot of people, yourself included.

If you marry, you usually take your vows seriously and see divorce as failure. I tell my Capricorn clients that life is not solely about success or failure, and that some relationships are a success until, perhaps, that relationship, like a temporary freelance contract, is complete so it ends. That's it. (If this sounds a little cold to you, you probably don't have a lot of Capricorn in your chart.) Life is like a long journey and some people, there from the very beginning, stay while others leave.

You Capricorn folk often seek status through advantageous marriages and partnerships. Capricorn men in particular tend to be traditional and fixed in their preferences. You are the type that seek a trophy wife. The Duchess of Cambridge is a Capricorn and has certainly achieved status on the world's stage by marrying the second in line to the British throne.

When one of my clients had trouble with her boyfriend, who was refusing to commit, I advised her to get super-fit. (She has plenty of Taurus in her full chart and Taurus needs to be fit for maximum energy levels.) I also suggested she 'do a Kate'. You see, as far as I can tell, when Prince William ended their relationship, Duchess Kate, the Capricorn, dusted herself off, dressed to impress and was photographed en route to, and exiting from, the very best clubs London has to offer. Eventually the prince couldn't take seeing her gorgeous photo in the papers over breakfast so he proposed. Prince William, by the way, has the Sun in Cancer, which is the direct opposite to his wife's Sun in Capricorn. Opposites can balance each other very nicely. They both have the Moon in Cancer and Mars in Libra, which is helpful as they have similar energy (Mars) and emotions (Moon).

I once had a gifted musician client with a Capricorn partner. He became very ill and needed to go into hospital. His partner refused to take any time off work to come to his aid, and even told his friends and family, who appealed to her, that she had a business to run and bills to pay. She viewed his illness as a total inconvenience. He eventually recovered and, needless to say, ended the relationship. Capricorn 'gone wrong' is so focused on work and so uncomfortable with emotion that they fail to offer emotional support to anyone who needs it. When we looked more deeply at her chart for my client, who needed closure, I realized that she had the Moon in Capricorn as well as the Sun. A double dose. When the Moon, which governs emotions, goes wrong, it can have a devastating impact. She was exhibiting all the classic 'gone wrong' Capricorn traits in the arena of emotions, so she was unable to support her partner: her solution was to continue building her empire and detach.

CAREER

Career, influence and power are fundamentally important to you Capricorn folk. You like to work for yourselves or in a traditional and stable environment, which offers the potential to progress, grow and, indeed, feed your ambition. Capricorns, along with your opposite sign, Cancer, like to build empires and you are usually very good at it. You don't seek out fame, like Leo, preferring respect and recognition for your achievements, which is very high on your priority list. For this reason you are suited to roles that allow you a certain level of command: you are natural bosses, CEOs, managers or company founders.

You have a natural sense of authority and a strength that is appealing to employers and employees alike, and you find it easy to gain people's trust. You tend to be rather dismissive of co-workers, though, and are not especially skilled in people management as you distrust kindness in the workplace and are lacking in emotional intelligence and compassion.

You are dedicated to your profession, however humble, and can always be relied upon to turn up and do your best. You persevere and are patient when climbing the ladder, but you expect success and give yourself a hard time if you have not achieved it by middle age. You also tend to be workaholics, and this can cause huge issues for you as it often alienates family and friends. It also leads to difficulties in later life when retirement is on the horizon.

If this is you, then know this: countless interviews with the dying have shown us that, when we are faced with our last breath, it is not lack of worldly success or our failure to spend enough time in the office that occupies our minds; it is regret at missing our child's first step, or being on a work trip when our partner sorely needed us. Please do not be someone who will eventually live with regret.

Work hard, but take a tip from my successful Capricorn friend: switch off your emails at a certain time, never work while you eat, take time off for family, and prioritize spending time with those you love. We all need to earn money but when does enough become enough?

HEALTH

You Capricorns seem to suffer particularly with your bones and joints, so you need to keep yourself supple and agile. While writing this, I was directed to the ancient book on my shelf that prescribes natural plant remedies for each of the signs (Nicholas Culpeper's *Complete Herbal*, introduced to me by my ever practical and beloved Taurus godmother). It suggests amaranth for Capricorn, and when I dug a bit deeper I discovered that this helps to boost bone strength and lower blood pressure, both of which Capricorn (or those with plenty of Capricorn in their charts) tends to suffer with.

Yoga would be wonderful for you – a double whammy: in addition to increasing your suppleness it would also allow you to disconnect from a purely pragmatic approach to your time and be in the moment. You spend so much time focused on working hard at everything you do that you need to learn how to relax and take things easy on many levels.

One of the most successful Capricorns I know switches off his emails at the weekend. He says that the sign of someone who has either not made it or fails to feel successful has his or her phone next to them at the dinner table or when having drinks with friends or family. Definitely food for thought!

THE FIX FOR CAPRICORN

1. **Lighten up.** Try your best not to take life so seriously. Allow yourself to be silly. Go to comedy clubs, fly a kite in the local park, find a hobby. Try anything that allows you to stop focusing on your career or responsibilities for a while.

2. **Let go.** Do as much as you can in all the areas of life that matter to you, then stop. Develop a trust in the flow of the universe, and avoid the need to control all situations (and certainly your loved ones).

3. **Own up** to your ambitions and laugh about them. Tell people that you are ambitious and are prone to trample on others. Make a joke of it. At least they will be prepared, and if you can laugh at yourself, others will laugh with you, not at you!

4. **Do not be so hard on yourself**, especially if you view aspects of your life as failure. Forgive your failings and know that life is often just a game. If you are happy, with people around you who love you, this is indeed success. It means more than millions in the bank.

5. **Try not to allow your need for status to get in the way.** It can prevent you from attracting true love, which is far more beneficial to you than any title or public image.

6. **Be open**, especially to learning new skills and for opportunities to change. Who you were a moment ago is not who you are now. You can be free from your own limited perception of who you really are. Find lighter signs, such as Sagittarius or Leo, in your full chart and channel their 'gone right' energy.

– AQUARIUS –
THE ACTIVIST

AIR SIGN

OPPOSITE OF LEO

ELEVENTH SIGN OF THE ZODIAC

ELEVENTH HOUSE

RULED BY SATURN/URANUS

Aquarius is an intellectual air sign and, like its fellow, Gemini, it's clever and logical. It's also bright, breezy and can be as light as the air. As well as smart, Aquarius 'gone right' is seriously insightful, almost psychic. It's governed by Saturn (associated with discipline, self-governance and life lessons) but also strongly associated with Uranus, which is known in astrology as the great awakener and signals areas where we need to become more aware. Aquarius is all about freedom, independence and triggering awareness.

Those folk with planets in Aquarius are often the revolutionaries of the Zodiac. They push for progressive change and assist in shifts in the collective consciousness: some people believe we are now living in their age. Many US astrologers say it started in the 1960s with the hippies' peace and love movement. Others feel it began in 2012, but I believe that it is strongly linked to the digital revolution, which started in the 1950s and has been speeding up ever since. Irrespective of when it began, we are all feeling the impact. In 2020, both Jupiter and Saturn will be in Aquarius and we can be sure that changes will be plain to see.

James Dean, the sultry film star, had the Sun in Aquarius, and one of his most famous films was *Rebel Without a Cause*. Very Aquarian! Aquarius people need a cause to get behind or may become obtuse and rebellious for the sake of it, which helps no one.

'Gone right', Aquarius folk are charming, sympathetic, kind and compassionate. You're exciting to be around, interesting, and interested in other people too; you usually make great listeners and trustworthy confidants. You're often in demand with your many friends for your insightful and straightforward advice. You have eclectic taste in everything, including people, and collect random groups of friends like bags of sweets. You love to mingle, mix and share experiences and ideas, especially if they are linked to common higher ideals. You are also highly inventive and, at times, nothing short of geniuses as you have the ability to think outside the box but your innovations are strongly driven by logic. It can be a fabulous combination.

'Gone wrong', the less appealing side of Aquarius presents itself. You often buck convention for the sake of being seen as a 'rebel', which becomes tiresome and draining. Your ingrained need to question everything, so often a strength, may mean you come over as contrary and difficult. This problem is magnified by the fact that you aren't always the most emotionally subtle people. In fact, you are at times shockingly direct, which can disturb the sensitive among us, or those who prefer polite trivia.

And then there's the other kind of Aquarius: not those who resist rules and authority and are ruled by freedom-loving Uranus, but those who conform, who have a 'gone wrong' tendency to be standoffish. You can be unforthcoming about yourselves and don't really do small-talk, which can make you difficult to get to know and creates the impression of coldness. You guys are ruled by Saturn, the planet that represents authority and establishment, and can be way too serious and aloof, thinking yourselves rather superior.

(Although, in my experience, even this less typical Aquarius is on track to rebel eventually. We'll see you at ninety years of age streaking on a golf course!)

Aquarius people of every stripe are inclined to be extreme and unpredictable, which can be delightful or difficult, depending on the situation. Extremely warm, extremely cold: you can be both in a matter of minutes. You lull people into a false sense of security and then, out of the blue, say something so random that the person opposite you has absolutely no idea who they've been talking to for the last hour. If they call you out about it, you will use your robotic memory to recall the whole conversation, then ask, just a little too innocently, which bit was confusing. It can all feel a little baffling to the person on the receiving end. Aquarius is scarily random.

Aquarius can be fanatical too, which is dangerous. If you are born under this sign and are fanatical about any cause or religion, you must tailor this trait before it gets out of hand and causes chaos. 'Chaos' is a word strongly associated with your sign.

Wolfgang Amadeus Mozart, the world-famous composer, was born under the sign of Aquarius. A child prodigy, who was already composing by the age of five, his career wasn't smooth. He was highly rebellious and, typical of his sign, gave respect only to those he felt earned it. He famously fought in public with Archbishop Colloredo of Vienna, who tried and failed to control him. Mozart was given a position at the court of Salzburg but left for greater things, which is very typical of his sign. Aquarians do not like to settle for comfortable, so while many people would have remained at court just for the status, Mozart set off to pursue his goal. He was determined to meet Joseph II, the Holy Roman Emperor, and did so. Afterwards the Emperor supported him with commissions and a part-time role at the imperial court. If the letters he wrote are anything to go by, Mozart also had a shocking sense of humour.

Aquarius folk love to laugh and poke fun, and if you make them laugh you will win them over, no matter what.

AQUARIUS
'GONE WRONG'

CONTRARY, DIFFICULT, CONTROLLING

Those Aquarius folk who try too hard to fit in make themselves unhappy and may come across as cold, difficult, contrary, hard to pin down and noncommittal, just like neighbouring Pisces. Your lack of tolerance when it comes to emotions means that you are capable of being extremely rude, obnoxious, detached, aloof and obtuse.

In the most extreme manifestation, you delight in causing chaos and creating rifts between people. An unhappy Aquarius becomes the very opposite of light, and it's difficult for them to dig themselves out. You create chaos merely to entertain yourselves and sow seeds of discord between others for fun. The worst of it is that you do it so cleverly that they have no idea they are caught up your cosmic web of chaos.

Aquarius can be one of the most controlling signs, even pipping Scorpio and Virgo to the post. They believe they have the awareness to know what is best for everyone (often they do). Usually it's their way or the highway.

THE LEARNING

If you have a strong Aquarius influence in your chart, find a higher cause to get behind and redirect that rebellious energy of yours into something worthwhile so that you are on track with your soul purpose. Try to be aware of when you are being controlling, contrary or difficult for the sake of it. Have compassion for people who may be trying to implement structure and rules. If you are among the Aquarian-led folk who delight in chaos, you must wake up now and get on track with your higher purpose, which is to serve and help humanity, not harm it. If you do not, you will live to regret the time you wasted being a trickster.

If you live or work with Aquarius, be direct with them. They can handle it and, besides, they dish it out often enough. Logic appeals, and they would prefer to hear the truth. You may get a rebellious kick back but it won't take long for things to settle down. If they are being contrary, offer them choice (this will prevent the rebellion); if they're being difficult, ask them how they would do things/ make the changes, which will make them stop and think.

COLD, EMOTIONALLY DETACHED

Aquarius 'gone wrong' is as cold as ice. You can be terrifying when you detach from the world. The person on the receiving end would be forgiven for thinking you'd left your body and a robot with no heart had stepped in.

You are very uncomfortable with unbridled emotion because you tend to look at everything from a rather detached and very logical standpoint. For you, it's all about the reasons why. You ask questions and analyse everything, picking apart an argument and finding the root cause of a person's behaviour before smashing down the gavel and delivering a damning, but very often accurate, assessment.

You hate having to answer to anyone and, even if you're doing nothing wrong, will refuse stubbornly to reply to any questions you deem inconsequential or invasive of your privacy. This may make you seem seriously evasive and means it's very difficult to get close to you. You typically have a plethora of acquaintances and contacts, but very few friends.

THE LEARNING

If you have a strong Aquarius influence in your chart, you must take other people's emotions into account. Have compassion. If they are overwhelmingly emotional, explain to them that you lack the tools to handle this behaviour and suggest they get help. Offer to do what you can to prevent the outbursts and try hard to make changes. We all have to answer to other people so try to be a little more patient (unless you are dealing with a paranoid, insecure partner, in which case direct them to get professional help). Stop seeing the need to compromise in relationships and make changes as a direct restriction on your individual self-expression.

If you live or work with Aquarius, evoke their compassion – it should not be hard: it's innate. If they detach and become cold, ask yourself if you are being unnecessarily emotional.

JUDGEMENTAL, STUBBORN, PRONE TO EXTREME VIEWS

You are usually the least judgemental of all the signs but you are extreme people so it can go either way and, occasionally, Aquarius goes very wrong in this regard.

Aquarius values smart and interesting people and prefers deep and meaningful interactions that serve a purpose: superficiality doesn't usually cut it with you guys. And though most of you would never judge someone on their accent or their clothes, you sure as hell will judge them if you find them neither interesting, clever nor funny. A favourite line is 'But does that really matter?' and if you decide someone is fake, shallow or dull, you will do anything to get rid of them. You can be so clinical it's almost brutal. In the worst-case scenario you are highly elitist, convinced your own views and your little clique are infinitely superior to anything or anyone else.

Once you *have* made a judgement, it's almost impossible to move you. You are a fixed sign and don't we know it. You can be stubborn, obstinate and immovable. You refuse to accept apologies or to forgive others, instead coldly cutting them from your life. You walk away from anyone who gets in your path – partners, friends, even family – then stubbornly blame them for whatever made you leave. Given your flash-quick minds and hyper-awareness, you can convince people of anything, so you must work with the truth and the facts, and avoid fanaticism in yourself and others.

THE LEARNING

If you have a strong Aquarius influence in your chart, make sure you have facts before you decide to dig in your heels. Try to have more patience with people who are seemingly superficial: it is usually due to insecurity and fear so compassion is key. If you are prone to extreme views, you need to educate yourself and research your conclusions. You have the ability to wake people up: do so only for the good of all. Remember that everything we say and do is like a seed planted: good seeds yield healthy fruit. Do not be elitist: we are all interconnected. When one suffers, so do we all, so make a pact to help all of humanity.

If you live or work with Aquarius and they are judgemental, present them with logical facts and they should see reason (eventually!). Try to encourage them to be more tolerant and compassionate – again, this is the key: they can usually see others' points of view but some need a few reminders. Be direct and straight but always honest: Aquarians read people and situations well so it's better not to have self-serving interests as a priority in getting them to modify their behaviour.

⊖ ELITIST ⊖

Aquarius 'gone right' are devout humanitarians who fight for equality, but 'gone wrong', they are the polar opposites, fighting for the one per cent to keep their status and obscene wealth to build an Elysium, which they hope will protect them from the rest of us when the balloon goes up.

THE LEARNING

If you have a strong Aquarius influence in your chart and wish to be happy on a soul level, it is vital that you give back and work to serve humanity. It is not enough to write songs about revolution and do nothing to bring it about: you need to get your hands dirty and help redress the imbalance. Stand up for what you believe in – volunteer at a soup kitchen, help at an animal refuge, raise funds for worthy causes or write blogs that inspire change where it is needed. You, more than any other sign, have the power to change the game, and when you get on track, your soul will feel real and lasting contentment.

If you live or work with Aquarius, accept that they are very often contrary and work with that. If you give them choice they will toe the line. If you attempt to control or trap them, they will drop mind bombs that rock any kind of structure you have attempted to build. They will cut you off and head for the clouds to regroup, or simply cause utter chaos. My son has Saturn in Aquarius (Saturn indicates the sign you must master) and he was, still is, a real rebel. Instead of enforcing rules, I give him choices and explain the possible outcomes for each, leaving him with the ultimate responsibility. Put anyone with strong Aquarius influences in a cage and they will blow the whole town up trying to break free.

AQUARIUS
'GONE RIGHT'

COMPASSIONATE, FOCUSED ON SERVING HUMANITY

'Gone right', Aquarius people are freedom-fighters and usually heavily involved in charitable causes, very focused on 'giving back' and driven to serve humanity. You make fearsome campaigners and activists. You're typically highly compassionate, but if you decide a person is needy, your sympathy has its limits. Needy does not attract Aquarius, and you lack tolerance for anyone who is self-centred or one-dimensional.

But once you align with a cause or a person, you will get behind it or them tirelessly. Your innate sense of nonconformity means you are not afraid to back someone no one else will. Given that you tend to go to extremes, sometimes you do and say things just to shock or wake people up – your favourite pastime, both literally and metaphorically!

THE LEARNING
It is vital for your well-being to feel you are part of some higher vision or cause but, given your 'gone wrong' inclination towards fanaticism, you must avoid becoming too extreme. For example, I do not condone the cruel production of fur, but neither do I approve

of activists hurting the people who wear or sell it. Whatever you decide to get behind, try to remain compassionate and tolerant.

—⊖ EGALITARIAN ⊖—

Aquarius is the anti-establishment sign and is generally drawn to humanitarian and progressive causes. You have no time for old-fashioned ideas about gender, class, race or anything else. Aquarius just sees people, and considers them all equal. You guys can connect with people from all sorts of varied backgrounds. Sociable, confident and illuminating, you are the natural connectors of the Zodiac, who match people and concepts: you love to make things 'pop'.

THE LEARNING
You must retain a level of tolerance for those less progressive than you. Do not fight someone who is fixed in their beliefs. Instead try gently to open their minds. Not everyone sees past race, class, creed or status so just accept that and have compassion. Remember, it is usually fear that prevents people from accepting others as equals. Keep connecting people and ideas and watch as they gel, then pop. Don't lose confidence because the occasional person is horrified by your progressive attitudes.

—⊖ FREE-SPIRITED, GENUINE ⊖—

Aquarius people have a reputation for being different, perhaps even 'out there', and in my experience it's well deserved and can be rather wonderful. (I would say that: I have the Sun, Jupiter, Venus and a few more planets in Aquarius!) Quirkiness is in the Aquarius DNA: 'gone right', you guys embrace your rather strange ways and passions and set about being who you want to be from the get-go. You're duty-bound not to care what others think. Totally unpredictable and eccentric, you are more likely to be found in an old curiosity shop than the mighty 'made in China' mall.

Aquarius is as multifaceted and layered as an onion. You have eclectic interests and skills and are comfortable wearing many different 'outfits', depending on who, or what, you are dealing with. Though you show many faces to the world, they are all authentically you. With Aquarius, what you see is what you get: 'gone right', nothing is faked.

THE LEARNING

Do not try to be different for the sake of it. Just be yourself and the rest will follow. Of course, there are the very Saturn-ruled conservative Aquarians, but even they delight in wearing odd socks. Be the free spirit that you are but focus on not hurting anyone else in the process. Society has put together some expectations to ensure that it works: do not buck all convention for the sake of it.

IN LOVE

At best, Aquarius is a dazzling, exciting and committed partner, who brings heaps of fun to the relationship. You prioritize being friends with your partner above everything else. You usually take your time to form a long-term bond and rarely pick anyone who doesn't also have a multi-faceted mind and life. Masters of long-distance love affairs, you are often just as stimulated by intelligence as you are by the physical. You usually have many friends of both sexes. Many people with Aquarius planets, especially Mars and

Moon, in their charts are bisexual: they fail to see the difference between men or women – they just see people.

On the 'gone wrong' side, many of you lack staying power and are unskilled in the art of commitment, seeing any form of compromise as a covert plan to trap you and limit your independence. You are always seeking the 'honeymoon' period and fresh, interesting connections with many people, so you may be seen as promiscuous and rebellious. 'Gone wrong' you are often the serious players of the Zodiac: if someone more exciting comes along you are capable of casting off your partner and getting over them very quickly while they spend years nursing a broken heart and shattered dreams. Cold!

Your lack of emotional intelligence can be a serious problem in relationships. You often do not know how to make people feel cared for or loved and can appear totally indifferent, trusting far too much in logic and rational thought. Of course, this is not the case if you have a more sensitive planet influencing your love life; or Cancer or Pisces as your rising sign, Moon or Venus in Pisces, for example.

Since you rarely experience jealousy, you do not respond well to jealousy or possessiveness in any form from your partner and do not react with tolerance when you recognize this trait in others.

If you're in a relationship with Aquarius, know that when you give them freedom and trust they will usually reward you with total loyalty and respect, never bad-mouthing you or talking about you negatively to others. They are usually very private people, who keep their problems to themselves until they have resolved them. This can make it hard to build deep intimacy and trust with them. They are used to being solo and this can be tough for you as they are fiercely independent. It may seem as if they shut you out of aspects of their intimate lives.

If you become jealous or possessive they will usually find the nearest escape and exit sharply. Most are not materialistic, though, so they will probably leave you with the house and all its contents in their bid for freedom, even if you have betrayed them. If you leave the door open for them, they will remain true and make the very best of partners; many stay friends with ex-partners, even after betrayals, as they are forgiving folk. You'd better get on with their friends, though: they, like their opposite sign, Leo, are dedicated to their true friends. If you try to control them you will eventually lose them for ever. This becomes a point of principle. They will cut you off, like a gangrenous limb.

If you are an emotional person they usually detach as they try to rationalize your meltdowns. They often lack the ability to handle them, so may seem cold and uncaring. In the worst-case scenario, if they think you are being needy, they will stubbornly refuse to comfort you, choosing instead to punish with silence, leave, or stray if they must stay.

I have recently been working with a client whose seemingly intolerant husband is Aquarius. He has eroded her confidence (sure, she allowed it) because she became insecure and needy. He refuses to give up his friendships with old female college friends, even though he has been intimate with a few. She is Scorpio, and has become insecure, resentful and jealous. These two signs are often a rather difficult union as Scorpio desires a soulmate dedicated just to them and Aquarius (selfishly, it seems) wants to remain free to connect with other people. Even if the Aquarius partner is faithful, they will not compromise their sense of freedom for anyone for very long. You need to evoke compassion to help an Aquarius 'gone wrong' to see your point of view, and make sure that you are not being insecure or needy.

On the other hand, if this sounds a little bleak, I have an Aquarian friend who has been married to his wife for ten years now. We all say that the stars indeed aligned at the time they met and that was that! She has Jupiter in Aquarius so understands him on a deep soul level, and they both give each other plenty of trust, freedom and respect. If Aquarius has nothing to rebel against they are devoted and can chill, and this couple are brilliant together. They often entertain and share a wide group of friends with varied interests, yet they always take enough alone time to keep their union alive and their bond strong.

CAREER

Aquarius is fantastically well suited to working with revolutionary causes and charitable organizations. This sign also governs the media industry and anything that connects the masses in some way, such as the digital world, new technologies and new inventions. Aquarius people are futurists and usually way ahead of their times, a trait they share with Pisces. Pisces has the vision and Aquarius has the awareness and the ability to think big. You make good software programmers, brokers, futures traders, media executives, astrologers and advertising professionals because you gauge future trends way ahead of the competition.

Aquarius thinks big: you guys see the big picture and this frequently makes you titans of industry and leaders in your field. Two of the biggest names in TV are both Aquarius: Oprah Winfrey and Ellen DeGeneres. Irrespective of how you feel about either of them, nobody can deny that both contribute to humanitarian causes.

Aquarius is usually popular in the workplace: you take everyone's needs into consideration. You never expect anyone to do anything that you would not do yourself, and you make congenial and thoughtful co-workers and progressive bosses.

You are great with people and highly intuitive, which makes you successful in any profession that involves dealing with humanity on a day-to-day basis. You make good salespeople, who can quickly satisfy customers and tune into their needs. You always serve others with a sense of humour and a positive outlook.

'Gone wrong', you serve only yourselves, caring little for anyone outside your group. You are the fanatical extremists, who work with a certain cold indifference towards anyone with differing views.

HEALTH

Aquarius is an intellectual air sign and you tend to suffer with mental afflictions, such as stress and anxiety. You have a certain nervous energy that you often don't know how to switch off, so you are prone to burnouts and meltdowns. I have several clients who have Mars (the planet that governs energy) in Aquarius and I have told them they needed to switch off from electricity to heal. I suggested that they sleep in a 'cave', removing televisions, laptops and mobile phones from their bedrooms as artificial light can trick the brain into staying awake; televisions and alarm clocks pump out electro-magnetic fields that are detrimental to relaxation. They should leave only a lamp in their bedrooms, and anything else that is essential. Without exception, all concluded that they slept more soundly.

If you are an Aquarius, or have this sign featuring prominently in your chart, you need to take time out from the constant bombardment of life or you run the risk of burning out. With this awareness you should never get to that stage but many I know with this sign have had mental breakdowns: they have an antenna that is constantly downloading information; it never turns off so they need to learn how to tune it out. Meditation is a lifesaver for you, as is getting outside into nature, without phones or other digital devices.

THE FIX FOR AQUARIUS

1. **Sleep in a cave.** Do not have anything plugged in when you sleep. A television in your bedroom is definitely not good either. Switch it all off or, better still, try not to have anything plugged in near your head.

2. **Know when to stop.** Do not push yourself to extremes, which causes you to lose your tolerance and compassion: you will likely short-circuit.

3. **Use your awareness** to tune in to a higher vibration of insight, kindness and compassion, and find the root cause of others' behaviour. This will enable you to be compassionate rather than cause chaos.

4. **Compromise in relationships.** Do not see other people's demands on you as a direct attempt to curb your individuality and limit your self-expression.

5. *Feng shui* **your space.** You are a natural and should be equipped to know how to clear a space of negative or stagnant energy. If not, look up 'space clearing' online and invest in some tools to assist you, such as frankincense, sage or *palo santo*.

6. Spend time alone. You need to replenish your energy and time alone will help with this. Explain to friends and partners that this is a basic emotional need so that they do not feel left out.

– PISCES –
THE VISION
♓

WATER SIGN

OPPOSITE OF VIRGO

TWELFTH SIGN OF THE ZODIAC

TWELFTH HOUSE

RULED BY NEPTUNE

Pisces folk have a gift for perceiving things that are hidden to most others. They're dreamers who see the big picture and are often able to make that vision reality. All in all, they're seriously cool people.

Let's take the life and works of a famous Pisces, Albert Einstein, as an example. His vision is the stuff of legend and there can be no better figure to show this sign in action. Einstein's revolutionary theory of relativity completely changed our understanding of the very fabric of the universe. He had issues with the formality and rigidity of the traditional education system, believing that its stringent approach stifled the creative process. This is typical of Pisces people, who abhor feeling restricted or forced to disconnect from their inner creativity. Einstein's love of music is well documented, and is shared with most Pisces or those with prominent Pisces in their birth charts. (Many great musicians were born under this sign – Chopin, Kurt Cobain, Nat King Cole, Johnny Cash, Aretha Franklin and Al Green to name just a few.) Research also shows that even when Einstein seemed to be in a committed union with one lover or another he was usually pining for someone else, another typical Pisces trait.

Michelangelo is another famous Pisces who was a true artistic genius. If you have ever seen the beautiful and awe-inspiring fresco on the ceiling of the Sistine Chapel in the Vatican, you will know that his vision was transformed into reality for all to behold. The story behind its conception illustrates several typical Pisces traits. Fresco was not a medium that Michelangelo was accustomed to and one of his fellow painters, Bramante (a competitive Aries with Saturn in Scorpio), knew it. Bramante suggested to the Pope that he should commission Michelangelo, hoping his rival would fail, but his plot backfired spectacularly. Michelangelo tried hard to refuse the commission but the Pope told him that 'God had spoken' and insisted he get to work. The fresco took four years to complete, and turned out to be one of the greatest achievements in Western art. Cardinal Biagio de Cesena, who had backed Bramante, caused Michelangelo no end of suffering throughout the years he spent on the project (suffering for the love of art is also a Pisces trait!) so the artist painted a portrait of Cesena in Hell, where he remains to this day. The lesson here is never provoke a Pisces. Once riled, their anger is colossal. And if they're also an artist, they might just immortalize you in a very unflattering form!

PISCES
'GONE WRONG'

FLAKY

Pisces rarely walk the middle ground: you are either the most reliable and committed people or simply flaky! You can be non-committal, slippery and a nightmare to deal with for mere mortals. One of my clients would regularly ground her Pisces son, only for him to slip out of his bedroom window and glide down the drain-pipe. Pisces people need clear boundaries, consistency, and to be shown exactly why their behaviour can be harmful. As a rule, you Pisces are kind at heart, so when you know how harmful your actions are to others you will usually try to clean up your act, which is endearing. When my client explained to her son that it made her anxious not to know where he was he began to take her feelings into consideration before thinking about slipping out again. Another Pisces client of mine is not so brilliant at diary management. It's always fifty-fifty as to whether he will honour our appointments. Some people would be horrified with this arrangement but I am always relaxed because I know that this is in his Pisces nature. I try to schedule his appointments for when I am at my desk working on other projects, just in case.

THE LEARNING

If you have a strong Pisces influence in your chart, you are learning about commitment in general and must be clear with what you can and cannot deliver. Making commitments and sticking to them wherever possible helps you to develop willpower, though you have to be realistic in your approach. For example, if you keep cancelling appointments, stop agreeing to them until you know you can definitely keep them. Pisces need to learn how to keep their promises or stop making them.

Strive to create structure and firm boundaries for yourself: learn how to use a diary to prioritize, then check it diligently before you over-commit to projects, meetings or engagements and create an achievable to-do list for days when you need to get things done. Try to manage your time by committing to a single activity for half an hour, and set an alarm to let you know when the time is up. Eventually time-management becomes a natural habit, but it takes effort to get there.

Try to be as honest as you possibly can to avoid getting stressed and attracting anger or disappointment from others. This all helps to strengthen your character and resolve.

If you live or work with Pisces, you need to paint the full picture for them by explaining how their behaviour negatively impacts on people around them. This encourages their empathy and increases understanding. Do not assume that they are already aware, as they can live in their own version of reality.

⊖ OVERLY STRONG-WILLED ⊖

As we've just seen, Pisces does not usually have strong willpower, but if you are one of those who is already aware of this, you may be over-compensating and going to the opposite extreme. Some Pisces I know are so determined not to be flaky and so anxious not to be taken advantage of by others that they become super-controlling and non-compromising. This is a trait you share with your opposite sign, Virgo.

THE LEARNING

If you have a strong Pisces influence in your chart and suspect you're more the controlling than the flaky kind, you first need to try to let go of your anxiety. It can feel terrifying to relinquish even a tiny bit of control but, as you probably know, it's also terrifying to feel that you're the person with all the responsibility. This can lead to feelings of being put-upon. If you admit to feeling vulnerable, this allows the universe and others to step up and help you. If you revert to controlling behaviour, this often has the reverse effect and annoys people. Try making small compromises with someone else's point of view, even if they take you out of your comfort zone. This requires practice (as with every pattern we try to change), but eventually you will prove to yourself that life is easier and better when you control what you can, then let go and trust more.

If you live or work with Pisces, step up at any opportunity to make small compromises that help them to move away from their controlling behaviours. Remember, this tendency reflects Pisces folk's attempt to resist their strong pull to flakiness. Have compassion: with encouragement, they can get closer to the middle ground!

—⊖ SENSITIVE ⊖—

Life can be very difficult for Pisces because you need to experience something personally to empathize with others. This can lead you into feeling like a victim or playing the martyr and make you quick to blame others for everything that goes wrong. If you fail to deliver, you often blame anything but your own shoddy sense of planning. You'll blame the transport, other people and anything else you can think of. Real growth comes from accepting responsibility and looking at what (if anything) you could have done to change the outcomes or prevent the patterns from repeating. Many Pisces folk blame bad experiences from their early years, such as distant or controlling parents, bullying at school or unfaithful partners for the way they are, but the more aware among you choose not to become victims of your past. You embrace the present with the knowledge that each and every one of us has the capacity to heal ourselves and become a different person, capable of creating a better life. This is a general life lesson for all of us, but one that typically resonates with Pisces folk: when we blame external events or other people for our failings we are actively choosing to refuse opportunities to grow.

Many of you see and feel things so intensely that you sense a need to escape the impact of your powerful visionary and prescient abilities. Pisces kids (and some grown-ups!) will disappear into a fantasy world: film, video games and any other form of interactive fiction. Adults are prone to slip into a haze of alcohol or drugs, or both. When problems arise or conflicts brew, instead of addressing a situation to bring about its resolution, you're inclined to ignore frantic attempts to contact you and hit the bottle or games console, or disappear into a cloud of marijuana smoke.

THE LEARNING

If you have a strong Pisces influence in your chart and feel the need to escape from painful feelings, do so, but look for a more helpful method such as a creative pastime: writing, painting or song. If you do drink to excess or indulge in other harmful activities regularly, you need to admit you have a problem, then see if you can limit this indulgence to one or perhaps two days a week. This will help you to develop willpower. And if you find you cannot control your drinking or other self-destructive behaviours (which is not uncommon for Pisces people), there are lots of peer support groups online and in your community, as well as professional help available. Do not just accept this as 'the way it is': make it the way it *was*.

Try to avoid harsh people, toxins and situations and embrace a gentler existence. The fix here is for you to build in regular time for spiritual activities such as meditation or yoga – anything that helps you to attune to your deeper self and find peace with the outer world. Some Pisces folk find particular solace in water-based activities – on a surfboard, for example, riding the waves – but whatever you choose, it is important to address the issues presented by family, colleagues, friends and lovers rather than avoiding them. Otherwise they will simply keep happening.

Try to remind yourself that if you keep falling into the habit of blaming others when things don't go right, or you've got too comfortable with your self-identity as a victim or a martyr, then ultimately the only person you're short-changing is you.

If you live or work with Pisces, try to bear in mind that their habit of ducking responsibility comes from a place of anxiety, not arrogance. Anything you can do to help them participate in putting things right, rather than running away, will be helpful to them and to you.

⊖ FIERCE TEMPER ⊖

If pushed to the limit, Pisces will explode in a furious rage. All the signs have a ruling planet, or a boss as I call it, and you Pisces people are governed by Neptune, lord and protector of the oceans and seas. Like Lord Neptune smashing his trident to create great waves, a Pisces temper can cause huge devastation. It takes a lot to rile you, but nobody should go there unless they're prepared for a tsunami powerful enough to wash them away. On the other hand, Neptunian babies can be gentle, healing and go with the flow.

THE LEARNING
If you have a strong Pisces influence in your chart, remember that you guys need to face issues gently, yet head on, as and when they

arise. You are learning about boundaries and often attract people and situations that test yours. You must not suppress or evade things as this leads to a build-up of resentment and anger that eventually triggers the tsunami, and by then it's often wholly inappropriate.

If you're dealing with a Pisces displaying this behaviour, give them space, then go back in (don't leave it too long!) and state your case calmly. Use the default setting of painting a full picture to show them how their rage impacts on you and others.

PISCES
'GONE RIGHT'

SPIRITUAL

Pisces are so in tune with the rhythms of life that everything flows for you and you just have that little bit of magic about you. You are spiritual and intuitive, some would say psychic. You very often have dreams that later come true and many of you have prescient abilities. My teacher used to call Pisces the 'mediums' or the 'go-betweens' for life, God and the universe.

All the best healers and psychics I know have Pisces featuring prominently in their birth charts. By 'healers', I don't just mean hands-on Reiki masters. I'm referring to all the people who have the drive to help others and are motivated to make the world a better place for everyone. My teacher used to say that all authentic healers have psychic abilities but not all psychics are healers. Throughout my life, I have found this to be true. Those who remain humble and heal people and conflict quietly are the real unsung healing heroes as far as I'm concerned.

Pisces 'gone right' always seems to know what to say to make you feel better and their thoughtfulness has the capacity to warm cold or hardened hearts. They are kind beyond belief and have an almost ethereal energy that reminds us all of the beauty to be found in real humanity.

THE LEARNING

If you have a strong Pisces influence in your chart, you need to learn how to protect yourself and how to keep your energy clean. (This is a need you share with fellow water signs, Cancer and Scorpio.) Again, it's all about boundaries. Knowing when to create space and how to say no both come in handy. Time alone to heal and recoup energy in an environment free from chaos works wonders for you when you are struggling. Soft lighting, gentle music, meditation and prayer help to maintain a strong connection to your higher self.

Being a sensitive and spiritual person does not mean that you allow others to walk all over you. Quite the opposite is true. Living a life grounded in spiritual values leads to self-respect, and endeavouring to treat others as you would wish to be treated empowers every one of us and raises the collective mood of humanity.

——○ CONNECTION WITH NATURE ○——

When you are in touch with nature, especially in the sea, you are in your element. I came to know about a brilliant man called Captain Paul Watson, a campaigner dedicated to saving our seas and marine wildlife from the environmental damage caused by mankind. I bet a friend that he had plenty of Pisces in his chart and I was right. He has Jupiter in Pisces.

THE LEARNING

You are ruled by Neptune, lord of the seas and you need water, like flowers need light: this is the way to heal you. The gentle sound of a bubbling stream or waves crashing in the ocean is like therapy to Pisces. If you are not fortunate enough to live by the sea, take breaks as often as you can to heal near it. I am generally not a fan of keeping animals in captivity but, looking at this as a sort of rescue, you could buy some fish from a pet shop and invest in a beautiful spacious tank. Watching them glide through the water without a care in the world would have the same relaxing impact as a massage.

'Gone right', Pisces is super-connected to wildlife and will do all they can to preserve vulnerable sea life and other animals. The very sensitive among them and those most true to their sign are often pioneering new ways to save the oceans and they certainly would not be seen dead wearing fur, such is their connection to suffering and nature in general.

Pisces 'gone right' is soothing, like raindrops in the heat of the desert: they bring a certain calm and cool to the rest of us mere mortals when we are in need.

IN LOVE

Pisces at their best are devoted lovers: you do all you can to make your partner's life easier, and dedicate yourself to making him or her happy and your relationship flow with ease. You are typically selfless but, depending on who you choose to open your heart to, this can leave you feeling that you have been taken advantage of if your partner is anything less than 100 per cent dedicated to you. You have high expectations that are difficult to meet.

When Pisces gets hurt your sensitivity can prevent you from trusting again. Other signs dust themselves off and carry on, but Pisces struggles to get over betrayal. This often holds you back, as love always results in some sort of pain, even when it is 'till death us do part'. If you've been wounded you need to accept, forgive and try to carry on being as open as you are when you are in love.

Pisces is prone to cheat on their partner or for their partner to cheat on them. You can be tempted away from your relationship by someone you feel might be better suited to you. You love the initial stages of romance, but when reality steps in, you often bail out. What really helps, whichever way round the dynamic is playing out, is compassion and forgiveness. For some couples an open relationship is the solution.

Pisces often lie to prevent conflict and simply run away from the results. When you do this you are passively taking control of situations by disappearing and refusing to give any sort of closure. Instead, try to create some space away from the situation, then, without leaving it for too long, tackle it honestly. Check that your motivation is pure, and move to heal the situation with integrity. If you can't face it directly, write a letter or ask a trustworthy mediator to help you.

If you are in a relationship with a Pisces, you must be present and do all you can to reassure them that you are devoted and committed to appease their fears. They need plenty of space, but the romance they bring to you after some alone-time makes it all worthwhile.

If you are dealing with a Pisces-led person who is struggling to open up, do not get angry as this makes them close off even more. Take a gentle approach and explain how their behaviour wounds you and damages them in the long run. Again, if you create space first and work to dispel any anger, you will avoid projecting your pain onto them and help them to recognize how harmful their behaviour is to both sides. You may not always succeed but the key lies in trying.

Do not chase a Pisces: once they make up their minds to go, they will slip through your fingers into the murky depths, like a slippery fish, out of your reach for ever. If you can cope with noncommittal behaviour then all is well, go with the flow, but if you know you need a steadier partner, do not fool yourself into thinking you can change them. Only they have the power to do that, and it requires hard work, discipline and commitment.

CAREER

You are often drawn to the creative industries: film, fashion, photography, design, music and television. That doesn't mean you all work in these fields, of course, and many of you with a strong Pisces presence in your chart will express your creativity in different ways. Pisces are also far-sighted, which enables you to pull solutions almost out of thin air. Those of you who are not in tune with the arts would do well to try to open the doors to these – often latent – gifts. Being realistic with your goals is the key to contentment. For example, if you're a Pisces looking to bring more creativity into your life but you need to pay the bills with a nine-to-five job, study something creative in your spare time and unleash the frustrated artist within.

You have vision and are keen to follow your dreams. The successful among you follow your heightened natural intuition. You invest, design and produce with relish, often mapping out paths for yourselves years beforehand and following that plan to the letter. Pisces don't want to lose themselves in someone else's fantasy. Others of you display the flip side of this propensity for dreaming: a tendency to get stuck imagining how life could be if you had the right career, rather than doing something about it.

You do best when you have a structured daily routine and for this reason many of you gravitate, at least at the beginning of your careers, towards industries that have strict rules and regimes. Either that or you create rigid structure for yourselves. A dear friend of mine was a policeman for a few years before suffering an injury. Afterwards he dedicated his life to his real passion: music. He secured a record deal and before long his music was featuring on Hollywood films. All very Pisces – he first worked in a sector that had rigid rules and structure, then moved into the arts and followed his dreams.

Pisceans frequently have a seriously disjointed sense of timing, so missing deadlines is nothing new for many of you. You procrastinate and count down to home time so you can reconnect with a bottle of wine and a binge on Netflix. If you are prone to do this, ask yourself what you can do to change your routine to become more present and reliable. Flick back to page 273 and refresh your memory on how you can learn to reduce flakiness. Search your heart for your passion and take steps to incorporate what you love to do into your daily life. (That goes for your downtime routines as well as your work.) Be prepared to make sacrifices if you need to change career and start again. Life is too short to wish even a single second away.

HEALTH

You need to get out of your head and into your body. Anything that allows you to feel at one with nature and the universe helps to boost your optimum health. Any water-based activity soothes Pisces: they love great open seas and are attracted to surfing, swimming, kayaking and waterskiing. Simply sitting by the ocean can revive you and give you fresh perspective.

Like the other water signs, Pisces folk are prone to depression, anxiety and feelings of hopelessness. You need to boost your serotonin levels in any way you can, without the help of medication, if possible. Exercise is important to all signs, but for Pisces it can give you the regular endorphin hit you need. Techniques such as meditation and mindfulness can also be particularly beneficial for Pisces: they allow you to connect with your intuition and your inner vision.

Despite your disposition towards escapism, you Pisces folk are happier when you stay in control. You need to be vigilant to make sure that your fears, or drugs and drink, do not become the rulers of your lives. I used to know the most brilliantly talented Pisces, one of the most creative people I have ever met. She was everything 'gone right' about Pisces. One tragic year she lost her parents and her partner, then turned to illegal drugs to escape the pain of her loss. Many people can shake off habits but Pisces and Scorpio, a fellow water sign, find it harder than most. Even with the support of her loved ones, she became lost to Neptunian confusion and an eternal high. If you know someone who over-indulges in this way, you can bet all the fine tea in Harrods that they have prominent Pisces planets featuring in their charts, regardless of their Sun sign.

THE FIX FOR PISCES

1. **To combat flakiness, buy a diary** or use an online scheduling tool and force yourself to use it, checking it every morning and every night before you go to bed.

2. **Don't over-commit.** Practise saying no, nicely, or buy yourself time.

3. **To manage your sensitivity,** look for a healthy way to duck (temporarily) out of painful situations. This might be five minutes of mindfulness or a creative hobby that can take the place of the daily wine drinking.

4. **Embrace the idea that you are not a victim** or a martyr but an independent adult in control of your life. The past is gone and the future is yours to create.

5. **Indulge your creativity.** Play an instrument. Tune in to your artistic and gentle nature.

6. **Avoid toxins and toxic people** who erode your sensitivity.

7. **Make regular trips to water.** A lake, river or the coast: anywhere near a body of water will soothe you. A swimming-pool will do at a push, although harsh chlorine is not particularly helpful!

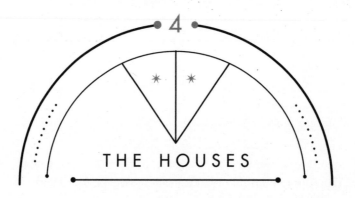

THE HOUSES

We're now getting to the final piece of the puzzle. I hope you're feeling enthused by the thrill of 'aha' moments and keen to start implementing changes in your life based on everything you're discovering. By now you're probably feeling confident about using your birth chart to pick up clues, and are more comfortable about training, then trusting your intuition.

Having focused so far on planets (the 'what') and signs (the 'how'), we are now turning to the third and final element in your chart: houses (the 'where').

You interpret charts by cross-referencing all three areas constantly, flipping between the chapters in this book to build a fuller picture and increase your understanding. We have already talked a fair bit about houses, especially in relation to the impact of generational planets, like Uranus, Neptune and Pluto. You may well already have picked up an idea of what the houses represent. But the purpose of this chapter is to add another dimension to your interpretations by looking at the context for how your combined planets and signs play out. So, the main question you're asking in this chapter is: 'Where [in which area of my life] will each planet and its sign play out for me?' It is worth mentioning again that astrology is a new language and, as with learning any language, you will become better and more skilled if you practise it.

HOW TO WORK
WITH THE HOUSES
IN YOUR CHART

To refresh your memory, the Zodiac is split into twelve signs; they all have ruling planets and they all reside in one of the twelve houses. We call this a default. Each house represents a different area of your life, such as assets and values, or spirituality. So, Aries is the first sign of the Zodiac, its ruling planet is Mars and its default setting is the first house. Taurus, the second sign, has its natural home in the second house, and its ruling planet is Venus. Gemini, ruled by Mercury, is the sign of the third house, and so on.

But, as you've already seen, the default setting does not always apply in your chart. Not everyone's planets, signs and houses stick together. All three elements move independently of one another to create the unique snapshot of the heavens at the precise moment of your birth that is your birth chart.

A quick reminder about the way planets (and their attached signs) fall in the houses. You will have noticed from looking at your own birth chart that perhaps the planets are not distributed evenly throughout it. Some houses may be empty and others crowded. This in itself is a big clue. If a house is crowded, that's a clear signal that you need to focus more attention on the parts of your character indicated by those planets, relating them to the areas of life represented by the house in which they fall.

An empty house doesn't mean that there's nothing going on for you in this area of your life. It might simply mean that you already have a lot of insight (conscious or unconscious) in this particular area. Perhaps, broadly speaking, you've got it figured out already.

Or it might mean that the lessons you need to learn are wrapped up in the house's resident sign.

So, look into the planetary activity in your houses, then figure out the sign ruling each house in your particular chart and go from there. Hunt for clues!

To identify each of your houses' resident signs, check the outer rim of the wheel of your chart, where you'll see that there's a sign symbol in each house. You always begin at nine o'clock on your chart, where the arrow tip is pointing to your rising sign, which is also the sign resident in your first house. Move round the chart anti-clockwise from there. The next sign in the outer rim is your second house's resident sign, and so on. You will need to refer back to the signs symbol key on page 12 if you do not know their natural order.

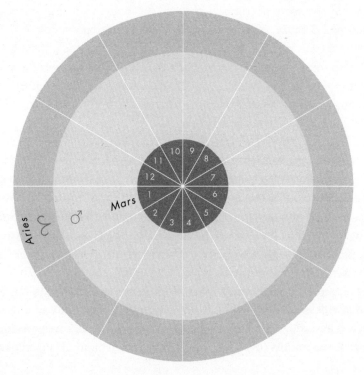

CHARLES CHAPLIN / 16 APRIL 1889, TUE

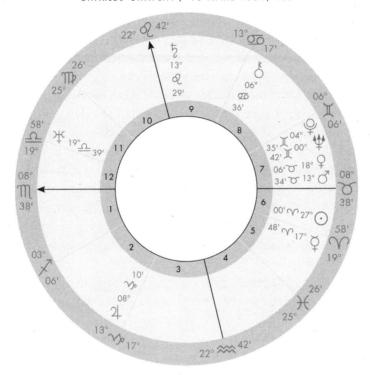

In the example chart above, you'll see that this person (Charlie Chaplin) has Scorpio ruling their first house, Sagittarius ruling their second, Moon in their first house, Jupiter in their second, no planets in their third and so on. So this person may also hunt for clues in the signs that rule the houses in their chart, then relate them to each house's associations, which are detailed below in 'Fast Track to the Houses' (page 295), with each house's default planet and sign.

As a quick example here, Charlie Chaplin has Sagittarius ruling his second house (Sagittarius focuses on the truth and timing in general) and the second house indicates how we build up our assets; Chaplin funded his owns films for the most part and obsessed over the timing of every move until he got it right. Only right will do for Sagittarius. That he has Jupiter, the ruler of Sagittarius, in the second gave him the ability (Jupiter represents skills and abilities) to express political truths of his time. But Jupiter also highlights where we are prone to go to extremes, and Chaplin was well known for being extreme when it came to his film production.

It's worth bearing in mind that, because the signs, planets and houses all have default settings, their traits and behaviours tend to overlap. Aries, Mars and the first house all have a lot in common, for example, so if you read something here that you think you've already read elsewhere in the book, it will be because the default setting is kicking in. That can be very powerful. For example, I have a client who is very Aquarius in his mannerisms even though he has Sun and Mercury in Aries. But in his chart those planets are both in his eleventh house (the default setting for Aquarius) and the Aquarius influence really comes through strongly in his case.

One final general point: the houses are not always equal. In theory a chart is divided into twelve equal-sized sections of thirty degrees. But if you have a house that is larger than the usual thirty degrees it is known as an 'interception'. (This can feel a bit confusing so, for the purpose of simplicity, let's keep it as straightforward as possible.)

An 'intercepted' house is a house that has been forced out of its natural placement in your chart by an excess of activity contained within it. It might be that the house contains a lot of planets, or that the planet and related signs it contains are particularly significant in your chart. But, essentially, intercepted houses mean that there is plenty to learn from them, along with the signs impacting upon them. My teacher used to say interceptions meant that something had gone a tad wrong with these signs and houses for us early in life or even in a past life, so we have a lot to figure out in this area in this lifetime. But as far as past lives go, we'll stay in the present!

Because each sign and house has an opposite, there will always be at least two signs and houses that are involved in an interception. For example, in David Bowie's chart, shown below, the first house (which in his case has Aquarius and Pisces resident) and the seventh house (Leo and Virgo) are intercepted. You can tell because they are bigger segments of the 'pie' and, as you can see, they're opposite one another.

So we would expect that Bowie had particular lessons to learn from studying the 'gone wrong' and 'gone right' traits of Aquarius and Pisces in relation to the areas of life associated with the first house (which, as you'll see from 'Fast Track to the Houses, on page 295, are all connected with the self, personality, persona and how you present yourself to the world). It would also be particularly instructive to pay close attention to Leo and Virgo's 'gone wrong' and 'gone right' traits and relate them to the areas of life associated with the seventh house (basically, the house of relationships). Intercepted signs tend to indicate that your early years held you back in some way from developing the 'gone right' traits of the signs in question. In Bowie's example, his intercepted Pisces may not have been able to rationalize or be practical at all in his first house (house of self). In the opposite house, where Virgo is intercepted, he may have been a perfectionist who focused on tiny details obsessively.

You may or may not have intercepted houses in your chart. If you do, just make a note to yourself that those particular houses, their resident signs and any planets that fall within them, will be especially rich in insights that have deeper meaning for you.

One note of extra explanation for those who have intercepted houses: it means that you will also have duplicate signs in the outer wheel of your chart (that is, you will see the same sign symbol featuring twice). That doesn't mean you need to count that sign twice. Just discount it the second time it comes up, move on to the next sign symbol in the outer rim of the chart and assign it to the next

DAVID BOWIE / NATAL / 8 JAN 1947

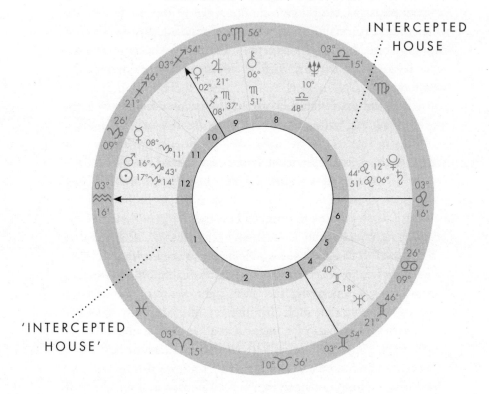

INTERCEPTED
HOUSE

'INTERCEPTED
HOUSE'

house you get to. Duplicate signs and their intercepted houses can show a way out of the difficulties caused by the interception. For example, a person with Cancer and Capricorn duplicated would do well to use as many Cancer and Capricorn 'gone right' traits as possible. They should bear in mind that Cancer shows where we need to build on our own security, where we need to 'feel safe'. Capricorn, by contrast, shows the life areas where we should become more organized and develop discernment.

Now pull up your birth chart again. You're going to work through the steps laid out below. At the end of the section on each house there is space for you to jot notes as you're reading about its associations. You will hopefully be well versed in this by now. The key is to reread and practise; the aim, as always, is to respond intuitively, as well as analytically, and make a note of anything that jumps out at you. There is also a table where you can complete your own personal summary of your interpretations when you combine each planet, sign and house in your chart.

STEP ONE.   Refresh your memory about what the planets represent and how the sign they fall in plays out for you. Refer back to your notes on each planet's impact on your chart.

STEP TWO.   Check to see which sign is ruling each house in your birth chart. Begin with the first house. Follow the line with an arrow tip that points to nine o'clock and you'll see that it's indicating a sign in the outer rim of your chart. That's the sign that rules your first house. (Remember, it may or may not be the default sign for the first house.) Continue to work round your chart anti-clockwise. Make a note of the sign in each house in the tables at the end of each house section.

STEP THREE. Read the information in this chapter about which areas of life the twelve houses represent, bearing in mind what you now know about the planets and signs that fall into each of those houses in your particular chart. Make notes about anything that seems relevant. Create space in your brain by writing things down.

STEP FOUR.   Complete your personal summary of the way the planets, signs and now the houses interconnect for you and try to formulate an overall interpretation for each house.

You may need to flip back to your previous summaries again and pull out the key words that connect with the planets and signs. There is absolutely no right or wrong way to do this exercise. It's yours to take ownership of. It relies heavily on your own intuition and offers only a framework. The aim is simply to start to bring together everything you've learned so far and build up your own overall interpretation.

Throughout the book you have been working with a lot of questions and issues thrown up by your chart. It's the job of the planets and their signs to trigger them, and you should feel as if your brain has been pinging as it lights up with clues.

With houses, it's more a matter of using the questions already flagged up by your planets and their signs in relation to where they can offer the most insight. To give you a simple example, if you have Chiron the wounded healer in the seventh house, which is the house strongly associated with relationships (among other things), it's highly likely that you have a vulnerability that requires some attention in this area of your life.

This chapter is short and simple. You have already done most of the hard brain work by identifying and interpreting your planets and signs. Now it's time to figure out in which areas of life they play out by reading about their houses. This chapter is all about tapping into your intuition to help you identify from the lists which specific area of your life is in play. Intuition is often a spontaneous first thought or idea based on subtle nudges. It is the stage prior to logic. It really comes into its own as you work with the houses, the final piece of the puzzle, the one that will offer you conclusions!

FAST TRACK
TO THE HOUSES!

FIRST HOUSE

The house of 'self': your persona, personality and self-identity. Your external presentation, how you appear to the world and the first impression you make on others (physical characteristics sometimes come into play). The associations of the first house are the same as those of the rising sign.

SECOND HOUSE

The house of assets and values, your personal finances; how you build resources; money matters and possessions; your values, what you value, and your attitude to wealth.

—⊖ THIRD HOUSE ⊖—

The house of mind and learning in general; communication with self and others; relationships with siblings; your immediate environment; short journeys.

—⊖ FOURTH HOUSE ⊖—

The house of security; home and family; your childhood and ancestral roots; your experience of mother and maternal influences in general; nurture and sensitivity.

—⊖ FIFTH HOUSE ⊖—

The house of love, fun and humour; your creative inspiration and self-expression; self-investment; children; drama and your ego.

—⊖ SIXTH HOUSE ⊖—

The house of your daily life, routines and habits; health in general; attitude to work and service; personal sacrifice and healing.

—⊖ SEVENTH HOUSE ⊖—

The house of relationships; romance; affairs; partnerships of all kinds; negotiations, peace and harmony.

—⊖ EIGHTH HOUSE ⊖—

The house of power, sex, drugs and rock 'n' roll; other people's resources; death and inheritance; transformation and our ability to change deeply; rituals of all types and the occult.

—⊖ NINTH HOUSE ⊖—

The house of spirituality and religion; long-distance travel; higher education; philosophy; law; publishing; expansion and luck.

—⊖ TENTH HOUSE ⊖—

The house of your relationship to commitment, status, authority and reputation; social status; career; government institutions; corporations; authority figures in general.

—⊖ ELEVENTH HOUSE ⊖—

The house of socializing, networking and connecting; friends and your connection to humanity in general; group associations; hopes and aspirations; ideals; the media industry.

—⊖ TWELFTH HOUSE ⊖—

The house of your spiritual leanings and natural connection to the universe; dreams and the unconscious; things that are hidden; music; dance; meditation; yoga and all things metaphysical, like your intuition.

HOUSES
IN DEPTH

FIRST
HOUSE

ASSOCIATED WITH: THE SELF IN GENERAL,
PARTICULARLY YOUR PERSONALITY

DEFAULT PLANET: MARS

DEFAULT SIGN: ARIES

—⊖ ASSOCIATIONS ⊖—

The first house's associations overlap almost completely with those of your rising sign, which is also its resident sign. (Quick reminder on how to identify your rising sign: check the symbol in the outer rim of your chart, the one with the arrow tip pointing to it at nine o'clock.)

The first house represents the self in general and your personality in particular. It usually gives a strong indication of the sign that you allow others to see, the sort of traits that make up people's first impression of you. In other words, your personality. If someone knocks on your door unexpectedly, the rising sign, or first house, is how you greet them before you get the chance to go to your wardrobe and choose an item to wear for the occasion. Your chart can be seen as your energy wardrobe; the rising sign is almost like nakedness. It also shows how we assert ourselves, which links back to Mars, its default planet.

HOW IT PLAYS OUT

Let's start by looking at the impact of the resident sign because it's particularly important in the case of the first house. For example, if a person has Aries ruling their first house (that is, Aries is their rising sign), it's particularly strong as it's in its default setting. The person would usually project themselves (and be seen) as assertive, dynamic and driven in some areas of life. Of course the 'gone wrong' scenario looks more like competitive, at worst aggressive or passive-aggressive, and prone to taking over.

If somebody has Leo in the first house they will usually wish to be seen as confident, bold and dazzling. A client I know with Leo rising is fun, very entertaining and creative, but constantly needs attention or to be validated and recognized for her achievements, all Leo traits! If a person has Cancer ruling the first house they will usually wish to be seen as gentle, kind and nurturing.

Planets in the first house carry extra lessons connected to selfhood and personality. I know a woman who has Moon in the first house (leave her sign out for a moment); she is very sensitive and kind and likes to present herself as a nurturing, mothering type. This works well for the most part but she tends to attract relationships that are needy (Moon represents our needs) so she literally needs to be needed, then is disappointed when her partner leaves her for something more balanced.

—⊖ HERE'S YOUR SPACE ⊖—

Study the first house in your birth chart. Is it empty or does it contain planets and signs? If it's empty, you'll need to pay extra attention to the house's ruling sign (on the outer rim of your chart.) Flip to its section in 'The Signs' (pages 97–285) and read about its 'gone wrong' and 'gone right' traits. Think about their associations with the first house. Then move on to consider how any planets (and their attached signs) that fall into this house for you might interact with the house's associations. Use the space below to jot down anything that jumps out at you.

Then, when you're ready, have a go at creating a summary of the combination of the entire planet/sign/house configuration from your own chart. Remember that once you have nailed this, you can do virtually anyone's chart! Use key words from previous summaries and let your intuition roam around to explore both 'gone wrong' and 'gone right' potentials. You won't necessarily have a lot to go on straight away, but don't worry: practice makes perfect! You may need to reread material and let thoughts and insights come to you in their own time. Be patient! Astrology is like painting: sometimes you need to let the paint dry before you go back in.

Finally, you might want to jot down any points that jump out at you as you're thinking and writing. There's a table below for you to do that. Remember that studying the 'gone right' traits of the planets and signs in this house will give you ideas for how to bring in more of what you want in your life and indicate what you need to move away from. You might find it helpful to look up the Fix for each sign, a simple summary of practical ways to master and nail it!

HOUSE	RESIDENT SIGN	WHICH PLANETS? IN WHICH SIGN?
First		
'Gone wrong' traits		
'Gone right' traits		

SECOND
HOUSE

ASSOCIATED WITH: ASSETS AND PERSONAL
FINANCES; VALUES, SELF-WORTH

DEFAULT PLANET: VENUS

DEFAULT SIGN: TAURUS

 ASSOCIATIONS

The second house indicates what a person finds valuable and worth-while. It is associated with assets, money and other things of material value but, thanks to the impact of its default ruling planet, Venus, also with what a person appreciates or is attracted to in a general sense. Some people prefer gadgets, shoes and clothes while others will admire and collect art or cherish the beauty of nature. The second house is also the house of personal values and self-worth.

Planets in this house usually show that a person is resourceful. The sign ruling it will show the ways in which a person's resourcefulness plays out and the sorts of traits they typically deploy in this arena. For example, a person with Mercury in the second house typically uses intelligence and communication ('gone right'!) to attract whatever they need and desire in life (Mercury being strongly associated with everything connected to the mind, including intelligence and communication).

HOW IT PLAYS OUT

So, for example, if you have several planets in the second house, it might be a warning sign that you're putting too much emphasis on material gain to boost self-worth.

If a person has Mars in the second house they are often driven and maybe even aggressive when it comes to making money. If someone has the Sun there, assets are usually important to that person above all else. If they have Mercury in the second house, they will use their communication skills to attract material gain and often spend their money on anything that will offer knowledge (books, courses and higher education). And so on.

Remember that if this house is empty of planets, you can check the sign symbol or symbols on the outer rim of your chart. There will be a lot of lessons for you to learn from the interplay between the house and the signs that rule it in your chart. And it can also be worthwhile, if you want a really structured approach, to check the house's sign for more clues. Taurus is the default sign of the second house, for example, and Taurus 'gone wrong' is particularly prone to become obsessed with worldly possessions and the status conferred by money. But whichever sign falls in your second house, investigating its 'gone wrong' and 'gone right' traits will also yield insights into your relationship with the areas highlighted in this house.

—— HERE'S YOUR SPACE ——

Study the second house in your birth chart. Is it empty or does it contain planets and signs? If it's empty, check the outer rim of your chart for the symbols, then look at its resident sign. Flip to its section in 'The Signs' (pages 97–285) and read about its 'gone wrong' and 'gone right' traits. Think about the associations with the second house. Consider how any planets that fall into this house for you, along with their associated signs, might play out in this particular area of your life. Use the table below to jot down anything that jumps out at you.

Move on to drawing up the combination of the entire planet/sign/house configuration from your own chart.

HOUSE	RESIDENT SIGN	WHICH PLANETS? IN WHICH SIGN?
Second		
'Gone wrong' traits		
'Gone right' traits		

THIRD
HOUSE

ASSOCIATED WITH: COMMUNICATION, INTELLIGENCE,
IDEAS, SHORT JOURNEYS, SIBLINGS

DEFAULT PLANET: MERCURY

DEFAULT SIGN: GEMINI

ASSOCIATIONS

The third house, like its ruling planet, Mercury, is strongly associated with everything connected to our minds. It holds the key to a
person's intelligence and opinions as well as the way they communicate. This is the house of ideas and, for example, a person with
Uranus (strongly associated with the ability to generate new ideas)
in this house will be brimming with inventive ideas and usually
happy to present them to an audience. People with planets in this
house, especially if there are a few, value intelligence highly and
tend to expect themselves to be clever, even brilliant. The thing is,
though, activity in the third house can often create an urge to learn
little and talk too much: if you have a lot going on in your third
house it's important to do the study or the research to back up your
ideas and opinions.

Siblings are usually very significant to people with third-house
activity. Some are close to their siblings, some fight and others are
nonplussed: whatever – a sibling relationship is the longest relationship we will ever have, from cradle to grave, and we must be at
peace with them. You have been given siblings for a reason that

involves learning, often loyalty and patience! By the way, if you have no siblings but still have activity in this house it usually means you have friends who are as close to you as siblings and with whom you are likely to share deep past-life connections.

The third house indicates short journeys, which are well starred, whereas the ninth is more about overseas travel. In both cases, travel is likely to provide an opportunity to grow and learn.

The takeaway lesson for people with planets in the third house is that true progress will come when you understand the impact that your communication and messages in general have upon the wider community.

HOW IT PLAYS OUT

One of my clients worked in digital advertising and had Mercury and the Sun in Gemini in the third house (the Gemini default setting). She was at the top of her game, but once we had worked together for some time she opened up about her deep soul longing to do something positive for humanity. She told me she was tired of using her intelligence to convince people to buy things they didn't need so we began to strategize a transition. She woke up! I encouraged her to use her Gemini and third-house skills to research a few brands that excited and inspired her, which she did. She now works with one and is much happier.

My own third house is ruled by Virgo so I need to make sure that I use Virgo 'gone right', which is all about healing, in my communications. 'Gone wrong' can be brutal: a sharp tongue like a samurai sword!

Another client works in entertainment and is seriously funny (classic Leo trait!). But she has Saturn (the planet that indicates areas or traits we must learn to master) in her third house so she first had to master the way she communicated her sense of fun, having been restricted in the fun arena when she was growing up. (This is often how Saturn exerts its influence. It is the planet of authority and often indicates an area that the person must learn how to master because they were restricted in some way or over-controlled in that area by authority figures, such as parents, in early life.)

─⊖ HERE'S YOUR SPACE ⊖─

Study the third house in your birth chart. Is it empty or does it contain planets and signs? If it's empty, what is the sign on the outer rim? Flip to its section in 'The Signs' (pages 97–285) and read about its 'gone wrong' and 'gone right' traits. Think about the associations with the third house and then consider how they might interact with any planets that fall into this house for you. Use the table below to jot down anything that jumps out at you.

Now draw up your summary for this planet/sign/house combination from your own chart.

HOUSE	RESIDENT SIGN	WHICH PLANETS? IN WHICH SIGN?
Third		
'Gone wrong' traits		
'Gone right' traits		

FOURTH
HOUSE

ASSOCIATED WITH: HOME AND FAMILY, SECURITY, FEELINGS,
YOUR CHILDHOOD AND ANCESTRAL ROOTS, YOUR EXPERIENCE
OF MOTHER AND MATERNAL INFLUENCES IN GENERAL

DEFAULT PLANET: MOON

DEFAULT SIGN: CANCER

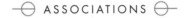

ASSOCIATIONS

The fourth house shows how a person relates to emotions and feelings in general and is strongly associated with family ties, commitment and security, as well as the experience you may have had with your mother, mothering and your childhood in general.

A person with a heavily populated fourth house often has lessons to learn about home and family. It can go either way: sometimes it shows a person who has had a sound and stable early home life, but frequently it correlates with an experience of insecurity or lack of stability at home when they were growing up. Unsurprisingly, this can sometimes lead them to become over-invested in this area of life. The fix is to create their own sense of security, home and family as soon as they can.

People with activity in the fourth house need a safe place to retreat to, unlike someone with more planets in the eleventh or ninth houses who will be happy living out of a suitcase or in several places at once. Fourth-house activity generally shows a strong need for security, whether that's financial security and immovable property or safe relationships. People with activity in in the fourth house tend to be risk-averse and are often homebodies.

The takeaway message for people with planets in the fourth house is the need to study the 'gone right' of the sign that rules it in order to to move on from the past and forgive emotional hurts; to figure out how to nurture themselves and others; and to avoid taking everything personally, becoming insecure or bitter.

⊖ HOW IT PLAYS OUT ⊖

Let's have a look first at the way the default setting of the fourth house (Moon, ruled by Cancer) might play out. A person with Cancer ruling their fourth would be working towards security in general: they would not be comfortable with an irregular income or light love affairs.

Sometimes this is all channelled healthily and manifests in someone who nurtures their relationships and creates safe havens for themselves and others. But it can make them very needy and lead them to demand constant emotional reassurance from their loved ones. If that is the case, they need to learn that real security begins within themselves. As ever, it can help to look to the 'Fix' of the sign that falls in their house, as well as the planets' 'gone right' traits, for guidance.

To give you a fuller picture, if a person has Mars (planet of energy and drive) in Cancer (associated with emotion and family) falling in this house, it usually means that they can be aggressive or too driven with their family (think 'tiger mums'). It also means that they could become angry when their emotions are triggered, especially if those triggers are connected to family life. If a person has the Sun in the fourth house, they are likely to need to feel proud of their families. Every person I know with Pluto in the fourth has had a turbulent childhood, leaving them with baggage that needs to be cleared away to allow for a kind of rebirth. (Pluto is the bulldozer of the horoscope, stripping away anything that's no longer useful.)

HERE'S YOUR SPACE

Have a look at the fourth house in your birth chart. Is it empty or does it contain planets and signs? If it's empty, what is the sign on the outer rim? Flip to its section in 'The Signs' (pages 97–285) and read all about its 'gone wrong' and 'gone right' traits. Try to relate it to the fourth house's associations. Then consider any planets (and their attached signs) that fall into this house for you. Use the table below to jot down anything that jumps out at you.

Now draw up your summary for this planet/sign/house configuration from your own chart.

HOUSE	RESIDENT SIGN	WHICH PLANETS? IN WHICH SIGN?
Fourth		
'Gone wrong' traits		
'Gone right' traits		

FIFTH HOUSE

ASSOCIATED WITH: EGO AND PRIDE, OUR RELATIONSHIP
WITH CREATIVITY, OUR VIEWS ON LOVE, CHILDREN,
FATHERS, PLAY AND FUN.

DEFAULT PLANET: THE SUN

DEFAULT SIGN: LEO

—⊖ ASSOCIATIONS ⊖—

The fifth house shows how a person loves and 'creates', how they go about attracting love and affection, and how they gain attention.

It is strongly associated with love and humility, as well as their opposites, ego and pride. In its most extreme manifestation, fifth-house activity 'gone wrong' can tip towards narcissism. Leo, this house's default sign, has a reputation for being the show-off of the Zodiac, highly attention-seeking and ego-driven. People with planets in the fifth house usually want to 'be' the show. It is the house of 'my': 'my' kids, 'my' style, 'my' project. Strong ties to 'father' are often shown here and, in my experience, many people who crave attention and seek love in inappropriate ways have 'Daddy issues'.

On a more positive note, it's also associated with creativity, a sense of fun and play. Children are important to people with fifth-house activity: 'gone right' they retain their own sense of childlike playfulness (not to be mistaken for childishness) and fun. They usually have incredible humour and creative prowess. 'Gone wrong', they recreate themselves through their children (they would be learning how to manage their ego and pride with regard to their children). But 'gone right', they will love them, help them shine in their own right, enjoy playing with them and appreciate their innocence.

The fifth house indicates our views on love and, in particular, how a person loves, depending on the sign involved. For example, someone with Taurus ruling this house may be nurturing and supportive of their partner ('gone right') or possessive and even jealous with and of them ('gone wrong').

The real lesson here lies with love and generosity. A person with a heavily populated fifth house must study the 'gone right' of the sign that plays out for them here to move on from selfish pursuits that serve only themselves. Their biggest weapon is their huge capacity for love, a sense of humour and their ability to not take themselves too seriously.

HOW IT PLAYS OUT

The default setting of the fifth house (Sun, ruled by Leo) has a tendency to manifest in ways that can be tough to be around. People with this setting can be self-centred, egotistical and attention-seeking (all classic fifth house 'gone wrong' traits) with a need for drama that relates back to a need for attention. Having said that, they are often hilarious (which allows them to get away with murder), have a great sense of fun and a genuine love of children (both strongly associated with Leo and the fifth house).

To give you a fuller picture, I have a friend with Uranus in Libra in the fifth house. He is unconventional and makes a good living in the media industry from his ideas (Uranus traits). His relationships were always erratic and his love life was unconventional (thanks to Uranus). He decided to work on his self-centred nature and attracted a long-lasting union. He is now happily married to a woman he dated long distance for years, who is from an entirely different culture. She keeps him on his toes and even forced him to learn her language. It's all very typical of his astrological placements. The fifth house is all about love (and, in one of its 'gone wrong' manifestations, selfishness). Uranus also indicates by sign the area in which we need to wake up, and Libra is strongly associated with relationships.

─⊖ HERE'S YOUR SPACE ⊖─

Take a look at the fifth house in your birth chart. Is it empty or populated with planets and signs? If it's empty, what is the sign on the outer rim? Flip to its section in 'The Signs' (pages 97–285) and read all about it's 'gone wrong' and 'gone right' traits. Think about the associations with the fifth house, then consider how they might interact with any planets that fall into this house for you. Use the table below to jot down anything that jumps out at you.

Now draw up your summary for this planet/sign/house configuration from your own chart.

HOUSE	RESIDENT SIGN	WHICH PLANETS? IN WHICH SIGN?
Fifth		
'Gone wrong' traits		
'Gone right' traits		

SIXTH
HOUSE

ASSOCIATED WITH: HEALTH, WELLBEING, PERSONAL
SACRIFICE AND HEALING, DAILY ROUTINES, PRODUCTIVITY,
ATTITUDE TO WORK AND OBSESSIONS

DEFAULT PLANET: MERCURY

DEFAULT SIGN: VIRGO

ASSOCIATIONS

The sixth house is associated with a person's attitude to health, healing and their fitness levels. If you have many planets in the sixth house, you must factor in your health when making any major decisions, and you will need to be fit on all levels.

The sixth house also shows how we view work. So, if a person has Moon in the sixth house, for their emotions (Moon is all about emotions) to be well balanced and nourished, they will need to feel productive and be proactive. This typically means that whatever they do to earn a living is vital for their well-being.

In my experience, people with plenty of activity in the sixth house are also prone to obsessive-compulsive disorders. The people who are obsessively clean, or check that their windows are locked ten times, will often have planets playing out in the sixth house or a strong Virgo influence in their charts with the 'gone wrong' traits playing a big role. Obsessive-compulsive disorders are all assigned to the sixth house or its default sign of Virgo.

The real lesson here is to figure out which area to focus on in order to enjoy optimum health and how to heal areas of your life that are unbalanced. A healthy work–life balance is vital for all of us, but it is of paramount importance for those who have planets in this house.

HOW IT PLAYS OUT

Look at what the planets in your sixth house represent and then the traits of the signs they fall in to draw lessons on the particular area of health and well-being that most affects you. For example, Mercury in the sixth indicates that you need to take care of your mind with practices that relax, train and tame it, such as meditation. With Mars in the sixth you would need to learn how best to manage and protect your energy.

I have a client who has suffered issues with his health regularly and he has many planets in the sixth house. I believe that some of his issues are psychosomatic and he tends to identify with his ailments, which doesn't help. The solution is to be mindful when making decisions to ensure that your well-being is taken into consideration: you are less likely to get away with pushing yourself to the brink, either energetically, physically or mentally.

Attitudes to work can play out here too. Most folk I know with even one planet in the sixth house have a strong work ethic. They do not sit around waiting for handouts or for other people to do all the heavy lifting. On the flip side, 'gone wrong' they can be hard work as opposed to hard-working!

HERE'S YOUR SPACE

Take a look at the sixth house in your birth chart. What's going on there for you? What is the sign on the outer rim? Flip to its section in 'The Signs' (pages 97–285) and read all about its 'gone wrong' and 'gone right' traits. Think about the associations with the sixth house and consider how they might interact with any planets that fall into this house for you. Use the table below to make notes.

Now draw up your summary for this planet/sign/house configuration from your own chart.

HOUSE	RESIDENT SIGN	WHICH PLANETS? IN WHICH SIGN?
Sixth		
'Gone wrong' traits		
'Gone right' traits		

SEVENTH
HOUSE

ASSOCIATED WITH: BALANCE, HARMONY, RELATIONSHIPS,
PARTNERSHIPS, AFFAIRS, ATTITUDE TO ROMANCE AND NEED
FOR LOVE

DEFAULT PLANET: VENUS

DEFAULT SIGN: LIBRA

—⊖ ASSOCIATIONS ⊖—

The seventh house is strongly associated with how a person views relationships, unions and partnerships and how much importance they place upon them. If, for example, a person has Moon in the seventh house, they may have an emotional need (Moon is all about emotions, and needs) for a partner to validate them.

The real lesson here is to make sure that *you* are the right one: not just hope for the right one to find and complete you, as if life were some Disney film. It's important to form honest relationships (taking compatibility into consideration) that are not based upon the need for another person to heal or make you whole. Romantic love is statistically proven to last only a maximum of eighteen months, if you are lucky. When this initial period passes the relationship should be based upon Libran ideals of equality, balance and peace.

—⊖ HOW IT PLAYS OUT ⊖—

I have a few clients who have Chiron, also known as the karmic wound and the wounded healer, in the seventh house, and they seem to struggle to sustain long-term intimate relationships. This certainly doesn't mean that they are destined to walk the Earth alone – far from it. It just means that they have a wound in the area of relationships and romance that needs working through and healing. This can play out in any number of ways but very often results in serious expectations being placed upon the other person and a continuing desire for the constant romance of the 'honeymoon' period. Sometimes, unfortunately, it manifests as their partner triggering deeply entrenched wounds. For example, if someone was abandoned by their mother, they may attract a partner who triggers wounds of abandonment.

If a person has the Sun in the seventh, they are destined to shine through their associations with others. (Remember, this house is associated with all kinds of partnerships, not just romantic ones.) However, Moon would mean that they have an emotional need for relationships and have much to learn from this area.

HERE'S YOUR SPACE

Take a look at the seventh house in your birth chart. Is it empty or full of activity? What is the resident sign? Flip to its section in 'The Signs' (pages 97–285) and read about its 'gone wrong' and 'gone right' traits. Let your mind ponder the associations with the seventh house, and with the areas of your character and life indicated by any planets that fall in this house for you. Use the table below to jot down anything that jumps out at you.

Now draw up your summary for this planet/sign/house configuration from your own chart.

HOUSE	RESIDENT SIGN	WHICH PLANETS? IN WHICH SIGN?
Seventh		
'Gone wrong' traits		
'Gone right' traits		

EIGHTH HOUSE

ASSOCIATED WITH: POWER, SEX, DRUGS AND ROCK 'N' ROLL;
DEPTH, REBIRTH, TRANSFORMATION AND OUR ABILITY TO
CHANGE DEEPLY; RITUALS OF ALL TYPES AND THE OCCULT;
ADDICTIONS; OTHER PEOPLE'S RESOURCES,
DEATH AND INHERITANCE

DEFAULT PLANETS: MARS AND PLUTO

DEFAULT SIGN: SCORPIO

ASSOCIATIONS

My astrology teacher used to call the eighth house the house of sex, drugs and rock 'n' roll. People with planets in the eighth house have to watch out for addictions. Their problem substance or issue could be any of the above (sex, drugs, rock 'n' roll). Or if Virgo rules their eighth house, say, they may be addicted to a healthy lifestyle, diet and fitness, which is not necessarily a bad thing (unless, of course, they are suffering with an eating disorder).

It's also the house of depth and seems to indicate that those with planets in it are likely to benefit from others' resources or an inheritance. This may not be as basic as money or property: an inheritance of talent would also count.

The real lessons here are to avoid addictions and any harmful toxins; to embrace depth, without the need of mind-altering drugs; and, also, to embrace joint partnerships and to be happy accepting assistance from others' resources, but to do so honestly and fairly.

People with activity in the eighth are intense, and this is fine, but they also need to know when to lighten up and relax.

HOW IT PLAYS OUT

In my experience, those with the Sun in the eighth are seriously deep humans. They're intense, not interested in superficiality on any level and, because it's the house associated with Scorpio, they are usually interested in all things Scorpio: power, sexuality and, of course, anything that is hidden from the average person's sight, such as the occult and rituals. We could perhaps call it the house of witchcraft and wizardry.

In general, anyone who has planets in the eighth house is likely to be drawn to powerful subjects and into looking at methods of transformation in their own lives or the lives of others.

A person with Sun in Pisces in the eighth house, for example, would have a very deep imagination. I have a client who works in film and he makes the most incredible visually and mentally stimulating movies. Pisces is all about imagination, and having his Sun (where he shines) in this house gives him depth and an interest in all things that transcend the superficial.

HERE'S YOUR SPACE

Take a look at the eighth house in your birth chart. Is it empty or is there a lot going on? What is the resident sign? Flip to its section in 'The Signs' (pages 97–285) and read about its 'gone wrong' and 'gone right' traits. Check in with the characteristics of any planets in this house and consider how they and their attached signs might interact with the house's associations. Use the table below to jot down anything that jumps out at you.

Now draw up your summary for this planet/sign/house configuration from your own chart.

HOUSE	RESIDENT SIGN	WHICH PLANETS? IN WHICH SIGN?
Eighth		
'Gone wrong' traits		
'Gone right' traits		

NINTH
HOUSE

ASSOCIATED WITH: INSPIRATION, STUDY AND
HIGHER EDUCATION; SPIRITUALITY AND RELIGION;
LONG-DISTANCE TRAVEL; PHILOSOPHY; LAW; PUBLISHING;
EXPANSION AND LUCK

DEFAULT PLANET: JUPITER

DEFAULT SIGN: SAGITTARIUS

ASSOCIATIONS

The ninth house is all about inspiration, learning, study and academia. If a person has planets falling in this house, it's important for them to carry out their studies at as high a level as possible, or they may fail to feel (or be) knowledgeable.

It's also the house of religion and, as I was telling a friend with Mars in Pisces in the ninth, it is important to ensure that, even if you have ambivalent or negative feelings about religion, you don't throw the baby out with the bathwater. He grew up in a very religious household and has chucked the whole lot into the bin, yet he craves spirituality. I was suggesting that perhaps he would find it worthwhile to hang on to the purity of the teachings and discard the rest. These days, many people have turned away from their religious upbringing and many more regard all religion as hypocritical nonsense. Yet, as my dear teacher used to say, it's important for us not to mistake the teacher for the teachings.

The real lesson here is to avoid fanaticism on every level, to study the areas that we are ignorant in and not to reject anything until we've looked into it for ourselves. The real messages in all religions are about love, compassion and treating others in the way that we would wish to be treated, should the shoe be on the other foot: this is the way of the spiritual warrior. I know quite a few spiritual warriors and they all have ninth-house activity.

HOW IT PLAYS OUT

It is vital that people who have planets in the ninth house do not remain ignorant, and keep open enough minds to allow them to explore possibilities. The ninth house is all about learning, and folk who have activity in the ninth should always try to learn about other cultures, even if it's just by travelling and seeking out foreign lands. Many with planets here speak other languages and forge new lives in countries other than their birthplace.

A few years ago I was teaching Dynamic Astrology as a weekly class at Shoreditch House in London, and one day I mentioned that, in my experience, those with Pluto (power) in the ninth house usually stood more in their power when in a foreign land. One fabulous Pisces smiled. He had Pluto in the ninth and said that his career as a graphic designer rocketed – indeed his whole life transformed for the better – when he took a risk and relocated from Brazil to London.

⊖ HERE'S YOUR SPACE ⊖

Take a look at the ninth house in your birth chart. Is it empty or populated with planets and signs? What is the resident sign? Flip to its section in 'The Signs' (pages 97–285) and read about its 'gone wrong' and 'gone right' traits. Remind yourself of the significance of any planets that fall in this house in your chart. Think about the ninth house's associations and see if they throw up any suggestions, answers or further clues. Use the table below to jot down anything that jumps out at you.

Now draw up your summary for this planet/sign/house configuration from your own chart.

HOUSE	RESIDENT SIGN	WHICH PLANETS? IN WHICH SIGN?
Ninth		
'Gone wrong' traits		
'Gone right' traits		

TENTH
HOUSE

ASSOCIATED WITH: YOUR RELATIONSHIP TO SUCCESS,
COMMITMENT, STATUS, AUTHORITY AND POWER; REPUTATION;
SOCIAL STATUS; CAREER; GOVERNMENT INSTITUTIONS;
CORPORATIONS; AUTHORITY FIGURES IN GENERAL

DEFAULT PLANET: SATURN

DEFAULT SIGN: CAPRICORN

—⊖ ASSOCIATIONS ⊖—

The tenth house is all about status and ambitions. It's a very serious
house, and if you have activity here then finding a career that works

for you is vital to your overall sense of achievement. This house is strongly associated with commitment and status, and most folk I know with planets here tend to be very serious about their careers and have the kind of relationships that involve a marriage certificate. Their public image is important to them so it's unlikely that they will settle with anyone who may embarrass then. They do take everything rather seriously.

Rules and authority are usually areas of focus for people with tenth-house activity, though that may not play out in the traditional sense, as in abiding by them for the sake of it. I have a friend with four planets in the tenth. He works in TV and is probably one of the most outspoken and rebellious producers I know, yet his time has come because the universal vibe and the powers that be are tired of sycophants . . . even if they don't know it yet.

The tenth house is the house of authority. I know so many successful folk who have Chiron (the karmic wound) in the tenth and, no matter how much they achieve, they never really feel successful. I tell them that perhaps this helps to keep their ego from growing like the weed it is. Tenth-house folk are authoritative, demanding and dedicated, and when they put their energy into something, they shoot to hit their targets.

The real lessons here are that you should not be too concerned with how others perceive you and not be too uptight with any public image: you just need to be content with who you are and how *you* perceive yourself.

HOW IT PLAYS OUT

Whichever sign rules the tenth house in your chart is the one whose 'gone right' energy you will need to tune in to in order to achieve success in this life. So if Pisces is ruling the tenth house, the world of the intangible is well starred for you. It could be film, video gaming, programming or coding. It could be the spiritual arena or the world of insight and intuition. Basically, it could be anything that involves some sort of a vision.

If you have Sun in the tenth it's likely that you are destined to shine in this life, or that you will gain attention in some way. I have a relative with Sun in the tenth and he got into lots of trouble for illegal graffiti as a young man. I told him that with his chart he was unlikely to get away with it as his Sun in the tenth put him in the spotlight (in this case, with authority figures). He didn't thank me at the time but years later we laughed about it and he has now cleaned up his act.

─○ HERE'S YOUR SPACE ○─

Take a look at the tenth house in your birth chart. What is going on here for you? Is it empty? If so, find the house's resident sign around the outer rim and read more about it (in 'The Signs', pages 97–285) for clues on how they impact on you in conjunction with the tenth house. If there are planets here, check their characteristics (see 'The Planets', pages 30–96), then find the signs they fall in, see which associations chime for you and use the table below to make notes on anything that stands out or feels significant.

Now draw up your summary for this planet/sign/house configuration from your own chart.

HOUSE	RESIDENT SIGN	WHICH PLANETS? IN WHICH SIGN?
Tenth		
'Gone wrong' traits		
'Gone right' traits		

ELEVENTH
HOUSE

ASSOCIATED WITH: AWARENESS, SOCIALIZING, GROUPS,
CAUSES, NETWORKING, CONNECTIONS IN GENERAL, MEDIA
AND INTELLECTUAL CONNECTIONS IN PARTICULAR

DEFAULT PLANET: URANUS

DEFAULT SIGN: AQUARIUS

 ASSOCIATIONS

The eleventh house is the house of humanity. It's all about how
we connect with others, as well as socializing and networking. Friendships are extremely important for everyone I know with planets in

the eleventh house, and these people need to embrace meaningful friendships to reach their full potential. They are usually fabulous connectors, facilitators and networkers, as they shimmy easily between diverse groups of purposeful people who have eclectic interests. They connect people, projects and ideas with a purpose in mind.

This house is also associated with inventiveness, and people with activity here are typically skilled at bringing ideas and concepts to the masses, usually with a higher cause in mind. The eleventh house is the house of 'doing good things for humanity'.

The real lessons of the eleventh house are that sincere friendships should be cultivated in order to achieve contentment of the soul; involvement in positive groups and causes that serve humanity is also well starred. That doesn't need to be boring: I have clients and friends who make riveting, eye-opening documentaries that raise awareness of issues, and I know plenty of successful folk who are also philanthropists and usually have planets in the eleventh.

As a rule, if you have activity in the eleventh house it is a particularly good idea for you to get involved in something with a higher vision than your daily work life (unless, of course, that work already involves doing some good for other beings or the planet!). You need to connect people and ideas without fear of being taken advantage of: the universe sees all.

─⊖ HOW IT PLAYS OUT ⊖─

I have Mars in the eleventh, and my friendship group, also known as the international #girlsquad, call me 'the connector'. I'm always saying something like 'I really feel that you ought to meet So-and-so,' and that's how it happens. I am driven to bring good people, ideas and concepts together, especially when they are likely to combine and create some good in the world. I'm also known to throw rather fun parties (though I say so myself!). If you have activity in this house then you're likely to love a party and find it easy to bring people and ideas together that have a habit of working out well.

I'm by no means the only one of our group who's drawn to the eleventh-house association of 'doing good things for humanity', though. When I checked I saw that every one of us has activity in this house and none of us are slouches when it comes to helping people or giving back.

One member of the squad has Mercury in the eleventh house. She works on TV as a presenter (which makes sense) and therefore communicates (Mercury) with the masses (eleventh house) through the media (also associated with the eleventh house). Dynamic Astrology really is like a code: you just have to see how it relates back to you and crack it!

Given that it's the house of friends and connections, those with lots of activity in their eleventh house may fail to embrace their potential to do good without these people to wake them up.

⊖ HERE'S YOUR SPACE ⊖

Take a look at the eleventh house in your birth chart. Is it empty? If so check its resident sign by looking at the outer rim. Read all about that sign's 'gone right' and 'gone wrong' traits (see 'The Signs', pages 97–285). Combine all of this with the eleventh house associations. If you have planets there check their characteristics, then identify the signs they fall in, keeping the house associations in mind. As ever, the table below is for you to jot down anything that springs to mind when you are combing for clues in the eleventh house, the resident sign and the planets.

Now draw up your summary for this planet/sign/house configuration from your own chart.

HOUSE	RESIDENT SIGN	WHICH PLANETS? IN WHICH SIGN?
Eleventh		
'Gone wrong' traits		
'Gone right' traits		

TWELFTH HOUSE

ASSOCIATED WITH: INTUITION AND THE SUBCONSCIOUS, HUMILITY, LOSS, ESCAPISM, THE HIDDEN REALMS, FAITH AND SECRETS; MUSIC; DANCE; MEDITATION; YOGA AND ALL THINGS METAPHYSICAL, THE SPIRITUAL ARENA IN GENERAL

DEFAULT PLANET: NEPTUNE

DEFAULT SIGN: PISCES

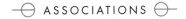

—⊖ ASSOCIATIONS ⊖—

The twelfth house is all about the subconscious and governs aspects of ourselves that often remain unknown until we embark upon the path to self-discovery and awareness.

The opposite of ego, this house is all about humility, grace and intuition. Those with placements in this house are often almost seer-like in their insights. I always feel that they are like the fairy folk who have had to toughen up to walk among humans.

People with activity in this house may often feel an acute sense of loss before they lose anything: this is due to their need for a connection to something greater than 'I'. They need to feel that there is a higher spiritual purpose to life to feel connected to their own version of God, the universe . . . and beyond.

They are also usually gentle and full of grace. They dream of a more idealistic world and need to learn the art of healthy retreat rather than disappearing to avoid conflict.

The real lessons here are to remain focused while still allowing yourself the time to dream. It is prudent to connect with a higher vision to understand the significance and insignificance of 'I'.

—⊖ HOW IT PLAYS OUT ⊖—

I have a client with Venus in Pisces in the twelfth. We always say that he has absolutely no ego, which is typical of the twelfth house 'gone right'. He is one of the most artistic people I know (courtesy of Venus and Pisces), but used to disappear for days on end and only came out on the other side, to the light of life, when he quit a rather unhealthy habit that had caused him to feel constantly unfocused and lost. Now that he is working on his self-improvement without the fog, he is much more present. People with activity in this house tend to wish to merge with the whole universe and to feel connected on some level.

Take a look at your twelfth house. Consider everything that is going on there for you. Which planets are inside and what sign do they fall in? Make a note of their characteristics and jot down a few traits that resonate with you as you are reading. If the twelfth house is empty, check the outer rim for the resident sign, then read all about that sign's traits (in 'The Signs', pages 97–285), keeping the twelfth house associations at the front of your mind. Use the table below to jot down your findings and think about how it all pieces together.

Now draw up your summary for this planet/sign/house configuration from your own chart.

HOUSE	RESIDENT SIGN	WHICH PLANETS? IN WHICH SIGN?
Twelfth		
'Gone wrong' traits		
'Gone right' traits		

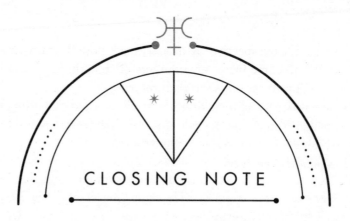

CLOSING NOTE

You've made it to the end of the book and the beginning of your journey into Dynamic Astrology. I hope that you have found plenty of clues in your chart that will enable you to embrace your most authentic self. This is the key to real and lasting happiness.

It is my sincerest wish that this book will help all of the sensitive people in our oh-so-*in*sensitive world, and inspire you all to stay beautiful, to find your inner star and to sit with that encapsulating light, no matter what life dishes out.

I care deeply about humanity, the planet and all its inhabitants (except the flies, spiders and snakes. But, hey, I never profess to be anything other than a flawed human being) and I believe that we are all stars with the capacity to shine like the magnificent Sun: stars, yes, we are!

There is nothing that arrests my attention or captures my heart more than simple kindness. It's all around us when we choose to see it. Good people walk among us, trying to help and unite us, reminding us that we are all brothers and sisters. We are family: connected by the stardust that created each and every one of us.

Astrology, the beautiful language of the stars, never ceases to amaze and move me. It soothes my heart in so many ways and for so many reasons, but mainly because it's the one language that unites us all, irrespective of money, background, status, race or creed. We all come from the remnants of stars that have exploded and, one day, to the stars we shall return.

Don't waste a moment of your precious life on anything other than magic. You are never, ever alone: we are all connected. I know that. I hope you do too.

Let's all help each other.

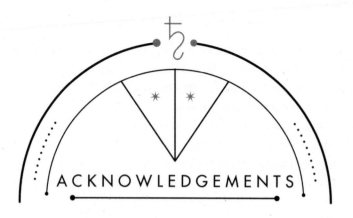

ACKNOWLEDGEMENTS

So many amazing people have inspired, educated and supported me through the twists and turns of my life, way too many to list them all but I'll make a humble attempt. Many of the people mentioned have supported me no end throughout the creation of this book.

First, thanks to my sisters Kathryn and Sara, and especially to my mother: your support and belief in me as a creative gives me the confidence to believe in myself and follow my dreams, as only Capricorn with Leo mid-heaven could. Thank you!

My beloved son Kam: you give me reason consistently to reach for the stars! I love you to the Moon and back. You're amazing.

My incredible Taurus godmother Marian: you are the most humble person I know, there is no one on Earth like you, and I'm so grateful to the universe for bringing you into my life.

To my incredible teachers, His Holiness the Seventeenth Galwang Karmapa, the late great Dr Akong Tulku Rinpoche, Lame Yeshe Rinpoche, Sir Tom Lucas, and to the man I know is raising a glass to me from his own star for sharing my take on the beautiful language, my Taurus teacher, the late Derek Hawkins.

Thanks to my best and oldest friends: Emma, you're the most loyal and funniest Leo I know, you never fail to make me laugh, and Sarah Jane, you and your Cancer Sun have supported me, counselled me and defended me for more years than I care to mention.

To Bob: we fight, laugh, cry and then create. You're the best friend anyone could hope for and I love you. You gotta turn down all that sixth-house Virgo stuff, though.

To my US family and friends, for your support and unfaltering belief in me: Janet, the Aquarius connector, Bonnie, Meredith and Jess, I love you like family; Pardis, you're hilarious, I love you like one of my sisters, and Hilary, what can I say? Thank the stars that connected us! You're a real star!

Julia, your wit, inspiration, mentoring, support and straight talk helped to change the game for me. Thank you for everything.

Emily, I still recall the very first time we met and I read your chart. You said, 'I just want everyone to be able to do that and to know what you know about astrology.' Your vision, smarts and determination made this book a reality! Thank you.

Helen, I still think it's your Moon in Aquarius that made you grasp astrology so fast. You helped make my words pop off the pages!

Adam, your handling of me is commendable: 'Carolyne, I think you might be the most interesting client I have ever worked with.' What a smooth Gemini understatement!

To my friend Ade (a.k.a. Retipuj), for all the last-minute urgent design work you sorted out for me. You always said yes and never complained once. Thank you!

Finally to my publisher: I'm so proud to have your iconic Penguin symbol on the cover. What kudos! Thank you.

Thank you to the universe!

May all beings be happy and free from suffering.